WATT

Other Works by Samuel Beckett

Published by Grove Press

Endgame
Happy Days
Krapp's Last Tape
    and Other Dramatic Pieces
Malone Dies
Molloy
Murphy
Proust
The Unnamable
Waiting for Godot
Watt
Molloy / Malone Dies / The Unnamable
    (in one volume)

WATT

By
Samuel Beckett

GROVE PRESS, INC. / NEW YORK
EVERGREEN BOOKS LTD. / LONDON

WATT

I

Mr Hackett turned the corner and saw, in the failing light, at some little distance, his seat. It seemed to be occupied. This seat, the property very likely of the municipality, or of the public, was of course not his, but he thought of it as his. This was Mr Hackett's attitude towards things that pleased him. He knew they were not his, but he thought of them as his. He knew were not his, because they pleased him.

Halting, he looked at the seat with greater care. Yes, it was not vacant. Mr Hackett saw things a little more clearly when he was still. His walk was a very agitated walk.

Mr Hackett did not know whether he should go on, or whether he should turn back. Space was open on his right hand, and on his left hand, but he knew that he would never take advantage of this. He knew also that he would not long remain motionless, for the state of his health rendered this unfortunately impossible. The dilemma was thus of extreme simplicity: to go on, or to turn, and return, round the corner, the way he

had come. Was he, in other words, to go home at once,
or was he to remain out a little longer?

Stretching out his left hand, he fastened it round
a rail. This permitted him to strike his stick against
the pavement. The feel, in his palm, of the thudding
rubber appeased him, slightly.

But he had not reached the corner when he
turned again and hastened towards the seat, as fast
as his legs could carry him. When he was so near the
seat, that he could have touched it with his stick, if he
had wished, he again halted and examined its occupants.
He had the right, he supposed, to stand and wait for
the tram. They too were perhaps waiting for the tram,
for a tram, for many trams stopped here, when requested, from without or within, to do so.

Mr Hackett decided, after some moments, that if
they were waiting for a tram they had been doing so for
some time. For the lady held the gentleman by the ears,
and the gentleman's hand was on the lady's thigh, and
the lady's tongue was in the gentleman's mouth. Tired
of waiting for the tram, said (1) Mr Hackett, they strike
up an acquaintance. The lady now removing her tongue
from the gentleman's mouth, he put his into hers. Fair
do, said Mr Hackett. Taking a pace forward, to satisfy
himself that the gentleman's other hand was not going
to waste, Mr Hackett was shocked to find it limply
dangling over the back of the seat, with between its
fingers the spent three quarters of a cigarette.

I see no indecency, said the policeman.

We arrive too late, said Mr Hackett. What a
shame.

Do you take me for a fool? said the policeman.

Mr Hackett recoiled a step, forced back his head
until he thought his throatskin would burst, and saw

---

(1) Much valuable space has been saved, in this work, that
would otherwise have been lost, by avoidance of the plethoric
reflexive pronoun after *say*.

at last, afar, bent angrily upon him, the red violent
face.

Officer, he cried, as God is my witness, he had
his hand upon it.

God is a witness that cannot be sworn.

If I interrupted your beat, said Mr Hackett, a
thousand pardons. I did so with the best intentions,
for you, for me, for the community at large.

The policeman replied briefly to this.

If you imagine that I have not your number, said
Mr Hackett, you are mistaken. I may be infirm, but
my sight is excellent. Mr Hackett sat down on the seat,
still warm, from the loving. Good evening, and thank
you, said Mr Hackett.

It was an old seat, low and worn. Mr Hackett's
nape rested against the solitary backboard, beneath it
unimpeded his hunch protruded, his feet just touched
the ground. At the ends of the long outspread arms the
hands held the armrests, the stick hooked round his
neck hung between his knees.

So from the shadows he watched the last trams
pass. oh not the last, but almost, and in the sky, and in
the still canal, the long greens and yellows of the summer
evening.

But now a gentleman passing, with a lady on his
arm, espied him.

Oh, my dear, he said, there is Hackett.

Hackett, said the lady. What Hackett?
Where?

You know Hackett, said the gentleman. You
must have often heard me speak of Hackett. Hunchy
Hackett. On the seat.

The lady looked attentively at Mr Hackett.

So that is Hackett, she said.

Yes, said the gentleman.

Poor fellow, she said.

Oh, said the gentleman, let us now stop, do you
mind, and wish him the time of evening. He advanced,

exclaiming, My dear fellow, my dear fellow, how are you?

Mr Hackett raised his eyes, from the dying day.

My wife, cried the gentleman. Meet my wife. My wife. Mr Hackett.

I have heard so much about you, said the lady, and now I meet you, at last. Mr Hackett!

I do not rise, not having the force, said Mr Hackett.

Why I should think not indeed, said the lady. She stooped towards him, quivering with solicitude. I should hope not indeed, she said.

Mr Hackett thought she was going to pat him on the head, or at least stroke his hunch. He called in his arms and they sat down beside him, the lady on the one side, and the gentleman on the other. As a result of this, Mr Hackett found himself between them. His head reached to the armpits. Their hands met above the hunch, on the backboard. They drooped with tenderness towards him.

You remember Grehan? said Mr Hackett.

The poisoner, said the gentleman.

The solicitor, said Mr Hackett.

I knew him slightly, said the gentleman. Six years, was it not.

Seven, said Mr Hackett. Six are rarely given.

He deserved ten, in my opinion, said the gentleman.

Or twelve, said Mr Hackett.

What did he do? said the lady.

Slightly overstepped his prerogatives, said the gentleman.

I received a letter from him this morning, said Mr Hackett.

Oh, said the gentleman, I did not know they might communicate with the outer world.

He is a solicitor, said Mr Hackett. He added, I am scarcely the outer world.

What rubbish, said the gentleman.

What nonsense, said the lady.

The letter contained an enclosure, said Mr Hackett, of which, knowing your love of literature, I would favour you with the primeur, if it were not too dark to see.

The primeur, said the lady.

That is what I said, said Mr Hackett.

I have a petrol-lighter, said the gentleman.

Mr Hackett drew a paper from his pocket and the gentleman lit his petrol-lighter.

Mr Hackett read:

TO NELLY

To Nelly, said the lady.

To Nelly, said Mr Hackett.

There was a silence.

Shall I continue? said Mr Hackett.

My mother's name was Nelly, said the lady.

The name is not uncommon, said Mr Hackett, even I have known several Nellies.

Read on, my dear fellow, said the gentleman.

Mr Hackett read:

TO NELLY

To thee, sweet Nell, when shadows fall
Jug-jug! Jug-jug!
I here in thrall
My wanton thoughts do turn.
Walks she out yet with Byrne?
Moves Hyde his hand amid her skirts
As erst? I ask, and Echo answers : Certes.

Tis well! Tis well! Far, far be it
Pu-we! Pu-we!
From me, my tit,
Such innocent joys to chide.
Burn, burn with Byrne, from Hyde
Hide naught — hide naught save what
  Is Greh'n's. IT hide from Hyde, with Byrne
burn not.

 It! Peerless gage of maidenhood!
 Cuckoo! Cuckoo!
 Would that I could
 Be certain in my mind
 Upon discharge to find
 Neath Cupid's flow'r, hey nonny O!
 Diana's blushing bud in statu quo.

 Then darkly kindle durst my soul
 Tuwhit! Tuwhoo!
 As on it stole
 The murmur to become
 Epithalamium,
 And Hymen o'er my senses shed
 The dewy forejoys of the marriage-bed.

 Enough —

Ample, said the lady.

A woman in a shawl passed before them. Her belly could dimly be seen, sticking out, like a balloon.

I was never like that, my dear, said the lady, was I?

Not to my knowledge, my love, said the gentleman.

You remember the night that Larry was born, said the lady.

I do, said the gentleman.

How old is Larry now? said Mr Hackett.

How old is Larry, my dear? said the gentleman.

How old is Larry, said the lady. Larry will be forty years old next March, D.V.

That is the kind of thing Dee always vees, said Mr Hackett.

I wouldn't go as far as that, said the gentleman.

Would you care to hear, Mr Hackett, said the lady, about the night that Larry was born?

Oh do tell him, my dear, said the gentleman.

Well, said the lady, that morning at breakfast Goff turns to me and he says, Tetty, he says, Tetty, my pet, I should very much like to invite Thompson, Cream and Colquhoun to help us eat the duck, if I felt sure you felt up to it. Why, my dear, says I, I never felt fitter in my life. Those were my words, were they not?

I believe they were, said Goff.

Well, said Tetty, when Thompson comes into the dining-room, followed by Cream and Berry (Coulquhoun I remember had a previous engagement), I was already seated at the table. There was nothing strange in that, seeing I was the only lady present. You did not find that strange, did you, my love?

Certainly not, said Goff, most natural.

The first mouthful of duck had barely passed my lips, said Tetty, when Larry leaped in my wom.

Your what? said Mr Hackett.

My wom, said Tetty.

You know, said Goff, her woom.

How embarrassing for you, said Mr Hackett.

I continued to eat, drink and make light conversation, said Tetty, and Larry to leap, like a salmon.

What an experience for you, said Mr Hackett.

There were moments, I assure you, when I thought he would tumble out on the floor, at my feet.

Merciful heavens, you felt him slipping, said Mr Hackett.

No trace of this dollar appeared on my face, said Tetty. Did it, my dear?

Not a trace, said Goff.

Nor did my sense of humour desert me. What
rolypoly, said Mr Berry, I remember, turning to me
with a smile, what delicious rolypoly, it melts in the
mouth. Not only in the mouth, sir, I replied, without
an instant's hesitation, not only in the mouth, my dear
sir. Not too osy with the sweet, I thought.

Not too what? said Mr Hackett.

Osy, said Goff. You know, not too osy.

With the coffee and liquors, labour was in full
swing, Mr Hackett, I give you my solemn word, under
the groaning board.

Swing is the word, said Goff.

You knew she was pregnant, said Mr Hackett.

Why er, said Goff, you see er, I er, we er —

Tetty's hand fell heartily on Mr Hackett's thigh.

He thought I was coy, she cried. Hahahaha.
Haha. Ha.

Haha, said Mr Hackett.

I was greatly worried I admit, said Goff.

Finally they retired, did you not? said Tetty.

We did indeed, said Goff, we retired to the
billiard-room, for a game of slosh.

I went up those stairs, Mr Hackett, said Tetty,
on my hands and knees, wringing the carpetrods as
though they were made of raffia.

You were in such anguish, said Mr Hackett.

Three minutes later I was a mother.

Unassisted, said Goff.

I did everything with my own hands, said Tetty,
everything.

She severed the cord with her teeth, said Goff,
not having a scissors to her hand. What do you think
of that?

I would have snapped it across my knee, if
necessary, said Tetty.

That is a thing I often wondered, said Mr
Hackett, what it feels like to have the string cut.

For the mother or the child? said Goff.

For the mother, said Mr Hackett. I was not found under a cabbage, I believe.

For the mother, said Tetty, the feeling is one of relief, of great relief, as when the guests depart. All my subsequent strings were severed by Professor Cooper, but the feeling was always the same, one of riddance.

Then you dressed and came downstairs, said Mr Hackett, leading the infant by the hand.

We heard the cries, said Goff.

Judge of their surprise, said Tetty.

Cream's potting had been extraordinary, extraordinary, I remember, said Goff. I never saw anything like it. We were watching breathless, as he set himself for a long thin jenny, with the black of all balls.

What temerity, said Mr Hackett.

A quite impossible stroke, in my opinion, said Goff. He drew back his queue to strike, when the wail was heard. He permitted himself an expression that I shall not repeat.

Poor little Larry, said Tetty, as though it were his fault.

Tell me no more, said Mr Hackett, it is useless.

These northwestern skies are really extraordinary, said Goff, are they not.

So voluptuous, said Tetty. You think it is all over and then pop! up they flare, with augmented radiance.

Yes, said Mr Hackett, there are protuberances and protuberances.

Poor Mr Hackett, said Tetty, poor *dear* Mr Hackett.

Yes, said Mr Hackett.

Nothing to the Glencullen Hacketts, I suppose, said Tetty.

It was there I fell off the ladder, said Mr Hackett.

What age were you then? said Tetty.

One, said Mr Hackett.

And where was your dear mother? said Tetty.

She was out somewhere, said Mr Hackett.

And your papa? said Tetty.

Papa was out breaking stones on Prince William's Seat, said Mr Hackett.

You were all alone, said Tetty.

There was the goat, I am told, said Mr Hackett.

He turned away from the ladder fallen in the dark yard and his gaze moved down over the fields and the low tottering walls, across the stream and up the further slope to the bluff already in shadow, and the summer sky. He slipped down with the little sunlit fields, he toiled up with the foothills to the dark bluff, and he heard the distant clink of the hammers.

She left you all alone in the yard, said Tetty, with the goat.

It was a beautiful summer's day, said Mr Hackett.

And what possessed her to slip off like that? said Goff.

I never asked her, said Mr Hackett. The pub, or the chapel, or both.

Poor woman, God forgive her, said Tetty.

Faith I wouldn't put it past him, said Mr Hackett.

Night is now falling fast, said Goff, soon it will be quite dark.

Then we shall all go home, said Mr Hackett.

On the far side of the street, opposite to where they sat, a tram stopped. It remained stationary for some little time, and they heard the voice of the conductor, raised in anger. Then it moved on, disclosing, on the pavement, motionless, a solitary figure, lit less and less by the receding lights, until it was scarcely to be distinguished from the dim wall behind it. Tetty was not sure whether it was a man or a woman. Mr Hackett was not sure that it was not a parcel, a carpet for example, or a roll of tarpaulin, wrapped up in dark paper and tied about the middle with a cord. Goff rose, without a word, and rapidly crossed the street. Tetty and Mr Hackett could see his eager gestures, for his coat was light in colour, and hear his voice, raised in remonstrance. But Watt moved no more, as far as they could see, than if he had been of stone, and if he spoke he spoke so low that they did not hear him.

Mr Hackett did not know when he had been more intrigued, nay, he did not know when he had been so intrigued. He did not know either what it was that so intrigued him. What is it that so intrigues me, he said, whom even the extraordinary, even the supernatural, intrigue so seldom, and so little. Here there is nothing in the least unusual, that I can see, and yet I burn with curiosity, and with wonder. The sensation is not disagreeable, I must say, and yet I do not think I could bear it for more than twenty minutes, or half an hour.

The lady also was an interested spectator.

Goff rejoined them, very cross. I recognised him at once, he said. He made use, with reference to Watt, of an expression that we shall not record.

For the past seven years, he said, he owes me five shillings, that is to say, six and ninepence.

He does not move, said Tetty.

He refuses to pay, said Mr Hackett.

He does not refuse to pay, said Goff. He offers me four shillings and fourpence. It is all the money he has in the world.

Then he would owe you only two and threepence, said Mr Hackett.

I cannot leave him without a penny in his pocket, said Goff.

Why not? said Mr Hackett.

He is setting out on a journey, said Goff. If I accepted his offer he would be obliged to turn back.

That might be the best thing for him, said Mr Hackett. Perhaps some day, when we are all dead,

looking back he will say, If only Mr Nesbit had accepted —

Nixon, my name is, said Goff.   Nixon.

If only Mr Nixon had accepted my four and
fourpence that night, and I had turned back, instead of
going on.

All lies, I suppose, in any case, said Mrs Nixon.

No no, said Mr Nixon, he is a most truthful man,
really incapable, I believe, of telling an untruth.

You might at least have accepted a shilling, said
Mr Hackett, or one and six.

There he is now, on the bridge, said Mrs Nixon.

He stood with his back towards them, from the
waist up faintly outlined against the last wisps of day.

You haven't told us his name, said Mr Hackett.

Watt, said Mr Nixon.

I never heard you mention him, said Mrs Nixon.

Strange, said Mr Nixon.

Known him long? said Mr Hackett.

I cannot really say I know him, said Mr Nixon.

Like a sewer-pipe, said Mrs Nixon.   Where are
his arms?

Since when can't you really say you know him?
said Mr Hackett.

My dear fellow, said Mr Nixon, why this sudden
interest?

Do not answer if you prefer not to, said Mr
Hackett.

It is difficult to answer, said Mr Nixon.   I seem
to have known him all my life, but there must have
been a period when I did not.

How is that, said Mr Hackett.

He is considerably younger than I, said Mr Nixon.

And you never mention him, said Mr Hackett.

Why, said Mr Nixon, I may very well have
mentioned him, there is really no reason why I should
not.   It is true—.   He paused.   He does not invite
mention, he said, there are people like that.

Not like me, said Mr Hackett.

He is gone, said Mrs Nixon.

Is that so, said Mr Nixon. The curious thing is, my dear fellow, I tell you quite frankly, that when I see him, or think of him, I think of you, and that when I see you, or think of you, I think of him. I have no idea why this is so.

Well well, said Mr Hackett.

He is on his way now to the station, said Mr Nixon. Why I wonder did he get down here.

It is the end of the penny fare, said Mrs Nixon.

That depends where he got on, said Mr Nixon.

He can scarcely have got on at a point remoter than the terminus, said Mr Hackett.

But does the penny fare end here, said Mr Nixon, at a merely facultative stop? Surely it ends rather at the station.

I think you are right, said Mr Hackett.

Then why did he get off here? said Mr Nixon.

Perhaps he felt like a little fresh air, said Mr Hackett, before being pent up in the train.

Weighed down as he is, said Mr Nixon. Come come.

Perhaps he mistook the stop, said Mrs Nixon.

But this is not a stop, said Mr Nixon, in the ordinary sense of the word. Here the tram stops only by request. And since nobody else got off, and since nobody got on, the request must have come from Watt.

A silence followed these words. Then Mrs Nixon said:

I do not follow you, Goff. Why should he not have requested the tram to stop, if he wished to do so?

There is no reason, my dear, said Mr Nixon, no earthly reason, why he should not have requested the tram to stop, as he undoubtedly did. But the fact of his having requested the tram to stop proves that he did not mistake the stop, as you suggest. For if he had mistaken the stop, and thought himself already at the railway station, he would not have requested the tram to stop. For the tram always stops at the station.

Perhaps he is off his head, said Mr Hackett.

He is a little strange at times, said Mr Nixon, but he is an experienced traveller.

Perhaps, said Mr Hackett, finding that he had a little time on his hands, he decided to while it away through the sweet cool evening air, rather than in the nasty railway station.

But he will miss his train, said Mr Nixon, he will miss the last train out, if he does not run.

Perhaps he wished to annoy the conductor, said Mrs Nixon, or the driver.

But a milder, more inoffensive creature does not exist, said Mr Nixon. He would literally turn the other cheek, I honestly believe, if he had the energy.

Perhaps, said Mr Hackett, he suddenly made up his mind not to leave town after all. Between the terminus and here he had time to reconsider the matter. Then, having made up his mind that it is better after all not to leave town just now, he stops the tram and gets down, for it is useless to go on.

But he went on, said Mr Nixon, he did not go back the way he came, but went on, towards the station.

Perhaps he is going home by a roundabout way, said Mrs Nixon.

Where does he live? said Mr Hackett.

He has no fixed address that I know of, said Mr Nixon.

Then his going on towards the station proves nothing, said Mrs Nixon. He may be fast asleep in Quin's hotel at the present moment.

With four and four in his pocket, said Mr Hackett.

Or on a bench somewhere, said Mrs Nixon. Or in the park. Or on the football field. Or on the cricket field. Or on the bowling green.

Or on the tennis courts, said Mr Nixon.

I think not, said Mr Hackett. He gets off the tram, determined not to leave town after all. But a little further reflexion shows him the folly of such a course. This would explain his attitude after the tram had moved on, and left him.

The folly of what course? said Mr Nixon.

Of turning back so soon, said Mr Hackett, before he was well started on his way.

Did you see the accoutrement? said Mrs Nixon. What had he on his head?

His hat, said Mr Nixon.

The thought of leaving town was most painful to him, said Mr Hackett, but the thought of not doing so no less so. So he sets off for the station, half hoping he may miss his train.

You may be right, said Mr Nixon.

Too fearful to assume himself the onus of a decision, said Mr Hackett, he refers it to the frigid machinery of a time-space relation.

Very ingenious, said Mr Nixon.

And what do you suppose frightens him all of a sudden? said Mrs Nixon.

It can hardly be the journey itself, said Mr Hackett, since you tell me he is an experienced traveller.

A silence followed these words.

Now that I have made that clear, said Mr Hackett, you might describe your friend a little more fully.

I really know nothing, said Mr Nixon.

But you must know something, said Mr Hackett. One does not part with five shillings to a shadow. Nationality, family, birthplace, confession, occupation, means of existence, distinctive signs, you cannot be in ignorance of all this.

Utter ignorance, said Mr Nixon.

He is not a native of the rocks, said Mr Hackett.

I tell you nothing is known, cried Mr Nixon. Nothing.

A silence followed these angry words, by Mr Hackett resented, by Mr Nixon repented.

He has a huge big red nose, said Mr Nixon grudgingly.

Mr Hackett pondered this.

You are not asleep, my dear, said Mr Nixon.

I grow drowsy, said Mrs Nixon.

Here is a man you seem to have known all your life, said Mr Hackett, who owes you five shillings for the past seven years, and all you can tell me is that he has a huge big red nose and no fixed address. He paused. He added, And that he is an experienced traveller. He paused. He added, And that he is considerably younger than you, a common condition I must say. He paused. He added, And that he is truthful, gentle and sometimes a little strange. He glared up angrily at Mr Nixon's face. But Mr Nixon did not see this angry glare, for he was looking at something quite different.

I think it is time for us to be getting along, he said, is it not, my dear.

In an instant the last flowers will be engulfed, said Mrs Nixon.

Mr Nixon rose.

Here is a man you have known as long as you can remember, said Mr Hackett, to whom you lent five shillings seven years ago, whom you immediately recognize, at a considerable distance, in the dark. You say you know nothing of his antecedents. I am obliged to believe you.

Nothing obliges you, said Mr Nixon.

I choose to believe you, said Mr Hackett. And that you are unable to tell what you do not know I am willing to believe also. It is a common failing.

Tetty, said Mr Nixon.

But certain things you must know, said Mr Hackett.

For example, said Mr Nixon.

How you met him, said Mr Hackett. In what circumstances he touched you. Where he is to be seen.

What does it matter who he is? said Mrs Nixon. She rose.

Take my arm, my dear, said Mr Nixon.

Or what he does, said Mrs Nixon. Or how he lives. Or where he comes from. Or where he is going to. Or what he looks like. What can it possibly matter, to us?

I ask myself the same question, said Mr Hackett.

How I met him, said Mr Nixon. I really do not remember, any more than I remember meeting my father.

Good God, said Mr Hackett.

In what circumstances he touched me, said Mr Nixon. I met him one day in the street. One of his feet was bare. I forget which. He drew me to one side and said he was in need of five shillings to buy himself a boot. I could not refuse him.

But one does not buy a boot, exclaimed Mr Hackett.

Perhaps he knew where he could have it made to measure, said Mrs Nixon.

I know nothing of that, said Mr Nixon. As to where he is to be seen, he is to be seen in the streets, walking about. But one does not see him often.

He is a university man, of course, said Mrs Nixon.

I should think it highly probable, said Mr Nixon.

Mr and Mrs Nixon moved off, arm in arm. But they had not gone far when they returned. Mr Nixon stooped and murmured in Mr Hackett's ear, Mr Nixon who did not like the sun to go down on the least hint of an estrangement.

Drink, said Mr Hackett.

Oh my goodness no, said Mr Nixon, he drinks nothing but milk.

Milk, exclaimed Mr Hackett.

Even water he will not touch, said Mr Nixon.

Well, said Mr Hackett wearily, I am obliged to you, I suppose.

Mr and Mrs Nixon moved off, arm in arm. But they had not gone far when they heard a cry. They stopped, and listened. It was Mr Hackett, crying, in the night, Pleased to have met you, Mrs Nisbet. Mrs Nixon, tightening her hold on Mr Nixon's arm, cried back, The pleasure is mine, Mr Hackett.

What? cried Mr Hackett.

She says the pleasure is hers, cried Mr Nixon.

Mr Hackett resumed his holds on the armrests. Pulling himself forward, and letting himself fall back, several times in rapid succession, he scratched the crest of his hunch against the backboard. He looked towards the horizon that he had come out to see, of which he had seen so little. Now it was quite dark. Yes, now the western sky was as the eastern, which was as the southern, which was as the northern.

Watt bumped into a porter wheeling a milkcan. Watt fell and his hat and bags were scattered. The porter did not fall, but he let go his can, which fell back with a thump on its tilted rim, rocked rattling on its base and finally came to a stand. This was a happy chance, for had it fallen on its side, full as it perhaps was of milk, then who knows the milk might have run out, all over the platform, and even on the rails, beneath the train, and been lost.

Watt picked himself up, little the worse for his fall, as usual.

The devil raise a hump on you, said the porter.

He was a handsome if dirty fellow. It is so difficult for railway porters to keep sweet and clean, with the work they have to do.

Can't you look where you're going? he said.

Watt did not cry out on this extravagant suggestion, let fall, it is only fair to say, in the heat of anger. He stooped to pick up his hat and bags, but straightened himself up without having done so. He did not feel at liberty to see to this matter until the porter had finished abusing him.

Mute on top of blind, said the porter.

Watt smiled and clasping his hands raised them to his breastbone and held them there.

Watt had watched people smile and thought he understood how it was done. And it was true that Watt's smile, when he smiled, resembled more a smile than a sneer, for example, or a yawn. But there was something wanting to Watt's smile, some little thing was lacking, and people who saw it for the first time, and most people who saw it saw it for the first time, were sometimes in doubt as to what expression exactly was intended. To many it seemed a simple sucking of the teeth.

Watt used this smile sparingly.

Its effect on the porter was to suggest to him words infinitely more disobliging than any he had already employed. But they were never spoken, by him, to Watt, for suddenly the porter seized his can and wheeled it rapidly away. The stationmaster, a Mr Lowry, was approaching.

This incident was of too common a kind to excite any great interest among those present. But there were connoisseurs on whom the exceptional quality of Watt was not lost, of his entry, his fall, his rise and subsequent attitudes. These were content.

Among these was the newsagent. He had seen all from his warm nest of books and periodicals. But now that the best was past he came out on the platform, with the intention of closing his stall, for the night. He therefore lowered and locked the corrugated apron. He seemed a man of more than usual acerbity, and to suffer from unremitting mental, moral and perhaps even physical pain. One noticed his cap, perhaps because of the snowwhite forehead and damp black curly hair on which it sat. The eye came always in the end to the scowling mouth and from there on up to the rest. His

moustache, handsome in itself, was for obscure reasons
unimportant. But one thought of him as the man who,
among other things, never left off his cap, a plain blue
cloth cap, with a peak and knob. For he never left off
his bicycle-clips either. These were of a kind that
caused his trouser-ends to stick out wide, on either side.
He was short and limped dreadfully. When he got
started he moved rapidly, in a series of aborted genu-
flexions.

He picked up Watt's hat and brought it to him,
saying, Your hat, sir, I think.

Watt looked at the hat. Was it possible that
this was his hat.

He put it on his head.

Now at the end of the platform the newsagent
came out of a door, wheeling his bicycle. He would
carry it down the winding stone stairs and then ride
home. There he would play a game of chess, between
masters, out of Mr Staunton's handbook. The next
morning he would carry his bicycle up the stairs again.
It was heavy, being a very good bicycle. It would have
been simpler to leave it below, but he preferred to have
it near him. This man's name was Evans.

Watt picked up his bags and got into the train.
He did not choose a compartment. It happened to be
empty.

On the platform the porter continued to wheel
cans, up and down. At one end of the platform there
was one group of cans, and at the other end there was
another. The porter chose with care a can in one group
and wheeled it to the other. Then he chose with care
a can in the other and wheeled it to the one. He is
sorting the cans, said Watt. Or perhaps it is a punishment for disobedience, or some neglect of duty.

Watt sat with his back to the engine, which
now, having got up steam, drew the long line of carriages
out of the station. Already Watt preferred to have his
back to his destination.

But he had not gone far when, conscious of eyes
upon him, he looked up and saw a large gentleman
sitting in the corner diagonally opposed to his. This
gentleman's feet rested on the wooden seat before him,
and his hands were in the pockets of his coat. The
compartment then was not so empty as Watt had at
first supposed.

My name is Spiro, said the gentleman.

Here then was a sensible man at last. He began
with the essential and then, working on, would deal
with the less important matters, one after the other,
in an orderly way.

Watt smiled.

No offence meant, said Mr Spiro.

Watt's smile was further peculiar in this, that it
seldom came singly, but was followed after a short time
by another, less pronounced it is true. In this it resembled the fart. And it even sometimes happened that a
third, very weak and fleeting, was found necessary,
before the face could be at rest again. But this was rare.
And it will be a long time now before Watt smiles again,
unless something very unexpected turns up, to upset
him.

My friends call me Dum, said Mr Spiro, I am so
bright and cheerful. D-U-M. Anagram of mud.

Mr Spiro had been drinking, but not more than
was good for him.

I edit *Crux*, said Mr Spiro, the popular catholic
monthly. We do not pay our contributors, but they
benefit in other ways. Our advertisements are extraordinary. We keep our tonsure above water. Our
prize competitions are very nice. Times are hard, water
in every wine. Of a devout twist, they do more good
than harm. For example : *Rearrange the fifteen letters
of the Holy Family to form a question and answer.
Winning entry: Has J. Jurms a po? Yes. Or: What do
you know of the adjuration, excommunication, mal-
ediction and fulminating anathematisation of the eels of*

Como, the hurebers of Beaune, the rats of Lyon, the slugs of Mâcon, the worms of Como, the leeches of Lausanne and the caterpillars of Valence?

Now the fields flew by, the hedges and the ditches, ghastly in the train's light, or appeared to do so, for in reality it was the train that moved, across a land for ever still.

Though we know what we know, said Mr Spiro, we are not partisan. I personally am a neo-John-Thomist, I make no bones about that. But I do not allow it to stand in the way of my promiscuities. *Podex non destra sed sinistra*—what pettiness. Our columns are open to suckers of every persuasion and freethinkers figure in our roll of honour. My own contribution to the supplementary redemption, *A Spiritual Syringe for the Costive in Devotion*, is so elastic, and unrigid, that a Presbyterian could profit by it, without discomfort. But why do I trouble you with this, you, a perfect stranger. It is because to-night I must speak, to a fellow wanderer. Where do you get down, sir?

Watt named the place.

I beg your pardon? said Mr Spiro.

Watt named the place again.

Then there is not a moment to lose, said Mr Spiro.

He drew a paper from his pocket and read:

Lourdes
Basses-Pyrénées
France

Sir
A rat, or other small animal, eats of a consecrated wafer.
1) *Does he ingest the Real Body, or does he not?*
2) *If he does not, what has become of it?*
3) *If he does, what is to be done with him?*

Yours faithfully
Martin Ignatius MacKenzie
(Author of The Chartered Accountant's Saturday Night)

Mr Spiro now replied to these questions, that is to say he replied to question one and he replied to question three. He did so at length, quoting from Saint Bonaventura, Peter Lombard, Alexander of Hales, Sanchez, Suarez, Henno, Soto, Diana, Concina and Dens, for he was a man of leisure. But Watt heard nothing of this, because of other voices, singing, crying, stating, murmuring, things unintelligible, in his ear. With these, if he was not familiar, he was not unfamiliar either. So he was not alarmed, unduly. Now these voices, sometimes they sang only, and sometimes they cried only, and sometimes they stated only, and sometimes they murmured only, and sometimes they sang and cried, and sometimes they sang and stated, and sometimes they sang and murmured, and sometimes they cried and stated, and sometimes they cried and murmured, and sometimes they stated and murmured, and sometimes they sang and cried and stated, and sometimes they sang and cried and murmured, and sometimes they cried and stated and murmured, and sometimes they sang and cried and stated and murmured, all together, at the same time, as now, to mention only these four kinds of voices, for there were others. And sometimes Watt understood all, and sometimes he understood much, and sometimes he understood little, and sometimes he understood nothing, as now.

The racecourse now appearing, with its beautiful white railing, in the fleeing lights, warned Watt that he was drawing near, and that when the train stopped next, then he must leave it. He could not see the stands, the grand, the members', the people's, so   ? when empty with their white and red, for they were too far off.

So he settled his bags under his hands and held himself in readiness, in readiness to leave the train, the moment it came to a standstill.

For Watt had once been carried past this station, and on to the next, through his not having prepar-

ed himself in time, to get down, when the train
stopped.

For this was a line so little frequented, especially
at this hour, when the driver, the stoker, the guard and
the station staffs all along the line, were anhelating
towards their wives, after the long hours of continence,
that the train would hardly draw up, when it would be
off again, like a bouncing ball.

Personally I would pursue him, said Mr Spiro,
if I were sure it was he, with all the rigour of the canon
laws. He took his legs off the seat. He put his head out
of the window. And pontifical decrees, he cried. A
great rush of air drove him back. He was alone, flying
through the night.

The moon was now up. It was not far up, but it
was up. It was of an unpleasant yellow colour. Long
past the full, it was waning, waning.

Watt's way of advancing due east, for example,
was to turn his bust as far as possible towards the north
and at the same time to fling out his right leg as far
as possible towards the south, and then to turn his bust
as far as possible towards the south and at the same time
to fling out his left leg as far as possible towards the
north, and then again to turn his bust as far as possible
towards the north and to fling out his right leg as far
as possible towards the south, and then again to turn
his bust as far as possible towards the south and to
fling out his left leg as far as possible towards the north,
and so on, over and over again, many many times, until
he reached his destination, and could sit down. So,
standing first on one leg, and then on the other, he
moved forward, a headlong tardigrade, in a straight line.
The knees, on these occasions, did not bend. They
could have, but they did not. No knees could better
bend than Watt's, when they chose, there was nothing
the matter with Watt's knees, as may appear. But when
out walking they did not bend, for some obscure reason.
Notwithstanding this, the feet fell, heel and sole together,

flat upon the ground, and left it, for the air's uncharted ways, with manifest repugnancy. The arms were content to dangle, in perfect equipendency.

Lady McCann, coming up behind, thought she had never, on the public road, seen motions so extraordinary, and few women had a more extensive experience of the public road than Lady McCann. That they were not due to alcohol appeared from their regularity, and dogged air. Watt's was a funambulistic stagger.

More than the legs the head impressed Lady McCann. For the movements of the legs could be accounted for, in a number of ways. And as she reflected on some of the ways, in which the movements of the legs could be accounted for, she recalled the old story of her girlhood days, the old story of the medical students and the gentlemen walking before them with stiff and open stride. Excuse me, sir, said one of the students, raising his cap, when they drew abreast, my friend here says it is piles, and I say it is merely the clap. We have all three then been deceived, replied the gentleman, for I thought it was wind myself.

It was therefore less the legs that puzzled Lady McCann, than the head, turning stiffly at every stride, on its stiff neck, under its hard hat, through a quarter of a circle at least. Where had she read that even so, from side to side, bears turn their heads, when baited? In Mr Walpole, perhaps.

Though not a rapid walker, because of old habit, perhaps, and of her feet, which were old and sore, Lady McCann saw all this in greater and in greater detail, with every step she took. For they were moving in the same direction, Lady McCann and Watt.

Though not a timorous woman as a rule, thanks to her traditions, catholic and military, Lady McCann preferred to halt and wait, leaning on her parasol, for the distance between them to increase. So, now halting, now advancing, she followed the high stamping mass,

at a judicious remove, until she came to her gate. Here,
faithful to the spirit of her cavalier ascendants, she
picked up a stone and threw it, with all her might,
which, when she was roused, was not negligible, at
Watt.   And it is to be supposed that God, always
favourable to the McCanns of   ?   , guided her
hand, for the stone fell on Watt's hat and struck it from
his head, to the ground.   This was indeed a providential
escape, for had the stone fallen on an ear, or on the
back of the neck, as it might so easily have done, as
it so nearly did, why then a wound had perhaps been
opened, never again to close, never, never again to close,
for Watt had a poor healing skin, and perhaps his blood
was deficient in   ?   . And he still carried,
after five or six years, and though he dressed it in a
mirror night and morning, on his right ischium a running sore of traumatic origin.

Beyond stopping, and laying down his bags, and
picking up his hat, and setting it on his head, and
picking up his bags, and setting himself, after one or
two false starts, again in motion, Watt, faithful to his
rule, took no more notice of this aggression than if it
had been an accident.   This he found was the wisest
attitude, to staunch, if necessary, inconspicuously, with
the little red sudarium that he always carried in his
pocket, the flow of blood, to pick up what had fallen,
and to continue, as soon as possible, on his way, or in
his station, like a victim of mere mischance.   But he
deserved no credit for this.   For it was an attitude
become, with frequent repetition, so part of his being,
that there was no more room in his mind for resentment
at a spit in the eye, to take a simple example, than if
his braces had burst, or a bomb fallen on his bum.

But he had not continued very far when, feeling
weak, he left the crown of the road and sat down on
the path, which was high, and edged with thick neglected grass.   He knew, as he did so, that it would not be
easy to get up again, as he must, and move on again,

as he must. But the feeling of weakness, which he had been expecting for some time, was such, that he yielded to it, and settled himself on the edge of the path, with his hat pushed back, and his bags beside him, and his knees drawn up, and his arms on his knees, and his head on his arms. The parts of the body are really very friendly at such times, towards one another. But this was a position that could not content him long, in the fresh night air, and soon he stretched himself out, so that one half of him was in the road, and the other on the path. Under the neck and under the distant palms he felt the cool damp grasses of the ditch's edge. And so he rested for a little time, listening to the little nightsounds in the hedge behind him, in the hedge outside him, hearing them with pleasure, and other distant nightsounds too, such as dogs make, on bright nights, at the ends of their chains, and bats, with their little wings, and the heavy daybirds changing to a more comfortable position, and the leaves that are never still, until they lie rotting in a wintry heap, and the breath that is never quiet. But this was a position that Watt, after a short time, found himself unable to sustain, and one of the reasons for that was perhaps this, that he felt the moon pouring its now whitening rays upon him, as though he were not there. For if there were two things that Watt disliked, one was the moon, and the other was the sun. So, settling his hat firmly on his head, and reaching forward for his bags, he rolled himself over into the ditch, and lay there, on his face, half buried in the wild long grass, the foxgloves, the hyssop, the pretty nettles, the high pouting hemlock, and other ditch weeds and flowers. And it was to him lying thus that there came, with great distinctness, from afar, from without, yes, really it seemed from without, the voices, indifferent in quality, of a mixed choir (1).

---

(1) What, it may be enquired, was the music of this threne? What at least, it may be demanded, did the soprano sing?

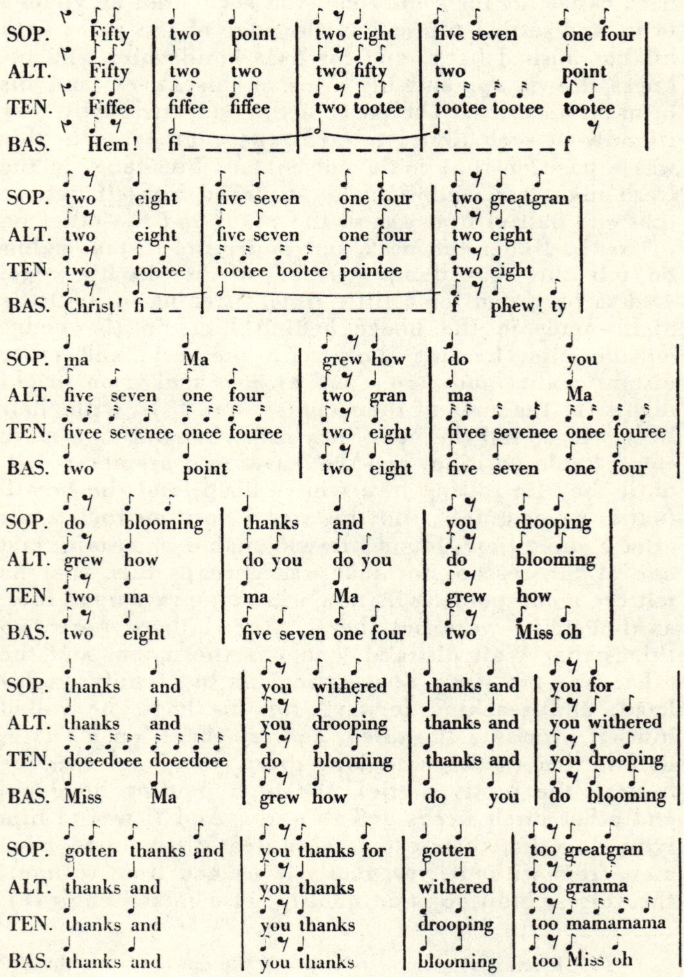
SOP. Fifty | two point | two eight | five seven one four |
ALT. Fifty | two two | two fifty | two point |
TEN. Fiffee | fiffee fiffee | two tootee | tootee tootee tootee |
BAS. Hem! | fi ______ | ______ | ______ f |
SOP. two eight | five seven one four | two greatgran
ALT. two eight | five seven one four | two eight |
TEN. two tootee | tootee tootee pointee | two eight |
BAS. Christ! fi __ | ____________ | f phew! ty |
SOP. ma Ma | grew how | do you |
ALT. five seven one four | two gran | ma Ma |
TEN. fivee sevenee onee fouree | two eight | fivee sevenee onee fouree |
BAS. two point | two eight | five seven one four |
SOP. do blooming | thanks and | you drooping |
ALT. grew how | do you do you | do blooming |
TEN. two ma | ma Ma | grew how |
BAS. two eight | five seven one four | two Miss oh |
SOP. thanks and | you withered | thanks and | you for |
ALT. thanks and | you drooping | thanks and | you withered |
TEN. doeedoee doeedoee | do blooming | thanks and | you drooping |
BAS. Miss Ma | grew how | do you | do blooming |
SOP. gotten thanks and | you thanks for | gotten | too greatgran |
ALT. thanks and | you thanks | withered | too granma |
TEN. thanks and | you thanks | drooping | too mamamama |
BAS. thanks and | you thanks | blooming | too Miss oh |

SOP. ma   Ma   grew   and the

ALT. ma   Ma   grew   and the

TEN. mamamama Mama   grew   and the   sa ------

BAS. Miss   Ma   grew and the   sa ------

SOP. and the   same   to   you

ALT. sa ------ me   to   you

TEN. ------ me   to   you

BAS. ------ me   Jesus!   to   you

This verse was followed by a second:

> *Fifty-one point one*
> *four two eight five seven one*
> *four two eight five seven one*
> *oh a bun a big fat bun*
> *a big fat yellow bun*
> *for Mr Man and a bun*
> *for Mrs Man and a bun*
> *for Master Man and a bun*
> *for Miss Man and a bun*
> *a big fat bun*
> *for everyone*
> *four two eight five seven one*
> *four two eight five seven one*
> *till all the buns are done*
> *and everyone is gone*
> *home to oblivion.*

The singing then ended.

Of these two verses Watt thought he preferred the former. Bun is such a sad word, is it not? And man is not much better, is it?

But by this time Watt was tired of the ditch, which he had been thinking of leaving, when the voices detained him. And one of the reasons why he was tired of the ditch was perhaps this, that the earth, whose contours and peculiar smell the vegetation at first had masked, now he felt it, and smelt it, the bare hard dark stinking earth. And if there were two things that Watt loathed, one was the earth, and the other was the sky. So he crawled out of the ditch, not forgetting his bags, and resumed his journey, with less difficulty than he had feared, at the point where it had been interrupted, by the feeling of weakness. This feeling of weakness Watt had left, together with his evening meal of goat's milk and insufficiently cooked cod, in the ditch, and it was with confidence that he now advanced, in the middle of the road, with confidence and with awe also, for the chimneys of Mr Knott's house were visible at last, in the light, of the moon.

The house was in darkness.

Finding the front door locked, Watt went to the back door. He could not very well ring, or knock, for the house was in darkness.

Finding the back door locked also, Watt returned to the front door.

Finding the front door locked still, Watt returned to the back door.

Finding the back door now open, oh not open wide, but on the latch, as the saying is, Watt was able to enter the house.

Watt was surprised to find the back door, so lately locked, now open. Two explanations of this occurred to him. The first was this, that his science of the locked door, so seldom at fault, had been so on this occasion, and that the back door, when he had found it locked, had not been locked, but open. And the second was this, that the back door, when he had found it locked, had in effect been locked, but had subsequently been opened, from within, or without, by some person, while he Watt had been employed in going, to and fro, from the back door to the front door, and from the front door to the back door.

Of these two explanations Watt thought he preferred the latter, as being the more beautiful. For if someone had opened the back door, from within, or without, would not he Watt have seen a light, or heard a sound? Or had the door been unlocked, from within, in the dark, by some person perfectly familiar with the premises, and wearing carpet slippers, or in his stocking-ed feet? Or, from without, by some person so skilful on his legs, that his footfalls made no sound? Or had a sound been made, a light shown, and Watt not heard the one nor seen the other?

The result of this was that Watt never knew how he got into Mr Knott's house. He knew that he got in by the back door, but he was never to know, never, never to know, how the backdoor came to be opened. And if the backdoor had never opened, but remained shut, then who knows Watt had never got into Mr Knott's house at all, but turned away, and returned to the station, and caught the first train back to town. Unless he had got in through a window.

No sooner had Watt crossed Mr Knott's threshold than he saw that the house was not in such darkness as he had at first supposed, for a light was burning in the kitchen.

When Watt reached this light he sat down beside it, on a chair. He set down his bags beside him, on the beautiful red floor, and he took off his hat, for he had reached his destination, discovering his scant red hair, and laid it on the table beside him. And a pretty picture they made, Watt's scalp and red-grey tufts, and the floor burning up, from below.

Watt saw, in the grate, of the range, the ashes grey. But they turned pale red, when he covered the lamp, with his hat. The range was almost out, but not quite. A handful of dry chips and the flames would spring, merry in appearance, up the chimney, with an organ note. So Watt busied himself a little while, covering the lamp, less and less, more and more, with his hat, watching the ashes greyen, redden, greyen, redden, in the grate, of the range.

Watt was so busy doing this, moving his hat to and fro behind him, that he neither saw, nor heard, the door open and a gentleman come in. So his surprise was extreme, when he looked up from his little game. For it was no more than that, an innocent little game, to while away the time.

Here then was something again that Watt would never know, for want of paying due attention to what was going on about him. Not that it was a knowledge that could be of any help to Watt, or any hurt, or cause him any pleasure, or cause him any pain, for it was not. But he found it strange to think, of these little changes, of scene, the little gains, the little losses, the thing brought, the thing removed, the light given, the light taken, and all the vain offerings to the hour, strange to think of all these little things that cluster round the comings, and the stayings, and the goings, that he would know nothing of them, nothing of what they had been, as long as he lived, nothing of when they came, of how they came, and how it was then, compared with before, nothing of how long they stayed, of how they stayed, and what difference that made, nothing of when they went, of how they went, and how it was then, compared with before, before they came, before they went.

The gentleman wore a fine full apron of green baize. Watt thought he had never seen a finer apron. In front there was a great pocket, or pouch, and in this the gentleman's hands were buried. Watt saw the little movements of the stuff, the little bulgings and crumplings, and the sudden indrawings, where it was nipped, between forefinger and thumb probably, for those are the nippers.

The gentleman gazed long at Watt, and then went away, without a word of explanation. Then Watt, for want of something to do, went back to his

little game, with the colours. But he soon gave over.
And the reason for that was perhaps this, that the
ashes would not redden any more, but remained grey,
even in the dimmest light.

Finding himself now alone, with nothing in
particular to do, Watt put his forefinger in his nose,
first in one nostril, and then in the other. But there
were no crusts in Watt's nose, to-night.

But in a short time the gentleman reappeared,
to Watt. He was dressed for the road, and carried a
stick. But no hat was on his head, nor any bag in
his hand.

Before leaving he made the following short
statement:

Haw! how it all comes back to me, to be sure.
That look! That weary watchful vacancy! The man
arrives! The dark ways all behind, all within, the long
dark ways, in his head, in his side, in his hands and
feet, and he sits in the red gloom, picking his nose,
waiting for the dawn to break. The dawn! The sun!
The light! Haw! The long blue days, for his head,
for his side, and the little paths for his feet, and all
the brightness to touch and gather. Through the grass
the little mosspaths, bony with old roots, and the trees
sticking up, and the flowers sticking up, and the fruit
hanging down, and the white exhausted butterflies, and
the birds never the same darting all day into hiding.
And all the sounds, meaning nothing. Then at night
rest in the quiet house, there are no roads, no streets
any more, you lie down by a window opening on refuge,
the little sounds come that demand nothing, ordain
nothing, explain nothing, propound nothing, and the
short necessary night is soon ended, and the sky blue
again over all the secret places where nobody ever comes,
the secret places never the same, but always simple and
indifferent, always mere places, sites of a stirring beyond
coming and going, of a being so light and free that it
is as the being of nothing. How I feel it all again,

after so long, here, and here, and in my hands, and in my eyes, like a face raised, a face offered, all trust and innocence and candour, all the old soil and fear and weakness offered, to be sponged away and forgiven! Haw! Or did I never feel it till now? Now when there is no warrant? Wouldn't surprise me. All forgiven and healed. For ever. In a moment. To-morrow. Six, five, four hours still, of the old dark, the old burden, lightening, lightening. For one is come, to stay. Haw! All the old ways led to this, all the old windings, the stairs with never a landing that you screw yourself up, clutching the rail, counting the steps, the fever of shortest ways under the long lids of sky, the wild country roads where your dead walk beside you, on the dark shingle the turning for the last time again to the lights of the little town, the appointments kept and the appointments broken, all the delights of urban and rural change of place, all the exitus and redditus, closed and ended. All led to this, to this gloaming where a middleaged man sits masturbating his snout, waiting for the first dawn to break. For of course he is not as yet familiar with the premises. Indeed it is a wonder to him, and will remain so, how having found the neighbourhood he found the gate, and how having found the gate he found the door, and how having found the door he passed beyond it. No matter, he is content. No. Let us not exaggerate. He is well pleased. For he knows he is in the right place, at last. And he knows he is the right man, at last. In another place he would be the wrong man still, and for another man, yes, for another man it would be the wrong place again. But he being what he has become, and the place being what it was made, the fit is perfect. And he knows this. No. Let us remain calm. He feels it. The sensations, the premonitions of harmony are irrefragable, of imminent harmony, when all outside him will be he, the flowers the flowers that he is among him, the sky the sky that he is above him, the earth trodden the earth

treading, and all sound his echo. When in a word he
will be in his midst at last, after so many tedious years
spent clinging to the perimeter. These first impressions,
so hardly won, are undoubtedly delicious. What a
feeling of security! They are transports that few are
spared, nature is so exceedingly accomodating, on the
one hand, and man, on the other. With what sudden
colours past trials and errors glow, seen in their new,
their true perspective, mere stepping-stones to this!
Haw! All is repaid, amply repaid. For he has arrived.
He even ventures to remove his hat, and set down his
bags, without misgiving. Think of that! He removes
his hat without misgiving, he unbuttons his coat and
sits down, proffered all pure and open to the long joys
of being himself, like a basin to a vomit. Oh, not in
idleness. For there is work to do. That is what is so
exquisite. Having oscillated all his life between the
torments of a superficial loitering and the horrors of
disinterested endeavour, he finds himself at last in a
situation where to do nothing exclusively would be an
act of the highest value, and significance. And what
happens ? For the first time, since in anguish and disgust
he relieved his mother of her milk, definite tasks of
unquestionable utility are assigned to him. Is not that
charming? But his regret, his indignation, are of short
duration, disappearing as a rule at the end of the third
or fourth month. Why is this? It is because of the
nature of the work to be performed, because of its
exceptional fruitfulness, because he comes to understand that he is working not merely for Mr Knott in
person, and for Mr Knott's establishment, but also,
and indeed chiefly, for himself, that he may abide, as
he is, where he is, and that where he is may abide
about him, as it is. Unable to resist these intenerating
considerations, his regrets, lively at first, melt at last,
melt quite away and pass over, softly, into the celebrated
conviction that all is well, or at least for the best. His
indignation undergoes a similar reduction, and calm

and glad at last he goes about his work, calm and glad
he peels the potato and empties the nightstool, calm
and glad he witnesses and is witnessed. For a time.
For the day comes when he says, Am I not a little out
of sorts, to-day? Not that he feels out of sorts, on the
contrary, he feels if possible even better disposed than
usual. Haw! He feels if possible even better disposed
than usual and he asks himself if he is not perhaps a
little seedy. The fool! He has learnt nothing. Nothing.
Pardon my vehemence. But that is a terrible day (to
look back on), the day when the horror of what has
happened reduces him to the ignoble expedient of
inspecting his tongue in a mirror, his tongue never so
rosy, in a breath never so sweet. It was a Tuesday
afternoon, in the month of October, a beautiful October
afternoon. I was sitting on the step, in the yard, looking
at the light, on the wall. I was in the sun, and the
wall was in the sun. I was the sun, need I add, and
the wall, and the step, and the yard, and the time
of year, and the time of day, to mention only these.
To be sitting, at so pleasant a conjuncture of one's
courses, in oneself, by oneself, that I think it will freely
be admitted is a way no worse than another, and better
than some, of whiling away an instant of leisure.
Puffing away at the same time at my tobacco-pipe,
which was as flat and broad that afternoon as an
apothecary's slice, I felt my breast swell, like a pelican's
I think it is. For joy? Well', no, perhaps not exactly
for joy. For the change of which I speak had not yet
taken place. Hymeneal still it lay, the thing so soon
to be changed, between me and all the forgotten horrors
of joy. But let us not linger on my breast. Look at
it now — bugger these buttons! — as flat and — ow! —
as hollow as a tambourine. You saw? You heard? No
matter. Where was I? The change. In what did it
consist? It is hard to say. Something slipped. There
I was, warm and bright, smoking my tobacco-pipe,
watching the warm bright wall, when suddenly

somewhere some little thing slipped, some little
tiny thing. Gliss — iss — iss — STOP ! I trust
I make myself clear. There is a great alp of
sand, one hundred metres high, between the pines
and the ocean, and there in the warm moonless night,
when no one is looking, no one listening, in tiny packets
of two or three millions the grains slip, all together,
a little slip of one or two lines maybe, and then stop,
all together, not one missing, and that is all, that is
all for that night, and perhaps for ever that is all, for
in the morning with the sun a little wind from the sea
may come, and blow them one from another far apart,
or a pedestrian scatter them with his foot, though that
is less likely. It was a slip like that I felt, that Tuesday
afternoon, millions of little things moving all together
out of their old place, into a new one nearby, and
furtively, as though it were forbidden. And I have
little doubt that I was the only person living to discover
them. To conclude from this that the incident was
internal would, I think, be rash. For my — how shall
I say? — my personal system was so distended at the
period of which I speak that the distinction between
what was inside it and what was outside it was not at
all easy to draw. Everything that happened happened
inside it, and at the same time everything that happened
happened outside it. I trust I make myself plain. I did
not, need I add, see the thing happen, nor hear it,
but I perceived it with a perception so sensuous that
in comparison the impressions of a man buried alive
in Lisbon on Lisbon's great day seem a frigid and
artificial construction of the understanding. The sun
on the wall, since I was looking at the sun on the wall
at the time, underwent an instantaneous and I venture
to say radical change of appearance. It was the same
sun and the same wall, or so little older that the
difference may safely be disregarded, but so changed
that I felt I had been transported, without my having
remarked it, to some quite different yard, and to some

quite different season, in an unfamiliar country. At the
same time my tobacco-pipe, since I was not eating a
banana, ceased so completely from the solace to which
I was inured, that I took it out of my mouth to make
sure it was not a thermometer, or an epileptic's dental
wedge. And my breast, on which I could almost feel the
feathers stirring, in the charming way breast feathers
have, relapsed into the void and bony concavity which my
dear tutor used to say reminded him of Crécy. For my
spine and sternum have always been concentric, ever
since I was a little nipper. It was then in my distress
that I had the baseness to call to my aid recent costiveness
and want of stomach. But in what did the change
consist? What was changed, and how? What was
changed, if my information is correct, was the sentiment
that a change, other than a change of degree, had taken
place. What was changed was existence off the ladder.
Do not come down the ladder, Ifor, I haf taken it away.
This I am happy to inform you is the reversed meta-
morphosis. The Laurel into Daphne. The old thing
where it always was, back again. As when a man,
having found at last what he sought, a woman, for
example, or a friend, loses it, or realises what it is.
And yet it is useless not to seek, not to want, for when
you cease to seek you start to find, and when you cease
to want, then life begins to ram her fish and chips
down your gullet until you puke, and then the puke
down your gullet until you puke the puke, and
then the puked puke until you begin to like it. The
glutton castaway, the drunkard in the desert, the lecher
in prison, they are the happy ones. To hunger, thirst,
lust, every day afresh and every day in vain, after the
old prog, the old booze, the old whores, that's the
nearest we'll ever get to felicity, the new porch and
the very latest garden. I pass on the tip for what
it is worth. But how did this sentiment arise, that a
change other than a change of degree had taken place?
And to what if to any reality did it correspond? And

to what forces is the credit for its removal to be attributed ? These are questions from which, with patience, it would be an easy matter to extract the next in order, and so descend, so mount, rung by rung, until the night was over. Unfortunately I have information of a practical nature to impart, that is to say a debt to pay, or a score to settle, before I depart. So I shall merely state, without enquiring how it came, or how it went, that in my opinion it was not an illusion, as long as it lasted, that presence of what did not exist, that presence without, that presence within, that presence between, though I'll be buggered if I can understand how it could have been anything else. But that and the rest, haw! the rest, you will decide for yourself, when your time comes. or rather you will leave undecided, to judge by the look of you. For do not imagine me to suggest that what has happened to me, what is happening to me, will ever happen to you, or that what is happening to you, what will happen to you, has ever happened to me, or rather, if it will, if it has, that there is any great chance of its being admitted. For in truth the same things happen to us all, especially to men in our situation, whatever that is, if only we chose to know it.

But I am worse than Mr Ash, a man I once knew to nod to. One evening I ran into him on Westminster Bridge. It was blowing heavily. It was also snowing heavily. I nodded, heavily. In vain. Securing me with one hand. he removed from the other with his mouth two pairs of leather gauntlets, unwound his heavy woollen muffler, unbuttoned successively and flung aside his great coat, jerkin, coat, two waistcoats, shirt, outer and inner vests, coaxed from a washleather fob hanging in company with a crucifix I imagine from his neck a gunmetal half-hunter. sprang open its case. held it to his eyes (night was falling). recovered in a series of converse operations his original form, said, Seventeen minutes past five exactly, as God is my witness, remember me to your wife (I never had one), let go my arm, raised his hat and hastened away. A moment later Big Ben (is that the name?) struck six. This in my opinion is the type of all information whatsoever, be it voluntary or solicited. If you want a stone, ask a turnover. If you want a turnover, ask plumpudding. This Ash was what I believe is still called an Admiralty Clerk of the Second Class and with that a sterling fellow. Such vermin pullulate. He died of premature exhaustion, the following week, oiled and houseled, leaving his half-hunter to his house-plumber. Personally of course I regret everything. Not a word, not a deed, not a thought, not a need, not a grief, not a joy, not a girl, not a boy, not a doubt, nor a trust, not a scorn, not a lust, not a hope, not a fear, not a smile, not a tear, not a name, not a face, no time, no place, that I do not regret, exceedingly. An ordure, from beginning to end. And yet, when I sat for Fellowship, but for the boil on my bottom... The rest, an ordure. The Tuesday scowls, the Wednesday growls, the Thursday curses, the Friday howls, the Saturday snores, the Sunday yawns, the Monday morns, the Monday morns. The whacks, the moans, the cracks, the groans, the welts, the squeaks, the belts, the shrieks, the pricks, the prayers, the kicks, the tears, the skelps, and the yelps. And the poor old lousy old earth, my earth and my father's and my mother's and my father's father's and my mother's mother's and my father's mother's and my mother's father's and my father's mother's father's and my mother's father's mother's and my father's mother's mother's and my mother's father's father's and my father's father's mother's and my mother's mother's father's and my father's father's father's and my mother's mother's mother's and other people's fathers' and mothers' and fathers' fathers' and mothers' mothers' and fathers' mothers' and mothers' fathers' and fathers' mothers' fathers' and

mothers' fathers' mothers' and fathers' mothers'
mothers' and mothers' fathers' fathers' and fathers'
fathers' mothers' and mothers' mothers' fathers' and
fathers' fathers' fathers' and mothers' mothers' mothers'.
An excrement. The crocuses and the larch turning
green every year a week before the others and the
pastures red with uneaten sheep's placentas and the long
summer days and the newmown hay and the wood-
pigeon in the morning and the cuckoo in the afternoon
and the corncrake in the evening and the wasps in the
jam and the smell of the gorse and the look of the
gorse and the apples falling and the children walking
in the dead leaves and the larch turning brown a week
before the others and the chestnuts falling and the
howling winds and the sea breaking over the pier and
the first fires and the hooves on the road and the
consumptive postman whistling *The Roses Are Blooming
in Picardy* and the standard oillamp and of course
the snow and to be sure the sleet and bless your heart
the slush and every fourth year the February débâcle
and the endless April showers and the crocuses and then
the whole bloody business starting all over again. A turd.
And if I could begin it all over again, knowing what
I know now, the result would be the same. And if I
could begin again a third time, knowing what I would
know then, the result would be the same. And if I could
begin it all over again a hundred times, knowing each
time a little more than the time before, the result
would always be the same, and the hundredth life as
the first, and the hundred lives as one. A cat's flux.
But at this rate we shall be here all night.

> *We shall be here all night,*
> *Be here all night shall we,*
> *All night we shall be here,*
> *Here all night we shall be.*
> *One dark, one still, one breath,*
> *Night here, here we, we night,*

One fleeing, fleeing to rest,
One resting on the flight.

Haw! You heard that one? A beauty. Haw! Hell!
Haw! So. Haw! Haw! Haw! My laugh, Mr — ?
I beg your pardon. Like Tyler? Haw! My laugh,
Mr Watt. Christian name, forgotten. Yes. Of all the
laughs that strictly speaking are not laughs, but modes
of ululation, only three I think need detain us, I mean
the bitter, the hollow and the mirthless. They correspond to successive, how shall I say successive...
suc...successive excoriations of the understanding, and
the passage from the one to the other is the passage
from the lesser to the greater, from the lower to the
higher, from the outer to the inner, from the gross
to the fine, from the matter to the form. The laugh
that now is mirthless once was hollow, the laugh that
once was hollow once was bitter. And the laugh that
once was bitter? Eyewater, Mr Watt, eyewater. But
do not let us waste our time with that, do not let us
waste *any more time* with that, Mr Watt. No. Where
were we. The bitter, the hollow and — Haw! Haw! —
the mirthless. The bitter laugh laughs at that which
is not good, it is the ethical laugh. The hollow laugh
laughs at that which is not true, it is the intellectual
laugh. Not good! Not true! Well well. But the
mirthless laugh is the dianoetic laugh, down the snout
— Haw! — so. It is the laugh of laughs, the *risus*
purus, the laugh laughing at the laugh, the beholding,
the saluting of the highest joke, in a word the laugh
that laughs — silence please — at that which is unhappy.
Personally of course I regret all. All, all, all. Not a
word, not a—. But have I not been over that already?
I have? Then let me speak rather of my present
feeling, which so closely resembles the feeling of sorrow,
so closely that I can scarcely distinguish between them.
Yes. When I think that this hour is my last on earth
on Mr Knott's premises, where I have spent so many

hours, so many happy hours, so many unhappy hours,
and — worst of all — so many hours that were neither
happy nor unhappy, and that before the cock crows, or
at very latest very little later, my weary little legs
must be carrying me as best they may away, my trunk
that is wearier still and my head that is weariest of all,
away far away from this state or place on which my
hopes so long were fixed, as fast as they can move in
and out the weary little fat bottom and belly away,
and the shrunk chest, and the poor little fat bald
head feeling as though it were falling off, faster and
faster through the grey air and further and further
away, in any one no matter which of the three hundred
and sixty directions open to a desperate man of average
agility, and often I turn, tears blinding my eyes, Haw!
without however pausing in my career (no easy matter),
perhaps longing to be turned into a stone pillar or a
cromlech in the middle of a field or on the mountain
side for succeeding generations to admire, and for cows
and horses and sheep and goats to come and scratch
themselves against and for men and dogs to make their
water against and for learned men to speculate regarding
and for disappointed men to inscribe with party slogans
and indelicate graffiti and for lovers to scratch their
names on, in a heart, with the date, and for now and
then a lonely man like myself to sit down with his back
against and fall asleep, in the sun, if the sun happened
to be shining. And consequently I feel a feeling that
closely resembles in every particular the feeling of
sorrow, sorrow for what has been, is and is to come,
as far as I personally am concerned, for with the
troubles and difficulties of other people I am in no
fit state for the time being to trouble my head, which
begins to feel as though it were falling off, than which
I think it will be readily allowed that for the intellectual
type of chap, Haw! like me few sensations can be
more painful, just as for the luxurious type of fellow
it would be the feeling of his private parts on the point

of falling off that would very likely be the most
worrying, and so on for the various other different
types of men. Yes, these moments together have changed
us, your moments and my moments, so that we are
not only no longer the same now as when they began
— ticktick! ticktick! — to elapse, but we know that
we are no longer the same, and not only know that
we are no longer the same, but know in what we are no
longer the same, you wiser but not sadder, and I sadder
but not wiser, for wiser I could hardly become without
grave personal inconvenience, whereas sorrow is a thing
you can keep on adding to all your life long, is it not,
like a stamp or egg collection, without feeling very
much the worse for it, is it not. Now when one man
takes the place of another man, then it is perhaps of
assistance to him who takes the place to know something of him whose place he takes, though to be
sure at the same time on the other hand the
inverse is not necessarily true, I mean that he
whose place is taken can hardly be expected
to feel any great curiosity about him who takes his
place. This interesting relation is I regret often
established by procuration. Consider for example the
increeping and outbouncing house and parlour maids
(I say house and parlour maids, but you know what
I mean), the latter having bounced out before the former
crept in, in such a way as to exclude all possibility of
encounter whether on the drive or on the way to and
from the tram-stop, bus-stop, railway-station, cabrank,
taxi-stand, bar parlour or canal. Now let the name of
the former of these two women be Mary, and that of
the latter Ann, or, better still, that of the former Ann
and that of the latter Mary, and let there exist a third
person, the mistress, or the master, for without some
such superior existence the existence of the house and
parlour maid, whether on the way to the house and
parlour, or on the way from the house and parlour, or
motionless in the house and parlour, is hardly con-

ceivable.   Then this third person, on whose existence
the existences of Ann and Mary depend, and whose
existence also in a sense if you like depends on the
existences of Ann and Mary, says to Mary, no, says to
Ann, for by this time Mary is afar off, in the tram,
the bus, the train, the cab, the taxi, the bar parlour
or canal, says to Ann, Jane, in the morning when Mary
had finished doing this, if Mary may be said to have ever
finished doing anything, then she began to do this, that
is to say she settled herself firmly in a comfortable semi-
upright posture before the task to be performed and
remained there quietly eating onions and peppermints
turn and turn about, I mean first an onion, then a
peppermint, then another onion, then another peppermint, then another onion, then another peppermint,
then another onion, then another peppermint, then
another onion, then another peppermint, then another
onion, then another peppermint, then another onion,
then another peppermint, then another onion, then
another peppermint, then another onion, then another
peppermint, and so on, while little by little the reason
for her presence in that place faded from her mind, as
with the dawn the figments of the id, and the duster,
whose burden up till now she had so bravely born,
fell from her fingers, to the dust, where having at once
assumed the colour (grey) of its surroundings it
disappeared until the following Spring.   An average of
anything from twenty-six to twenty-seven splendid
woollen dusters per mensem were lost in this way by
our Mary during her last year of service in this unfortunate house.   Now what, it may well be asked, can
the fancies have been that so ravished Mary from a
sense of her situation?   Dreams of less work and higher
wages?   Erotic cravings?   Recollections of childhood?
Menopausal discomfort?   Grief for a loved one defunct
or departed for an unknown destination ?   Daltonic
visualisations of the morning paper's racing programme?
Prayers for a soul?   She was not a woman to confide.

And indeed I think I am correct in saying that she
was opposed to conversation on principle as such.
Whole days, and even entire weeks, would glide away
without Mary's having opened her gob for any purpose
other than the reception of her five fingers fastened
firmly on a fragment of food, for to the spoon, the
knife, and even the fork, considered as aids to ingestion,
she had never been able to accustom herself, in spite
of excellent references. Her appetite, on the other hand,
was quite exceptional. Not that the food absorbed by
Mary, over a given period, was greater in mass, or
richer in vitamens, than the normal healthy person's
allowance for the same time. No. But her appetite
was exceptional in this, that it knew no remission. The
ordinary person eats a meal, then rests from eating
for a space, then eats again, then rests again, then eats
again, then rests again, then eats again, then rests
again, then eats again, then rests again, then eats again,
then rests again, then eats again, then rests again, and
in this way, now eating, and now resting from eating,
he deals with the difficult problem of hunger, and indeed
I think I may add thirst, to the best of his ability and
according to the state of his fortune. Let him be a
small eater, a moderate eater, a heavy eater, a vegetarian,
a naturist, a cannibal, a coprophile, let him look
forward to his eating with pleasure or back on it with
regret or both, let him eliminate well or let him eliminate
ill, let him eructate, vomit, break wind or in other
ways fail or scorn to contain himself as a result of an
ill-adapted diet, congenital affliction or faulty training
during the impressionable years, let him, Jane, I say,
be one or more or all or more than all of these, or let
him on the other hand be none of these, but something
quite different, as would be the case for example if he
were on hunger strike or in a catatonic stupor or obliged
for some reason best known to his medical advisers to
turn for his sustenance to the clyster, the fact remains,
and can hardly be denied, that he proceeds by what we

call meals, whether taken voluntarily or involuntarily, with pleasure or pain, successfully or unsuccessfully, through the mouth, the nose, the pores, the feedtube or in an upward direction with the aid of a piston from behind is not of the slightest importance, and that between these acts of nutrition, without which life as it is generally understood would be hard set to continue, there intervene periods of rest or repose, during which no food is taken, unless it be every now and then from time to time an occasional snack, quick drink or light collation, rendered if not indispensable at least welcome by an unforeseen acceleration of the metabolic exchanges due to circumstances of an imprevisible kind, as for example the backing of a loser, the birth of a child, the payment of a debt, the recovery of a loan, the voice of conscience, or any other shock to the great sympathetic, causing a sudden rush of chyme, or chile, or both, to the semidigested slowly surely earthward struggling mass of sherrywine, soup, beer, fish, stout, meat, beer, vegetables, sweet, fruit, cheese, stout, anchovy, beer, coffee and benedictine, for example, swallowed lightheartedly but a few short hours before to the strains as likely as not of a piano and cello. Whereas Mary ate all day long, that is to say from early dawn, or at least from the hour at which she woke, which to judge from the hour at which she rose, or rather at which she first appeared in the bowels of this unhappy home, was in no way premature, to late at night, for she retired to rest with great punctuality every evening at eight o'clock, leaving the dinner things on the table, and fell at once into an exhausted sleep, if her snores, of which as I have often been heard to remark I never heard the like, were not simulated, which I for my part will never believe, seeing as how they continued with undiminished sonority all night long, from which I may add I am inclined to suspect that Mary, like so many women, slept on the flat of her back, a dangerous and detestable practice in my opinion, though I know there are times when it is

difficult, not to say impossible, to do otherwise. Ahem!
Now when I say that Mary ate all day, from her opening
her eyes in the morning to her closing them at night,
in sleep, I mean that at no moment during this period
was Mary's mouth more than half empty, or, if you prefer,
less than half full, for to the habit generally received
of finishing one mouthful before initiating the next Mary
had never, notwithstanding her remarkable papers, been
able to adapt herself. Now when I say that at no moment
of Mary's waking hours was Mary's mouth more than
half empty, or less than half full, I do not mean that
it was always so, for on close and even on casual
inspection it would have been found, nine times out of
ten, full to overflowing, which goes far towards explaining Mary's indifference to the pleasures of conversation.
Now when speaking of Mary's mouth I make use of the
expression full to overflowing, I do not merely mean to
say that it was so full, nine tenths of the time, that it
threatened to overflow, but in my thought I go further
and I assert, without fear of contradiction, that it was
so full, nine tenths of the time, that it did overflow, all
over this ill-fated interior, and traces of this exuberance,
in the form of partially masticated morcels of meat,
fruit, bread, vegetables,nuts and pastry I have frequently
found in places as remote in space, and distinct in
purpose, as the coal-hole, the conservatory, the American
Bar, the oratory, the cellar, the attic, the dairy and, I
say it with shame, the servants' W.C., where a greater
part of Mary's time was spent than seemed compatible
with a satisfactory, or even tolerable, condition of the
digestive apparatus, unless we are to suppose that she
retired to that place in search of a little fresh air, rest
and quiet, for a woman more attached to rest and quiet
I have never, I say it without fear of exaggeration, known
or even heard of. But to return to where we left her, I
see her still, propped up in a kind of stupor against one
of the walls in which this wretched edifice abounds, her
long grey greasy hair framing in its cowl of scrofulous

mats a face where pallor, languor, hunger, acne, recent dirt, immemorial chagrin and surplus hair seemed to dispute the mastery.   Flitters of perforated starch entwine an ear. Under the rusty cotton frock, plentifully embossed with scabs of slobber, two cuplike depressions mark the place of the bosom and a conical protuberance that of the abdomen. Between on the one hand a large pouch or bag, containing the forenoon's supplies, cunningly dissimulated in the tattered skirt, and on the other Mary's mouth, Mary's hands flash to and fro, with a regularity that I do not hesitate to compare with that of piston-rods. At the moment that the one hand presses, with open palm, between the indefatigable jaws, a cold potato, onion, tart or sandwich, the other darts into the pouch and there, unerringly, fastens on a sandwich, onion, tart or cold potato, as Mary wills.   And the former, on its way down to be filled, meets the latter on its way up to be emptied, at a point equidistant from their points of departure, or arrival. And save for the flying arms, and champing mouth, and swallowing throat, not a muscle of Mary stirs, and over all the dreaming face, which may strike you, Jane, as strange, but, believe me, Jane, I invent nothing. Now with regard to Mary's limbs, ahem, of which I think I am correct in saying that no mention has yet been made, winter and summer... Winter and summer. And so on. Summer! When I lie dying, Mr Watt, behind the red screen, you know, perhaps that is the word that will sound, summer, and the words for summer things. Not that I ever much cared for them. But some call for the priest, and others for the long days when the sun was a burden. It was summer when I landed here. And now I shall finish and you will hear my voice no more, unless we meet again elsewhere, which considering the probable state of our health is not likely. For then I shall rise, no, I am not seated, then I shall go, just as I am, in the things I stand up in, if you can call this standing up, with not so much as a toothbrush in my pocket to brush my tooth with, morning and evening, or a penny in my purse to buy me a bun in the heat of noonday, without a hope, a friend, a plan, a prospect or a hat to my head to take off to the kind ladies and gentlemen, and make my way as best I may down the path to the gate, for the last time, in the grey of the morning, and pass out with a nod on the hard road and up on the hard path and so go, putting my better foot foremore to the best of my abilities, and the dusty uncut privet brushing my cheek, and so on, and on, hotter and hotter, weaker and weaker, until someone takes pity on me, or God has mercy on me, or better still both, or failing these I fall unable to rise by the way and am taken into custody black with flies by a passing man in blue, leaving you here in my place, with before you all I have behind me, and all I have before me, haw! all I have before me. It was summer. There were three men in the house: the master, whom as you well know we call Mr Knott; a senior retainer named Vincent, I believe; and a junior, only in the sense that he was of more recent acquisition, named, if I am not mistaken, Walter. The first is here, in his bed, or at least in his room. But the second, I mean Vincent, is not here any more, and the reason for that is this, that when I came in he went out. But the third, I mean Walter, is not here any more either, and the reason for that is this, that when Erskine came in he went out, just as Vincent went out when I came in. And I, I mean Arsene, am not here any more either, and the reason for that is this, that when you came in I went out, just as when I came in Vincent went out and as Walter went out when Erskine came in. But Erskine, I mean the second last to come and the next to go, Erskine is here still, sleeping and little dreaming what the new day holds in store, I mean promotion and a new face and the end in sight. But another evening shall come and the light die away out of the sky and the colour from the earth—

Now the day is over,
Night is drawing nigh—igh,
Shadows of the evening
Steal across the sky—

haw! I began a little low perhaps, and the door open
on the wind or the rain or the sleet or the hail or the
snow or the slush or the storm or the warm still scents
of summer or the still of the ice or the earth awakening
or the hush of harvest or the leaves falling through the
dark from various altitudes, never two coming to earth
at the same time, then bowling red and brown and
yellow and grey briskly for an instant, yes, through the
dark, for an instant, then running together in heaps,
here a heap, and there a heap, to be paddled in by
happy boys and girls on their way home from school
looking forward to Hallow's E'en and Guy Fawkes and
Christmas and the New Year, haw! yes, happy girls
and boys looking forward to the happy New Year, and
then perhaps carted off in old barrows and used as
dung the following spring by the poor, and a man come,
shutting the door behind him, and Erskine go. And then
another night fall and another man come and Watt go,
Watt who is now come, for the coming is in the shadow
of the going and the going is in the shadow of the coming, that is the annoying part about it. And yet there
is one who neither comes nor goes, I refer I need hardly
say to my late employer, but seems to abide in his place,
for the time being at any rate, like an oak, an elm, a
beech or an ash, to mention only the oak, the elm, the
beech and the ash, and we nest a little while in his
branches. Yet come he did once, otherwise how would
he be here, and go sooner or later I suppose he must,
though you wouldn't think it to look at him. But
appearances are often deceptive as my poor old mother,
heaving a sigh, used to say to my poor old father (for
I am not illegitimate) in my hearing (for they always
spoke freely before me), a sentiment to which I can still

hear my poor old father, with a sigh, assent, saying,
Thanks be to God, an opinion in which in tones that
haunt me still my poor old mother would acquiesce,
sighing, saying, Amen. Or is there a coming that is
not a coming to, a going that is not a going from, a
shadow that is not the shadow of purpose, or not? For
what is this shadow of the going in which we come, this
shadow of the coming in which we go, this shadow of
the coming and the going in which we wait, if not the
shadow of purpose, of the purpose that budding
withers, that withering buds, whose blooming is a
budding withering? I speak well, do I not, for a man in
my situation? And what is this coming that was not our
coming and this being that is not our being and this
going that will not be our going but the coming and being
and going in purposelessness? And though in purposelessness I may seem now to go, yet I do not, any more
than in purposelessness then I came, for I go now with
my purpose as with it then I came, the only difference
being this, that then it was living and now it is dead,
which is what you might call what I think the English
call six of one and half a dozen of the other, do they not,
might you not? Or do I confuse them with the Irish?
But to return to Vincent and Walter, they were very
much your heighth, breadth and width, that is to say
big bony shabby seedy haggard knockkneed men, with
rotten teeth and big red noses, the result of too much
solitude they used to say, just as I am very much
Erskine's and Erskine very much mine, that is to say
little fat shabby seedy juicy or oily bandylegged men,
with a little fat bottom sticking out in front and a little
fat belly sticking out behind, for what would a little
fat bottom sticking out in front be without a little fat
belly sticking out behind? For though it is rumoured
that Knott would prefer to have no one at all about him,
to look after him, yet since he is obliged to have someone
at all about him, to look after him, being quite incapable
of looking after himself, then the suggestion is that what

he likes best is the minimum number of small fat shabby
seedy juicy bandylegged potbellied potbottomed men
about him, to look after him, or, failing this, the fewest
possible big bony seedy shabby haggard knockkneed
rottentoothed rednosed men about him, to take care of
him, though at the same time it is freely hinted that
in default of either of these he would be perfectly
content to have men of quite a different stamp or mould
about him, as unlike physically you and Vincent and
Walter as Erskine and me, if that is conceivable, to
fuss over him, as long as they were seedy and shabby
and few in number, for to seediness and shabbiness
and fewness in number he is greatly attached, if he can
be said to be greatly attached to anything, though I
have heard it confidently asserted that if he could not
have seediness and shabbiness and fewness in number
he would be only too delighted to do without them,
about him, to make much of him. But that he has
never had any but on the one hand big bony seedy
shabby haggard knockkneed rottentoothed rednosed
men like you and on the other small fat seedy shabby
juicy or oily bandylegged potbellied potbottomed men
like me, about him, to attend to him, seems certain,
unless it be so long ago that all trace of them is lost.
For Vincent and Walter were not the first, ho no, but
before them were Vincent and another whose name I
forget, and before them that other whose name I forget
and another whose name I also forget, and before them
that other whose name I also forget and another whose
name I never knew, and before them that other whose
name I never knew and another whose name Walter
could not recall, and before them that other whose
name Walter could not recall and another whose name
Walter could not recall either, and before them that
other whose name Walter could not recall either and
another whose name Walter never knew, and before them
that other whose name Walter never knew and another
whose name even Vincent could not call to mind, and

before them that other whose name even Vincent could
not call to mind and another whose name even Vincent
could not call to mind either, and before them that
other whose name even Vincent could not call to mind
either and another whose name even Vincent never
knew, and so on, until all trace is lost, owing to the
shortness of human memory, one always ousting the
other, though perhaps ousting is not the word, just
as you ousted me, and Erskine Walter, and I Vincent,
and Walter that other whose name I forget, and Vincent
that other whose name I also forget, and that other
whose name I forget that other whose name I never
knew, and that other whose name I also forget that
other whose name Walter could not recall, and that
other whose name I never knew that other whose name
Walter could not recall either, and that other whose
name Walter could not recall that other whose name
Walter never knew, and that other whose name Walter
could not recall either that other whose name even
Vincent could not call to mind, and that other whose
name Walter never knew that other whose name even
Vincent could not call to mind either, and that other
whose name even Vincent could not call to mind that
other whose name even Vincent never knew, and so
on, until all trace is lost, on account of the vanity of
human wishes. But that all those of whom all trace
is not lost, even though their names be forgotten, were,
if not big, bony, seedy, shabby, haggard, knockkneed,
rottentoothed and rednosed, at least small, fat, seedy,
shabby, oily, bandylegged, potbellied and potbottomed,
seems certain, if any reliance is to be placed on oral
tradition as handed down by word of mouth from one
fleeting generation to the next, or, as is more usual, to
the next but one. This, if it does not prove beyond
all manner of doubt that of all those of whom all trace
is lost not one was a body quite different from us,
does tend to support the hypothesis so often emitted
that there is something about Mr Knott that draws

towards him, to be about him and take care of him, two
types of men, and two only, on the one hand the big
bony seedy shabby haggard knockkneed type, with the
decayed teeth and the big red nose, and on the other
the small fat seedy shabby oily or juicy bandylegged
type, with the little fat bottom and belly sticking out
in opposite directions, or, alternatively, that there is
something in these two types of men that draw them
to Mr Knott, to be about him and watch over him,
though at the same time it is quite possible that if we
were in a position to examine the skeleton of one of
those of whom not only the name but all trace is
lost, of him for example whose name even that other
whose name even Vincent (if that was his name) never
knew never knew, we might find him to have been quite
a different type of chap, neither big nor small, bony nor
fat, seedy nor shabby, haggard nor juicy, rottentoothed
nor potbellied, rednosed nor potbottomed, quite quite
possible, if not quite quite probable. Now though I knew
at the outset that I should not have the time to go into
these matters as fully as I should wish, or they deserve,
yet I felt, perhaps wrongly, that it was my duty to
mention them, if only in order for you clearly to understand that about Mr Knott, attentive to his wants, if
speaking of Mr Knott one may speak of wants, two
men and so far as we know never more and never fewer
have always been to be found, and that of these two
it is not always necessary, as far as we can judge, that
one should be bony and so on, and the other fat and
so forth, as is now the case with you and Arsene, forgive
me, with you and Erskine, for both may be bony and
so on, as was the case with Vincent and Walter, or
both may be fat and so forth, as was the case with
Erskine and me, but that it is necessary, as far as can
be ascertained, that of these two men for ever about
Mr Knott in tireless assiduity turning, the one or the
other or both should be either bony and so on or fat
and so forth, though if we could go back in pure time

as easily as we can in pure space the possibility, if not
the probability, is not excluded of our finding two or
less than two or even more than two men or women or
men and women as little bony and so on as fat and so
forth eternally turning about Mr Knott in tireless love.
But to go into this matter as longly and as deeply and
as fully as I should like, and it deserves, is unfortunately
out of the question. Not that space is wanting, for
space is not wanting. Not that time is lacking, for time
is not lacking. But I hear a little wind come and go,
come and go, in the bushes without, and in the henhouse
the cock in his sleep uneasily stirs. And I think I
have said enough to light that fire in your mind that
shall never be snuffed, or only with the utmost difficulty, just as Vincent did for me, and Walter for
Erskine, and as you perhaps will do for another, though
that is not certain, to judge by the look of you. Not
that I have told you all I know, for I have not, being
now a good-natured man, and of good will what is
more, and indulgent towards the dreams of middle age,
which were my dreams, just as Vincent did not tell
me all, nor Walter Erskine, nor the others the others,
for here we all seem to end by being good-natured
men, and of good will, and indulgent towards the
dreams of middle age, which were our dreams, whatever
may escape us now and then in the way of bitter and
I blush to say even blasphemous words and expressions,
and perhaps also because what we know partakes in
no small measure of the nature of what has so happily
been called the unutterable or ineffable, so that any
attempt to utter or eff it is doomed to fail, doomed,
doomed to fail. Why even I myself, strolling all alone
in some hard earned suspension of labour in this charming garden, have tried and tried to formulate this
delicious haw! and I may add quite useless wisdom so
dearly won, and with which I am so to speak from the
crown of my head to the soles of my feet imbued, so
that I neither eat nor drink nor breathe in and out nor

do my doodles but more sagaciously than before, like Theseus kissing Ariadne, or Ariadne Theseus, towards the end, on the seashore, and tried in vain, notwithstanding the beauties of the scene, bower and sward, glade and arbour, sunshine and shadow, and the pleasant dawdling motion carrying me about in the midst of them, hither and thither, with unparalleled sagacity. But what I could say, or at least a part, and I trust not the least diverting, I think I have said, and as far as it lay in my power to take you, under the circumstances, I think I have taken you, all things considered. And now for a little along the way that lies between you and me Erskine will go by your side, to be your guide, and then for the rest you will travel alone, or with only shades to keep you company, and that I think you will find, if your experience at all resembles mine, the best part of the outing or at least the least dull, even though the light falls fast, and far below the stumbling feet. Now for what I have said ill and for what I have said well and for what I have not said, I ask you to forgive me. And for what I have done ill and for what I have done well and for what I have left undone, I ask you also to forgive me. And I ask you to think of me always — bugger these buttons — with forgiveness, as you desire to be thought of with forgiveness, though personally of course it is all the same to me whether I am thought of with forgiveness, or with rancour, or not at all. Goodnight.

But he had not been long gone when he appeared again, to Watt. He stood sideways in the kitchen doorway, looking at Watt, and Watt saw the housedoor open behind him and the dark bushes and above them at a great distance something that he thought was perhaps the day again already. And as Watt fixed his eyes on what he thought was perhaps the day again already, the man standing sideways in the kitchen doorway looking at him became two men standing sideways in two kitchen doorways looking at him. But

II

Mr Knott was a good master, in a way.

Watt had no direct dealings with Mr Knott, at this period. Not that Watt was ever to have any direct dealings with Mr Knott, for he was not. But he thought, at this period, that the time would come when he would have direct dealings with Mr Knott, on the first floor. Yes, he thought that time would come for him, as he had thought it had ended for Arsene, and for Erskine just begun.

For the moment all Watt's work was on the ground floor. Even the first floor slops that he emptied, it was Erskine who carried them down, every morning, in a pail. The first floor slops could have been emptied, quite as conveniently, if not more conveniently, and the pail rinsed, on the first floor, but they never were, for reasons that are not known. It is true that Watt had instructions to empty these slops, not in the way that slops are usually emptied, no, but in the garden, before sunrise, or after sunset, on the violet bed in violet time, and on the pansy bed in pansy time, and on the rose bed in rose time, and on the celery banks in celery time, and on the seakale pits in seakale time, and in the tomato house in tomato time, and so on, always in the garden, in the flower garden, and in the vegetable garden, and in the fruit garden, on some young growing thirsty thing at the moment of its most need, except of course in time of frost, or when the snow was on the ground, or when the water was on the ground. Then his instructions were to empty the slops on the dunghill.

But Watt was not so foolish as to suppose that this was the real reason why Mr Knott's slops were not emptied away on the first floor, as they could so easily have been. This was merely the reason offered to the understanding.

It was remarkable that no such instructions existed touching the second floor slops, that is to say, Watt's slops, and Erskine's slops. These, when they had been carried down, Erskine's by Erskine, and Watt's by Watt, Watt was free to dispose of as he pleased. But he was given nevertheless to understand that their commixture with those of the first floor, if not formally forbidden, was not encouraged.

So Watt saw little of Mr Knott. For Mr Knott was seldom on the ground floor, unless it was to eat a meal, in the dining-room, or to pass through it, on his way to and from the garden. And Watt was seldom on the first floor, unless it was when he came down to begin his day, in the morning, and then again at evening, when he went up, to begin his night.

Even in the dining-room Watt did not see Mr Knott, although Watt was responsible for the dining-room, and for the service there of Mr Knott's meals. The reasons for this may appear when the time comes to treat of that complex and delicate matter, Mr Knott's food.

This is not to say that Watt never saw Mr Knott at this period, for he did, to be sure. He saw him from time to time, passing through the ground floor on his way to the garden from his quarters on the first floor, and on his way back from the garden to his quarters, and he saw him also in the garden itself. But these rare appearances of Mr Knott, and the strange impression they made on Watt, will be described please God at greater length, at another time.

Callers were few. Tradesmen called, of course, and beggars, and hawkers. The postman, a charming man, called Severn, a great dancer and lover of greyhounds, seldom called. But he did sometimes, always in the evening, with his light eager step and his dog by his side, to deliver a bill, or a begging letter.

The telephone seldom rang, and when it did it was about some indifferent matter touching the plumbing, or the roof, or the food supplies, that Erskine could deal with, or even Watt, without troubling their master.

Mr Knott saw nobody, heard from nobody, as far as Watt could see. But Watt was not so foolish as to draw any conclusion from this.

But these fleeting acknowledgements of Mr Knott's establishment, like little splashes on it from the outer world, and without which it would have been hard set to keep going, will it is to be hoped be considered in greater detail, later on, and how some were of moment to Watt, and how some were of none. In particular the appearance of the gardener, a Mr Graves, at the backdoor, twice and even three times every day, should be gone into with the utmost care, though there is little likelihood of its shedding any light on Mr Knott, or on Watt, or on Mr Graves.

But even there where there was no light for Watt, where there is none for his mouthpiece, there may be light for others. Or was there perhaps some light for Watt, on Mr Knott, on Watt, in such relations as those with Mr Graves, or with the fishwoman, that he left unspoken. That is by no means impossible.

Mr Knott never left the grounds, as far as Watt could judge. Watt thought it unlikely that Mr Knott could leave the grounds, without it's coming to his notice. But he did not reject the possibility of Mr Knott's leaving the grounds, without his being any the wiser. But the unlikelihood, on the one hand of Mr Knott's leaving the grounds, and on the other of his doing so without exciting the general comment, seemed very great, to Watt.

On only one occasion, during Watt's period of service on the ground floor, was the threshold crossed by a stranger, by other feet that is than Mr Knott's, or Erskine's, or Watt's, for all were strangers to Mr Knott's establishment, as far as Watt could see, with the exception of Mr Knott himself, and his personnel at any given moment.

This fugitive penetration took place shortly after Watt's arrival. On his answering the door, as his habit was, when there was a knock at the door, he found standing before it, or so he realized later, arm in arm, an old man and a middleaged man. The latter said:

We are the Galls, father and son, and we are come, what is more, all the way from town, to choon the piano.

They were two, and they stood, arm in arm, in this way, because the father was blind, like so many members of his profession. For if the father had not been blind, then he would not have needed his son to hold his arm, and guide him on his rounds, no, but he would have set his son free, to go about his own business. So Watt supposed, though there was nothing in the father's face to show that he was blind, nor in his attitude either, except that he leaned on his son in a way expressive of a great need of support. But he might have done this, if he had been halt, or merely tired, on account of his great age. There was no family likeness between the two, as far as Watt could make out, and nevertheless he knew that he was in the

presence of a father and son, for had he not just been
told so. Or were they not perhaps merely stepfather
and stepson. We are the Galls, stepfather and stepson
— those were perhaps the words that should have been
spoken. But it was natural to prefer the others. Not
that they could not very well be a true father and son,
without resembling each other in the very least, for
they could.

How very fortunate for Mr Gall, said Watt, that
he has his son at his command, whose manner is all
devotion and whose mere presence, when he might
obviously be earning an honest penny elsewhere,
attests an affliction characteristic of the best tuners,
and justifies emoluments rather higher than the
usual.

When he had led them to the music-room, and left
them there, Watt wondered if he had done right. He
felt he had done right, but he was not sure. Should
he not perhaps rather have sent them flying about their
business? Watt's feeling was that anyone who demanded,
with such tranquil assurance, to be admitted to
Mr Knott's house, deserved to be admitted, in the
absence of precise instructions to the contrary.

The music-room was a large bare white room.
The piano was in the window. The head, and neck,
in plaster, very white, of Buxtehude, was on the mantel-
piece. A ravanastron hung, on the wall, from a nail,
like a plover.

After a short time Watt returned to the music-
room, with a tray, of refreshments.

Not Mr Gall Senior, but Mr Gall Junior, was
tuning the piano, to Watt's great surprise. Mr Gall
Senior was standing in the middle of the room, perhaps
listening. Watt did not take this to mean that Mr Gall
Junior was the true piano-tuner, and Mr Gall Senior
simply a poor blind old man, hired for the occasion,
no. But he took it rather to mean that Mr Gall Senior,
feeling his end at hand, and anxious that his son should

follow in his footsteps, was putting the finishing touches
to a hasty instruction, before it was too late.

While Watt looked round, for a place to set down
his tray, Mr Gall Junior brought his work to a close.
He reassembled the piano case, put back his tools in
their bag, and stood up.

The mice have returned, he said.

The elder said nothing. Watt wondered if he had
heard.

Nine dampers remain, said the younger, and an
equal number of hammers.

Not corresponding, I hope, said the elder.

In one case, said the younger.

The elder had nothing to say to this.

The strings are in flitters, said the younger.

The elder had nothing to say to this either.

The piano is doomed, in my opinion, said the
younger.

The piano-tuner also, said the elder.

The pianist also, said the younger.

This was perhaps the principal incident of Watt's
early days in Mr Knott's house.

In a sense it resembled all the incidents of note
proposed to Watt during his stay in Mr Knott's house,
and of which a certain number will be recorded in this
place, without addition, or subtraction, and in a sense
not.

It resembled them in the sense that it was not
ended, when it was past, but continued to unfold,
in Watt's head, from beginning to end, over and
over again, the complex connexions of its lights and
shadows, the passing from silence to sound and from
sound to silence, the stillness before the movement
and the stillness after, the quickenings and retardings,
the approaches and the separations, all the shifting
detail of its march and ordinance, according to the
irrevocable caprice of its taking place. It resembled
them in the vigour with which it developed a

purely plastic content, and gradually lost, in the nice processes of its light, its sound, its impacts and its rhythm, all meaning, even the most literal.

Thus the scene in the music-room, with the two Galls, ceased very soon to signify for Watt a piano tuned, an obscure family and professional relation, an exchange of judgments more or less intelligible, and so on, if indeed it had ever signified such things, and became a mere example of light commenting bodies, and stillness motion, and silence sound, and comment comment.

This fragility of the outer meaning had a bad effect on Watt, for it caused him to seek for another, for some meaning of what had passed, in the image of how it had passed.

The most meagre, the least plausible, would have satisfied Watt, who had not seen a symbol, nor executed an interpretation, since the age of fourteen, or fifteen, and who had lived, miserably it is true, among face values all his adult life, face values at least for him. Some see the flesh before the bones, and some see the bones before the flesh, and some never see the bones at all, and some never see the flesh at all, never never see the flesh at all. But whatever it was Watt saw, with the first look, that was enough for Watt, that had always been enough for Watt, more than enough for Watt. And he had experienced literally nothing, since the age of fourteen, or fifteen, of which in retrospect he was not content to say, That is what happened then. He could recall, not indeed with any satisfaction, but as ordinary occasions, the time when his dead father appeared to him in a wood, with his trousers rolled up over his knees and his shoes and socks in his hand; or the time when in his surprise at hearing a voice urging him, in terms of unusual coarseness, to do away with himself, he narrowly escaped being knocked down, by a dray; or the time when alone in a rowing-boat, far from land, he suddenly smelt flowering

currant; or the time when an old lady of delicate
upbringing, and advantageous person, for she was
amputated well above the knee, whom he had pursued
with his assiduities on no fewer than three distinct
occasions, unstrapped her wooden leg, and laid aside
her crutch. Here no tendency appeared, on the part
of his father's trousers, for example, to break up into
an arrangement of appearances, grey, flaccid and
probably fistular, or of his father's legs to vanish in
the farce of their properties, no, but his father's legs
and trousers, as then seen, in the wood, and subsequently brought to mind, remained legs and trousers,
and not only legs and trousers, but his father's legs
and trousers, that is to say quite different from any
of the legs and trousers that Watt had ever seen, and
he had seen a great quantity, both of legs and of trousers,
in his time. The incident of the Galls, on the contrary,
ceased so rapidly to have even the paltry significance
of two men, come to tune a piano, and tuning it, and
exchanging a few words, as men will do, and going,
that this seemed rather to belong to some story heard
long before, an instant in the life of another, ill told,
ill heard, and more than half forgotten.

So Watt did not know what had happened. He
did not care, to do him justice, what had happened.
But he felt the need to think that such and such a
thing had happened then, the need to be able to say,
when the scene began to unroll its sequences, Yes,
I remember, that is what happened then.

This need remained with Watt, this need not
always satisfied, during the greater part of his stay in
Mr Knott's house. For the incident of the Galls father
and son was followed by others of a similar kind,
incidents that is to say of great formal brilliance and
indeterminable purport.

Watt's stay in Mr Knott's house was less agreeable,
on this account, than it would have been, if such
incidents had been unknown, or his attitude towards

them less anxious, that is to say, if Mr Knott's house had been another house, or Watt another man. For outside Mr Knott's house, and of course grounds, such incidents were unknown, or so Watt supposed. And Watt could not accept them for what they perhaps were, the simple games that time plays with space, now with these toys, and now with those, but was obliged, because of his peculiar character, to enquire into what they meant, oh not into what they really meant, his character was not so peculiar as all that, but into what they might be induced to mean, with the help of a little patience, a little ingenuity.

But what was this pursuit of meaning, in this indifference to meaning? And to what did it tend? These are delicate questions. For when Watt at last spoke of this time, it was a time long past, and of which his recollections were, in a sense, perhaps less clear than he would have wished, though too clear for his liking, in another. Add to this the notorious difficulty of recapturing, at will, modes of feeling peculiar to a certain time, and to a certain place, and perhaps also to a certain state of the health, when the time is past, and the place left, and the body struggling with quite a new situation. Add to this the obscurity of Watt's communications, the rapidity of his utterance and the eccentricities of his syntax, as elsewhere recorded. Add to this the material conditions in which these communications were made. Add to this the scant aptitude to receive of him to whom they were proposed. Add to this the scant aptitude to give of him to whom they were committed. And some idea will perhaps be obtained of the difficulties experienced in formulating, not only such matters as those here in question, but the entire body of Watt's experience, from the moment of his entering Mr Knott's establishment to the moment of his leaving it.

But before passing from the Galls father and son to matters less litigious, or less tediously litigious, it seems advisable that the little that is known, on this subject, should be said. For the incident of the Galls father and son was the first and type of many. And the little that is known about it has not yet all been said. Much has been said, but not all.

Not that many things remain to be said, on the subject of the Galls father and son, for they do not. For only three or four things remain to be said, in this connexion. And three or four things are not really many, in comparison with the number of things that might have been known, and said, on this subject, and now never shall.

What distressed Watt in this incident of the Galls father and son, and in subsequent similar incidents, was not so much that he did not know what had happened, for he did not care what had happened, as that nothing had happened, that a thing that was nothing had happened, with the utmost formal distinctness, and that it continued to happen, in his mind, he supposed, though he did not know exactly what that meant, and though it seemed to be outside him, before him, about him, and so on, inexorably to unroll its phases, beginning with the first (the knock that was not a knock) and ending with the last (the door closing that was not a door closing), and omitting none, uninvoked, at the most unexpected moments, and the most inopportune. Yes, Watt could not accept, as no doubt Erskine could not accept, and as no doubt Arsene and Walter and Vincent and the others had been unable to accept, that nothing had happened, with all the clarity and solidity of something, and that it revisited him in such a way that he was forced to submit to it all over again, to hear the same sounds, see the same lights, touch the same surfaces, and so on, as when they had first involved him in their unintelligible intricacies. If he had been able to accept it, then perhaps it would not have revisited him, and this would have been a great saving of vexation, to put it mildly. But he could not accept it, could not bear it. One wonders sometimes where Watt thought he was. In a culture-park?

But if he could say, when the knock came, the knock become a knock, or the door become a door, in his mind, presumably in his mind, whatever that might mean, Yes, I remember, that is what happened then, if then he could say that, then he thought that then the scene would end, and trouble him no more, as the appearance of his father with his trousers rolled up and his shoes and socks in his hands troubled him no more, because he could say, when it began, Yes, yes, I remember, that was when my father appeared to me, in the wood, dressed for wading. But to elicit something from nothing requires a certain skill and Watt was not always successful, in his efforts to do so. Not that he was always unsuccessful either, for he was not. For if he had been always unsuccessful, how would it have been possible for him to speak of the Galls father and son, and of the piano they had come all the way from town to tune, and of their tuning it, and of their passing the remarks they had passed, the one to the other, in the way he did? No, he could never have spoken at all of these things, if all had continued to mean nothing, as some continued to mean nothing, that is to say, right up to the end. For the only way one can speak of nothing is to speak of it as though it were something, just as the only way one can speak of God is to speak of him as though he were a man, which to be sure he was, in a sense, for a time, and as the only way one can speak of man, even our anthropologists have realised that, is to speak of him as though he were a termite. But if Watt was sometimes unsuccessful, and sometimes successful, as in the affair of the Galls father and son, in foisting a meaning there where no meaning appeared, he was most often neither the one, nor the other. For Watt considered, with reason, that he was successful, in this enterprise, when he could

evolve, from the meticulous phantoms that beset him,
a hypothesis proper to disperse them, as often as this
might be found necessary. There was nothing, in this
operation, at variance with Watt's habits of mind.
For to explain had always been to exorcize, for Watt.
And he considered that he was unsuccessful, when he
failed to do so. And he considered that he was neither
wholly successful, nor wholly unsuccessful, when the
hypothesis evolved lost its virtue, after one or two
applications, and had to be replaced by another, which
in its turn had to be replaced by another, which in due
course ceased to be of the least assistance, and so on.
And that is what happened, in the majority of cases.
Now to give examples of Watt's failures, and of Watt's
successes, and of Watt's partial successes, in this connexion, is so to speak impossible. For when he speaks,
for example, of the incident of the Galls father and
son, does he speak of it in terms of the unique hypothesis
that was required, to deal with it, and render it in-
nocuous, or in terms of the latest, or in terms of some
other of the series? For when Watt spoke of an incident
of this kind, he did not necessarily do so in terms of
the unique hypothesis, or of the latest, though this at
first sight seems the only possible alternative, and the
reason why he did not, why it is not, is this, that when
one of the series of hypotheses, with which Watt laboured
to preserve his peace of mind, lost its virtue, and had
to be laid aside, and another set up in its place, then
it sometimes happened that the hypothesis in question,
after a sufficient period of rest, recovered its virtue and
could be made to serve again, in the place of another,
whose usefulness had come to an end, for the time
being at least. To such an extent is this true, that one
is sometimes tempted to wonder, with reference to two
or even three incidents related by Watt as separate and
distinct, if they are not in reality the same incident,
variously interpreted. As to giving an example of the
second event, namely the failure, that is clearly quite

out of the question. For there we have to do with events that resisted all Watt's efforts to saddle them with meaning, and a formula, so that he could neither think of them, nor speak of them, but only suffer them, when they recurred, though it seems probable that they recurred no more, at the period of Watt's revelation, to me, but were as though they had never been.

Finally, to return to the incident of the Galls father and son, as related by Watt, did it have that meaning for Watt at the time of its taking place, and then lose that meaning, and then recover it? Or did it have some quite different meaning for Watt at the time of its taking place, and then lose that meaning, and then receive that, alone or among others, which it exhibited, in Watt's relation? Or did it have no meaning whatever for Watt at the moment of its taking place, were there neither Galls nor piano then, but only an unintelligible succession of changes, from which Watt finally extracted the Galls and the piano, in self-defence? These are most delicate questions. Watt spoke of it as involving, in the original, the Galls and the piano, but he was obliged to do this, even if the original had nothing to do with the Galls and the piano. For even if the Galls and the piano were long posterior to the phenomena destined to become them, Watt was obliged to think, and speak, of the incident, even at the moment of its taking place, as the incident of the Galls and the piano, if he was to think and speak of it at all, and it may be assumed that Watt would never have thought or spoken of such incidents, if he had not been under the absolute necessity of doing so. But generally speaking it seems probable that the meaning attributed to this particular type of incident, by Watt, in his relations, was now the initial meaning that had been lost and then recovered, and now a meaning quite distinct from the initial meaning, and now a meaning evolved, after a delay of varying length, and with greater or less pains, from the initial absence of meaning.

One more word on this subject.

Watt learned towards the end of this stay in Mr Knott's house to accept that nothing had happened, that a nothing had happened, learned to bear it and even, in a shy way, to like it. But then it was too late.

That then is that in which the incident of the Galls father and son resembled other incidents, of which it was merely the first in time, other incidents of note. But to say, as has been said, that the incident of the Galls father and son had this aspect in common with all the subsequent incidents of note, is perhaps to go a little too far. For not all the subsequent incidents of note, with which Watt was called upon to deal, during his stay in Mr Knott's house, and of course grounds, presented this aspect, no, but some meant something from the very beginning, and continued to mean it, with all the tenacity of, for example, the flowering currant in the rowing-boat, or the capitulation of the one-legged Mrs Watson, right up to the end.

As to that in which the incident of the Galls father and son differed from the subsequent incidents of its category, that is no longer clear, and cannot therefore be stated, with profit. But it may be taken that the difference was so nice as with advantage to be neglected, in a synopsis of this kind.

Watt thought sometimes of Arsene. He wondered what had become of the duck. He had not seen her leave the kitchen with Arsene. But then he had not seen Arsene leave the kitchen either. And as the bird was nowhere to be found, in the house or in the garden, Watt supposed she must have slipped away, with her master. He wondered also what Arsene had meant, nay, he wondered what Arsene had said, on the evening of his departure. For his declaration had entered Watt's ears only by fits, and his understanding, like all that enters the ears only by fits, hardly at all. He had realised, to be sure, that Arsene was speaking, and in a sense to him, but something had prevented

him, perhaps his fatigue, from paying attention to
what was being said and from enquiring into what was
being meant. Watt was now inclined to regret this, for
from Erskine no information was to be obtained. Not
that Watt desired information, for he did not. But he
desired words to be applied to his situation, to Mr Knott,
to the house, to the grounds, to his duties, to the stairs,
to his bedroom, to the kitchen, and in a general way
to the conditions of being in which he found himself.
For Watt now found himself in the midst of things
which, if they consented to be named, did so as it were
with reluctance. And the state in which Watt found
himself resisted formulation in a way no state had ever
done, in which Watt had ever found himself, and Watt
had found himself in a great many states, in his day.
Looking at a pot, for example, or thinking of a pot,
at one of Mr Knott's pots, of one of Mr Knott's pots, it
was in vain that Watt said, Pot, pot. Well, perhaps
not quite in vain, but very nearly. For it was not a
pot, the more he looked, the more he reflected, the
more he felt sure of that, that is was not a pot at all.
It resembled a pot, it was almost a pot, but it was not
a pot of which one could say, Pot, pot, and be comforted.
It was in vain that it answered, with unexceptionable
adequacy, all the purposes, and performed all the
offices, of a pot, it was not a pot. And it was just this
hairbreadth departure from the nature of a true pot that
so excruciated Watt. For if the approximation had
been less close, then Watt would have been less
anguished. For then he would not have said, This is
a pot, and yet not a pot, no, but then he would have
said, This is something of which I do not know the
name. And Watt preferred on the whole having to
do with things of which he did not know the name,
though this too was painful to Watt, to having to do
with things of which the known name, the proven name,
was not the name, any more, for him. For he could
always hope, of a thing of which he had never known

the name, that he would learn the name, some day,
and so be tranquillized. But he could not look forward
to this in the case of a thing of which the true name
had ceased, suddenly, or gradually, to be the true name
for Watt. For the pot remained a pot, Watt felt sure
of that, for everyone but Watt. For Watt alone it was
not a pot, any more.

Then, when he turned for reassurance to himself,
who was not Mr Knott's, in the sense that the pot was,
who had come from without and whom the without would
take again (1), he made the distressing discovery that
of himself too he could no longer affirm anything that
did not seem as false as if he had affirmed it of a stone.
Not that Watt was in the habit of affirming things of
himself, for he was not, but he found it a help, from
time to time, to be able to say, with some appearance
of reason, Watt is a man, all the same, Watt is a man,
or, Watt is in the street, with thousands of fellow-
creatures within call. And Watt was greatly troubled
by this tiny little thing, more troubled perhaps than
he had ever been by anything, and Watt had been
frequently and exceedingly troubled, in his time, by
this imperceptible, no, hardly imperceptible, since he
perceived it, by this indefinable thing that prevented
him from saying, with conviction, and to his relief,
of the object that was so like a pot, that it was a pot,

---

(1) Watt, unlike Arsene, had never supposed that Mr Knott's
house would be his last refuge. Was it his first? In a sense it
was, but it was not the kind of first refuge that promised to be
the last. It occurred to him, of course, towards the end of his
stay, that it might have been, that he might have made it, this
transitory refuge, the last, if he had been more adroit, or less
in need of rest. But Watt was very subject to fancies, towards
the end of his stay under Mr Knott's roof. And it was also under
the pressure of a similar eleventh hour vision, of what might have
been, that Arsene expressed himself on this subject, in the way
he did, on the night of his departure. For it is scarcely credible
that a man of Arsene's experience could have supposed, in
advance, of any given halt, that it was to be the last halt.

and of the creature that still in spite of everything presented a large number of exclusively human characteristics, that it was a man. And Watt's need of semantic succour was at times so great that he would set to trying names on things, and on himself, almost as a woman hats. Thus of the pseudo-pot he would say, after reflexion, It is a shield, or, growing bolder, It it a raven, and so on. But the pot proved as little a shield, or a raven, or any other of the things that Watt called it, as a pot. As for himself, though he could no longer call it a man, as he had used to do, with the intuition that he was perhaps not talking nonsense, yet he could not imagine what else to call it, if not a man. But Watt's imagination had never been a lively one. So he continued to think of himself as a man, as his mother had taught him, when she said, There's a good little man, or, There's a bonny little man, or, There's a clever little man. But for all the relief that this afforded him, he might just as well have thought of himself as a box, or an urn.

It was principally for these reasons that Watt would have been glad to hear Erskine's voice, wrapping up safe in words the kitchen space, the extraordinary newel-lamp, the stairs that were never the same and of which even the number of steps seemed to vary, from day to day, and from night to morning, and many other things in the house, and the bushes without and other garden growths, that so often prevented Watt from taking the air, even on the finest day, so that he grew pale, and constipated, and even the light as it came and went and the clouds that climbed the sky, now slow, now rapid, and generally from west to east, or sank down towards the earth on the other side, for the clouds seen from Mr Knott's premises were not quite the clouds that Watt was used to, and Watt had a great experience of clouds, and could distinguish the various sorts, the cirrhus, the stratus, the tumulus and the various other sorts, at a glance. Not that the fact of Erskine's

naming the pot, or of his saying to Watt, My dear
fellow, or, My good man, or, God damn you, would
have changed the pot into a pot, or Watt into a man,
for Watt, for it would not. But it would have shown
that at least for Erskine the pot was a pot, and Watt
a man. Not that the fact of the pot's being a pot, or
Watt's being a man, for Erskine, would have caused
the pot to be a pot, or Watt to be a man, for Watt, for
it would not. But it would perhaps have lent a little
colour to the hope, sometimes entertained by Watt,
that he was in poor health, owing to the efforts of his
body to adjust itself to an unfamiliar milieu, and that
these would be successful, in the end, and his health
restored, and things appear, and himself appear, in
their ancient guise, and consent to be named, with the
time-honoured names, and forgotten. Not that Watt
longed at all times for this restoration, of things, of
himself, to their comparative innocuousness, for he did
not. For there were times when he felt a feeling closely
resembling the feeling of satisfaction, at his being so
abandoned, by the last rats. For after these there
would be no more rats, not a rat left, and there were
times when Watt almost welcomed this prospect, of
being rid of his last rats, at last. It would be lonely,
to be sure, at first, and silent, after the gnawing, the
scurrying, the little cries. Things and himself, they
had gone with him now for so long, in the foul weather,
and in the less foul. Things in the ordinary sense, and
then the emptinesses between them, and the light high
up before it reached them, and then the other thing, the
high heavy hollow jointed unstable thing, that trampled
down the grasses, and scattered the sand, in its pursuits.
But if there were times when Watt envisaged this
dereliction with something like satisfaction, these were
rare, particularly in the early stages of Watt's stay in
Mr Knott's house. And most often he found himself
longing for a voice, for Erskine's, since he was alone
with Erskine, to speak of the little world of Mr Knott's

establishment, with the old words, the old credentials. There was of course the gardener, to speak of the garden. But could the gardener speak of the garden, the gardener who went home every evening, before nightfall, and did not return next morning until the sun was well up, in the sky? No, the gardener's remarks were not evidence, in Watt's opinion. Only Erskine could speak of the garden, as only Erskine could speak of the house, usefully, to Watt. And Erskine never spoke, either of the one, or of the other. Indeed Erskine never opened his mouth, in Watt's presence, except to eat, or belch, or cough, or keck, or muse, or sigh, or sing, or sneeze. It is true that during the first week hardly a day passed that Erskine did not address himself to Watt, on the subject of Watt's duties. But in the first week Watt's words had not yet begun to fail him, or Watt's world to become unspeakable. It is true also that from time to time Erskine would come running to Watt, all in a fluster, with some quite ridiculous question, such as, Did you see Mr Knott?, or, Has Kate come? But this was much later. Perhaps some day, said Watt, he will ask, Where is the pot?, or, Where did you put that pot? These questions, absurd as they were, constituted nevertheless an acknowledgement of Watt that Watt was not slow to appreciate. But he would have appreciated it more if it had come earlier, before he had grown used to his loss of species.

The song that Erskine sang, or rather intoned, was always the same. It was:

?

Perhaps if Watt had spoken to Erskine, Erskine would have spoken to Watt, in reply. But Watt was not so far gone as all that.

Watt's attention was extreme, in the beginning, to all that went on about him. Not a sound was made, within earshot, that he did not capture and, when necessary, interrogate, and he opened wide his eyes to all that passed, near and at a distance, to all that came and went and paused and stirred, and to all that brightened and darkened and grew and dwindled, and he grasped, in many cases, the nature of the object affected, and even the immediate cause of its being so. To the thousand smells also, which time leaves behind, Watt paid the closest attention. And he provided himself with a portable spittoon.

This constant tension of some of his most noble faculties tired Watt greatly. And the results, on the whole, were meagre. But he had no choice, at first.

One of the first things that Watt learned by these means was that Mr Knott sometimes rose late and retired early, and sometimes rose very late and retired very early, and sometimes did not rise at all, nor at all retire, for who can retire who does not rise? What interested Watt here was this, that the earlier Mr Knott rose the later he retired, and that the later he rose the earlier he retired. But between the hour of his rising and the hour of his retiring there seemed no fixed correlation, or one so abstruse that it did not exist, for Watt. For a long time this was a source of great wonder, to Watt, for he said, Here is one who seems on the one hand reluctant to change his state, and on the other impatient to 'do so. For on Monday, Tuesday and Friday he rose at eleven and retired at seven, and on Wednesday and Saturday he rose at nine and retired at eight, and on Sunday he did not rise at all, nor at all retire. Until Watt realised that between Mr Knott risen and Mr Knott retired there was so to speak nothing to choose. For his rising was not a rising from sleep to vigil, nor his setting a setting from vigil to sleep, no, but they were a rising and a setting from and to and to and from a state that was neither sleep nor vigil, nor vigil nor sleep. Even Mr Knott could hardly be expected to remain day and night in the same position.

Mr Knott's meals gave very little trouble.

On Saturday night a sufficient quantity of food was prepared and cooked to carry Mr Knott through the week.

This dish contained foods of various kinds, such as soup of various kinds, fish, eggs, game, poultry, meat cheese, fruit, all of various kinds, and of course bread and butter, and it contained also the more usual beverages, such as absinthe, mineral water, tea, coffee, milk, stout, beer, whiskey, brandy, wine and water, and it contained also many things to take for the good of the health, such as insulin, digitalin, calomel, iodine, laudanum, mercury, coal, iron, camomille and worm-powder, and of course salt and mustard, pepper and sugar, and of course a little salicylic acid, to delay fermentation.

All these things, and many others too numerous to mention, were well mixed together in the famous pot and boiled for four hours, until the consistence of a mess, or poss, was obtained, and all the good things to eat, and all the good things to drink, and all the good things to take for the good of the health were inextricably mingled and transformed into a single good thing that was neither food, nor drink, nor physic, but quite a new good thing, and of which the tiniest spoonful at once opened the appetite and closed it, excited and stilled the thirst, compromised and stimulated the body's vital functions, and went pleasantly to the head.

It fell to Watt to weigh, to measure and to count, with the utmost exactness, the ingredients that composed this dish, and to dress for the pot those that required dressing, and to mix them thoroughly together without loss, so that not one could be distinguished from another, and to put them on to boil, and when boiling to keep them on the boil, and when boiled to take them off the boil and put out to cool, in a cool place. This was a task that taxed Watt's powers, both of mind and of body, to the utmost, it was so delicate, and rude. And in warm weather it sometimes happened, as he mixed, stripped to the waist, and plying with both hands the great iron rod, that tears would fall, tears of mental fatigue, from his face, into the pot, and from his chest, and out from under his arms, beads of moisture, provoked by his exertions, into the pot also. His moral reserves also were severely tried, so great was his sense of responsibility. For he knew, as though he had been told, that the receipt of this dish had never varied, since its establishment, long long before, and that the choice, the dosage and the quantities of the elements employed had been calculated, with the most minute exactness, to afford Mr Knott, in a course of fourteen full meals, that is to say, seven full luncheons, and seven full dinners, the maximum of pleasure compatible with the protraction of his health.

This dish was served to Mr Knott, cold, in a bowl, at twelve o'clock noon sharp and at seven p.m. exactly, all the year round.

That is to say that Watt carried in the bowl, full, to the dining-room at those hours, and left it on the table. An hour later he went back and took it away, in whatever state Mr Knott had left it. If the bowl still contained food, then Watt transferred this food to the dog's dish. But if it was empty, then Watt washed it up, in readiness for the next meal.

So Watt never saw Mr Knott at mealtime. For Mr Knott was never punctual, at his meals. But he was seldom later than twenty minutes, or half an hour. And whether he emptied the bowl, or did not, it never took him more than five minutes to do so, or seven minutes at the outside. So that Mr Knott was never in the dining-room when Watt brought in the bowl, and he was never there either when Watt went back, to take the bowl away. So Watt never saw Mr Knott, never never saw Mr Knott, at mealtime.

Mr Knott ate this dish with a little plated trowel, such as confectioners and grocers use, and tea-merchants.

This arrangement represented a great saving of labour. Coal was also economized.

To whom, Watt wondered, was this arrangement due? To Mr Knott himself? Or to some other person, to a past domestic perhaps of genius for example, or a professional dietician? And if not to Mr Knott himself, but to some other person (or of course persons), did Mr Knott know that such an arrangement existed, or did he not?

Mr Knott was never heard to complain of his food, though he did not always eat it. Sometimes he emptied the bowl, scraping its sides, and bottom, with the trowel, until they shone, and sometimes he left the half of it, or some other fraction, and sometimes he left the whole of it.

Twelve possibilities occurred to Watt, in this connexion:

1. Mr Knott was responsible for the arrangement, and knew that he was responsible for the arrangement, and knew that such an arrangement existed, and was content.

2. Mr Knott was not responsible for the arrangement, but knew who was responsible for the arrangement, and knew that such an arrangement existed, and was content.

3. Mr Knott was responsible for the arrangement, and knew that he was responsible for the arrangement, but did not know that any such arrangement existed, and was content.

4. Mr Knott was not responsible for the arrangement, but knew who was responsible for the arrangement, but did not know that any such arrangement existed, and was content.

5. Mr Knott was responsible for the arrangement, but did not know who was responsible for the arran-

gement, nor that any such arrangement existed, and was content.

6. Mr Knott was not responsible for the arrangement, nor knew who was responsible for the arrangement, nor that any such arrangement existed, and was content.

7. Mr Knott was responsible for the arrangement, but did not know who was responsible for the arrangement, and knew that such an arrangement existed, and was content.

8. Mr Knott was not responsible for the arrangement, nor knew who was responsible for the arrangement, and knew that such an arrangement existed, and was content.

9. Mr Knott was responsible for the arrangement, but knew who was responsible for the arrangement, and knew that such an arrangement existed, and was content.

10. Mr Knott was not responsible for the arrangement, but knew that he was responsible for the arrangement, and knew that such an arrangement existed, and was content.

11. Mr. Knott was responsible for the arrangement, but knew who was responsible for the arrangement, but did not know that any such arrangement existed, and was content.

12. Mr. Knott was not responsible for the arrangement, but knew that he was responsible for the arrangement, but did not know that any such arrangement existed, and was content.

Other possibilities occurred to Watt, in this connexion, but he put them aside, and quite out of his mind, as unworthy of serious consideration, for the time being. The time would come, perhaps, when they would be worthy of serious consideration, and then, if he could, he would summon them to his mind, and consider them seriously. But for the moment they did not seem worthy of serious consideration, so he put them quite out of his mind, and forgot them.

Watt's instructions were to give what Mr Knott
left of this dish, on the days that he did not eat it all,
to the dog.

Now there was no dog in the house, that is to
say, no house-dog, to which this food could be given,
on the days that Mr Knott did not require it.

Watt, reflecting on this, heard a little voice say,
Mr Knott, having once known a man who was bitten
by a dog, in the leg, and having once known another
man who was scratched by a cat, in the nose, and
having once known a fine healthy woman who was
butted by a goat, in the loins, and having once known
another man who was disembowelled by a bull, in the
bowels, and having once frequented a canon who was
kicked by a horse, in the crotch, is shy of dogs, and
other four-footed friends, about the place, and of his
inarticulate bipedal brothers and sisters in God hardly
less so, for he once knew a missionary who was trampled
to death by an ostrich, in the stomach, and he once
knew a priest who, on leaving with a sigh of relief the
chapel where he had served mass, with his own hands,
to more than a hundred persons, was shat on, from
above, by a dove, in the eye.

Watt never knew quite what to make of this
particular little voice, whether it was joking, or whether
it was serious.

So that it was necessary that a dog from outside
should call at the house at least once every day, on
the off chance of its being given part, or all, of
Mr Knott's lunch, or dinner, or both, to eat.

Now in this matter great difficulties must have
been encountered, notwithstanding the large numbers of
hungry and even starving dogs with which the neighbourhood abounded, and doubtless had always abounded,
for miles around, in every direction. And the reason
for that was perhaps this, that the number of times
that the dog went full away was small compared with
the number of times that it went away half empty, and

the number of times that it went away half empty was
small compared with the number of times that it went
away as empty as it came. For it was more usual for
Mr Knott to eat all his food than to eat only a part,
and to eat only a part than to eat none at all, much
much more usual. For while it is true that Mr Knott
very often rose very late and retired very early, yet
the number of times was very great on which Mr Knott
rose just in time to eat his lunch, and ate his dinner
just in time to retire. The days on which he neither
rose nor retired, and so left both his lunch and his
dinner untouched, were of course wonderful days, for
the dog. But they were very rare.

Now will of its own free will the average hungry
or starving dog be constant in its attendance, under
such conditions? No, the average hungry or starving dog,
if left to its own devices, will not, for it would not be
worth its while.

Add to this that the dog's attendance was
required, not at any odd hour of the day or night that
it might fancy to drop in, no, but between certain
definite limiting hours, and these were, eight o'clock
p.m. and ten o'clock p.m. And the reason for that was
this, that at ten o'clock the house was shut up for the
night, and it was not known, until eight o'clock, if
Mr Knott had left anything, or all, or nothing, of his
food for the day. For though as a general rule Mr Knott
ate every atom, both of his lunch and of his dinner,
in which case the dog got nothing, yet what was to
prevent him from eating every atom of his lunch, but
no dinner, or only part of his dinner, in which case
the dog got the uneaten dinner, or portion of dinner,
or from eating no lunch, or only part of his lunch, and
yet every atom of his dinner, in which case the dog
got the uneaten lunch, or portion of lunch, or from
eating only part of his lunch, and then again only part
of his dinner, in which case the dog benefited by the
two uneaten portions, or from not touching either his

lunch or his dinner, in which case the dog, if it neither delayed nor precipitated his arrival, went away with its belly full at last.

By what means then were the dog and the food to be brought together, on those days on which, Mr Knott having left all or part of his food for the day, all or part of the food was available for the dog? For Watt's instructions were formal: On those days on which food was left over, the food left over was to be given to the dog, without loss of time.

This was the problem that must have faced Mr Knott, in the far distant past, at the moment of his setting up house.

This was one of the many problems that must have faced Mr Knott then.

Or if not Mr Knott, then another, of whom all trace is lost. Or if not another, then others, of whom no trace remains.

Watt now passed on to the manner in which this problem had been solved, if not by Mr Knott, then by that other, and if neither by Mr Knott nor by that other, then by those others, in a word, to the manner in which this problem had been solved, this problem of how to bring the dog and food together, by Mr Knott, or by him, or by them, whom it had faced, in that far distant past, when Mr Knott set up his establishment, for that it could have been solved by some person or persons whom it had never faced seemed improbable, highly improbable, to Watt.

But before he passed on to this, he paused to reflect that the solution of this problem of how to bring the dog and food together in the way described had perhaps been arrived at by the same person or persons by whom the solution of the problem of how Mr Knott's food was to be prepared had been arrived at, so long before.

And when he had paused to reflect on this, he paused a little longer, before passing on to the solution that seemed to have prevailed, to consider some at least of those that did not seem to have prevailed.

But before pausing a little longer to do this, he hastened to remark that those solutions that did not seem to have prevailed might have been considered, and set aside, as unsatisfactory, by the author or authors of the solution that did seem to have prevailed, or might not.

1. An exceptional hungry or starving dog might have been sought out, that for reasons best known to itself would have considered it worth its while to call at the house, in the manner required.

But the chances of such a dog's existing were small.

But the likelihood of finding such a dog, if it did exist, was slight.

2. An ill-nourished local dog might have been selected, to which with the consent of its proprietor all or part of Mr Knott's food might have been brought, by one of Mr Knott's men, on the days that Mr Knott left all or part of his food, for the day.

But then one of Mr Knott's men would have had to put on his coat and hat and turn out, as likely as not in the pitch dark, and in torrents of rain in all probability, and grope his way in the dark in the pours of rain, with the pot of food in his hand, a wretched and ridiculous figure, to where the dog lay.

But was there any guarantee of the dog's being in, when the man arrived? Might not the dog have gone out, for the night?

But was there any guarantee, supposing the dog to be in when the man arrived, of the dog's being hungry enough to eat the pot of food, when the man arrived with the pot of food? Might not the dog have satisfied its hunger, during the day? Or was there any assurance, supposing the dog to be out when the man arrived, of the dog's being hungry enough, when it came in, in the morning, or during the night, to eat the pot of food that the man had brought? Might not the dog have satisfied its hunger, during the night, and indeed left the house with no other purpose?

3. A messenger might have been employed, a man, or a boy, or a woman, or a girl, to call at the house every evening at say eight fifteen o'clock in the evening, and on those evenings on which food was available for the dog to take that food to a dog, to any dog, and to stand over that dog until it had eaten the food, and if it could not or would not finish the food to take what remained of the food to another dog, to any other dog, and to stand over that other dog until it had eaten what remained of the food, and if it could not or would not finish what remained of the food to take what still remained of the food to another dog, to any other dog, and so on, until all the food was eaten, and not an atom remained, and then to bring back the pot empty.

(This person might have been further employed to clean the boots, and the shoes, either before leaving the house with the pot full, though of course it was not full at all, or on returning to the house with the pot empty, or simply on learning that there was no food available for the dog, that day. This would have greatly relieved the gardener, a Mr Graves, and enabled him to give to the garden the time that he gave to the boots, and to the shoes. And is it not strange most strange that one says of a thing that it is full, when it is not full at all, but not of a thing that it is empty, if it is not empty? And perhaps the reason for that is this, that when one fills, one seldom fills quite full, for that would not be convenient, whereas when one empties one empties completely, holding the vessel upside down, and rinsing it out with boiling water if necessary, with a kind of fury.)

But was there any guarantee that the messenger would indeed give the food to a dog, or dogs, in accordance with his instructions? What was to prevent the messenger from eating the food himself, or from selling all or part of the food to some other party, or from giving it away, or from emptying it away into the nearest ditch or hole, to save time, and trouble?

But what would happen if the messenger, through indisposition, or drunkenness, or carelessness, or idleness, failed to call at the house on an evening on which food was available for the dog?

But might not even the most hardy, the most sober, the most conscientious of messengers, knowing all the local dogs, their habits and their homes, their colours and their shapes, have still some food got, in the old pot, when ten o'cluck strock, from the old clock, and then how would he bring back the pot, the trusty messenger, if the pot was not empty in time, for the following morning would be too late, for Mr Knott's pots and pans were not allowed to stay out, over night.

But was a dog the same thing as the dog? For in Watt's instructions there was no mention of a dog, but only of the dog, which could only mean that what was required was not any dog, but one particular dog, that is to say, not one dog one day, and the next another, and perhaps the next a third, no, but every day the same, every day the same poor old dog, as long as the dog lived. But a fortiori were several dogs the same thing as the dog?

4. A man possessed of a famished dog might have been sought out, whose business brought him, accompanied by his dog, past Mr Knott's house every evening of the year, between the hours of eight and ten. Then on those evenings on which food was available for the dog, in Mr Knott's window, or some other conspicuous window, a red light would be set, or perhaps better a green, and on all other evenings a violet light, or perhaps better no light at all, and then the man (and no doubt after a little time the dog too) would lift up his eyes to the window as he passed, and seeing a red light, or a green light, would hasten to the housedoor and stand over his dog until his dog had eaten all the food that Mr Knott had left, but seeing a violet light,

or no light at all, would not hasten to the door, with his dog, but continue on his way, down the road, with his dog, as though nothing had happened.

But was it likely that such a man existed?

But was it likely, if he did, that he could be found?

But if he did, and he were found, might he not confound, in his mind, as he passed before the house, on his way home, if he were homeward bound, or on his way out, if he were outward bound, for whither can a man be bound, if bound he be, but on the one hand homeward, and on the other outward, might he not confound, in his mind, the red light with the violet, the violet with the green, the green with the none, the none with the red, and when there was no food him for come ratatat knocking at the door, and when there was for him some food onward plod along the road, followed by his faithful emaciated dog?

But might not Erskine, or Watt, or some other Erskine, or some other Watt, set in the window the wrong light, or the no light, by mistake, or the right light, or the no light, when it was too late, out of forgetfulness, or procrastination, and the man and dog come running to the door, when there was nothing, or onward plod, when there was something?

But would not this greatly add to the worries, the responsibilities, and the exertions, already so heavy, of Mr Knott's servants?

So Watt considered, not only some of those solutions that had not apparently prevailed, but also some of those objections that were perhaps the cause of their not having done so, distributed as follows:

Solution	*Number of Objections*
1st	2
2nd	3
3rd	4
4th	5

Number of Solutions   *Number of Objections*
4 14
3 9
2 5
1 2

Passing on then to the solution that seemed to have prevailed, Watt found it to be roughly this, that a suitable local dogowner, that is to say a needy man with a famished dog, should be sought out, and on him settled a handsome annuity of fifty pounds payable monthly, in consideration of his calling at Mr Knott's house every evening between eight and ten, accompanied by his dog in a famished condition, and on those days on which there was food for his dog of his standing over his dog, with a stick, before witnesses, until the dog had eaten all the food until not an atom remained, and of his then taking himself and his dog off the premises without delay; and that a younger famished dog should by this man at Mr Knott's expense be acquired and held in reserve, against the day when the first famished dog should die, and that then again another famished dog should in the same way be procured and held in readiness, against the inevitable hour when the second famished dog should pay nature's debt, and so on indefinitely, there being thus two famished dogs always available, the one to eat the food left over by Mr Knott in the manner described until it died, and the other then for as long as it lived to do the same, and so on indefinitely; and further that a similar young local but dogless man should be sought out, against the day when the first local man should die, to take over and exploit, in the same way and on the same terms, the two surviving famished dogs thus left without a master, and without a home; and that then again another young local dogless man should in the same way be secured, against the dread hour of the second local's man dissolution, and so on indefinitely,

there being thus two famished dogs and two needy local
men for ever available, the first needy local man to
own and exploit the two famished dogs in the manner
described as long as he lived, and the other then, as
long as he drew breath, to do the same, and so on
indefinitely; and that lest, as might very well happen,
one of the two famished dogs, or both the famished
dogs, should fail to survive their master, and follow
him at once to the grave, a third, a fourth, a fifth and
even a sixth famished dog should be acquired and
suitably maintained at Mr Knott's expense in some
convenient place in a famished condition, or that better
still there should be at Mr Knott's expense on some
favourable site established a kennel or colony of
famished dogs from which at any time a well-bred well-
trained famished dog could be withdrawn and set to
work, in the manner described; and that on the off
chance of the second poor young local man's passing
over, into the beyond, at the same time as the first
poor local man, or even before, and stranger things are
of hourly occurrence, a third, a fourth, a fifth and even
a sixth poor young local dogless man or even woman
should be sought out and by fair words and occasional
gifts of money and old clothes as far as possible secured
to Mr Knott's service eventually in the manner described,
or better still that a suitable large needy local family
of say the two parents and from ten to fifteen children
and grand-children passionately attached to their birthplace should be sought out, and by a handsome small
initial lump sum to be paid down and by a liberal
annual pension of fifty pounds to be paid monthly and
by occasional seasonable gifts of loose change and tight
clothes and by untiring well-timed affectionate words
of advice and encouragement and consolation, attached
firmly for good and all in block, their children and
their children's children, to Mr Knott's service, in all
matters touching this matter of the dog required to eat
the food that Mr Knott left, and exclusively in these,

and that to their care the kennel or colony of famished
dogs set up by Mr Knott in order that there should
never be wanting a famished dog to eat his food on
those days that he did not eat it himself should be once
and for all handed over, for the matter of the kennel
was one that touched the matter of the dog. And this
seemed to Watt roughly the way in which the solution
to the problem of how Mr Knott's food was to be given
to the dog had been reached, and though of course for
some time it can have been no more than a tissue now
dilating now contracting of thoughts in a skull, very
likely very soon it was much more than this, for
immense impoverished families abounded for miles
around in every conceivable direction, and must have
always done so, and very likely very soon a real live
famished dog as large as life was coming night after
night as regular as clockwork to Mr Knott's back door,
led by and probably preceding an unmistakeable speci-
men of local indigent proliferation, for everyone to see,
and admire; and the pension being paid, and every now
and then when least expected a half-crown bestowed,
or a florin, or a shilling, or a sixpence, or a threepence,
or a penny, or a halfpenny, and the castoff clothes,
of which Mr Knott, who was a great caster-off of clothes,
had a large store, being handed over, now a coat, now a
waistcoat, now a greatcoat, now a raincoat, now a
trousers, now a knickerbockers, now a shirt, now a vest,
now a pant, now a combination, now a braces, now a belt,
now a collar, now a tie, now a scarf, now a muffler, now
a hat, now a cap, now a stocking, now a sock, now a boot
and now a shoe, and the good words of counsel, of encouragement and comfort spoken, and lavished the little
acts of kindness and of love, just when they were most
needed, and' the kennel of famished dogs handed over
and in full swing, for all the world to see, and admire.

The name of this fortunate family was Lynch,
and at the moment of Watt's entering Mr Knott's service,
this family of Lynch was made up as follows.

There was Tom Lynch, widower, aged eighty-five years, confined to his bed with constant undiagnosed pains in the caecum, and his three surviving boys Joe, aged sixty-five years, a rheumatic cripple, and Jim, aged sixty-four years, a hunchbacked inebriate, and Bill, widower, aged sixty-three years, greatly hampered in his movements by the loss of both legs as the result of a slip, followed by a fall, and his only surviving daughter May Sharpe, widow, aged sixty-two years, in full possession of all her faculties with the exception of that of vision. Then there was Joe's wife née Doyly-Byrne, aged sixty-five years, a sufferer from Parkinson's palsy but otherwise very fit and well, and Jim's wife Kate née Sharpe aged sixty-four years, covered all over with running sores of an unidentified nature but otherwise fit and well. Then there was Joe's boy Tom aged forty-one years, unfortunately subject alternately to fits of exaltation, which rendered him incapable of the least exertion, and of depression, during which he could stir neither hand nor foot, and Bill's boy Sam, aged forty years, paralysed by a merciful providence from no higher than the knees down and from no lower than the waist up, and May's spinster daughter Ann, aged thirty-nine years, greatly reduced in health and spirits by a painful congenital disorder of an unmentionable kind, and Jim's lad Jack aged thirty-eight years, who was weak in the head, and the boon twins Art and Con aged thirty-seven years, who measured in height when in their stockinged feet three feet and four inches and who weighed in weight when stripped to the buff seventy-one pounds all bone and sinew and between whom the resemblance was so marked in every way that even those (and they were many) who knew and loved them most would call Art Con when they meant Art, and Con Art when they meant Con, as least as often as, if not more often than, they called Art Art when they meant Art, and Con Con when they meant Con. And then there was young Tom's wife Mag née

even fivepence a time, that depended, or a bottle of ale,
and Jack's other son Tom aged fourteen years, who
some said took after his father because of the weakness
of his head and others said took after his mother because of the weakness of his chest and some said took
after his paternal grandfather Jim because of his taste
for strong spirits and others said took after his paternal
grandmother Kate because of a patch he had on the
sacrum the size of a plate of weeping excema and some
said took after his paternal greatgrandfather Tom because of the cramps he had in the stomach. And then
finally to pass on to the rising generation there were
Sean's two little girls Rose and Cerise, aged five and four
respectively, and these innocent little girlies were
bleeders like their papa and mama, and indeed it was
very wrong of Sean, knowing what he was and knowing
what Kate was, to do what he did to Kate, so that she
conceived and brought forth Rose, and indeed it was
very wrong of her to let him, and indeed it was very
wrong of Sean again, knowing what he was and what
Kate was and now what Rose was, to do again what he
did again to Kate, so that Kate conceived again and
brought forth Cerise, and indeed it was very wrong of
her again to let him again, and then there were Simon's
two little boys, Pat and Larry, aged four and three
respectively, and little Pat was rickety with little arms
and legs like sticks and a big head like a balloon and a
big belly like another, and so was little Larry, and the
only difference between little Pat and little Larry was
this, allowing for the slight difference in age, and name,
that little Larry's legs were even more like sticks than
little Pat's, whereas little Pat's arms were even more like
sticks than little Larry's, and that little Larry's belly
was a little less like a balloon than little Pat's, whereas
little Pat's head was a little less like a balloon than little
Larry's.

Five generations, twenty-eight souls, nine hundred
and eighty years, such was the proud record of the

Lynch family, when Watt entered Mr Knott's service (1).

Then a moment passed and all was changed. Not that there was death, for there was not. Nor that there was birth, for there was not either. But puff puff breath again they breathed, in and out, the twenty-eight, and all was changed.

As by the clouding the unclouding of the sun the sea, the lake, the ice, the plain, the marsh, the mountain-side, or any other similar natural expanse, be it liquid, or be it solid.

Till changing changing in twenty over twenty-eight equals five over seven times twelve equals sixty over seven equals eight months and a half approximately, if none died, if none were born, a thousand years!

If all were spared, the living spared, the unborn spared.

In eight months and a half, from the date of Watt's entering Mr Knott's service.

But all were not spared.

For Watt had not been four months with Mr Knott when Liz the wife of Sam lay down and expelled a child, her twentieth, with the greatest of ease as may well be imagined, and for some days after this agreeably surprised all those who knew her (and they were many) by the unusual healthiness of her appearance and by a flow of good spirits quite foreign to her nature, for for many years she had passed rightly for more dead than alive, and she suckled the infant with great enjoyment and satisfaction apparently, the flow of milk being remarkably abundant for a woman of her age and habit of body, which was exsanguious, and then after five or six or perhaps even seven days of this kind of thing grew suddenly weak and to the great astonishment of her husband Sam, her sons Blind Bill and Maim Mat, her married daughters Kate and Ann and their

_____

(1) The figures given here are incorrect. The consequent calculations are therefore doubly erroneous.

husbands Sean and Simon, her niece Bridie and her nephew Tom, her sisters Mag and Lil, her brothers-in-law Tom and Jack, her cousins Ann, Art and Con, her aunts-in-law May and Mag, her aunt Kate, her uncles-in-law Joe and Jim, her father-in-law Bill and her grandfather-in-law Tom, who were not expecting anything of the kind, grew weaker and weaker, until she died.

This loss was a great loss to the family Lynch, this loss of a woman of forty goodlooking years.

For not only was a wife, a mother, a mother-in-law, an aunt, a sister, a sister-in-law, a cousin, a niece-in-law, a niece, a niece-in-law, a daughter-in-law, a granddaughter-in-law and of course a grandmother, snatched from her grandfather-in-law, her father-in-law, her uncles-in-law, her aunt, her aunts-in-law, her cousins, her brothers-in-law, her sisters, her niece, her nephew, her sons-in-law, her daughters, her sons, her husband and of course her four little grandchildren (who however exhibited no sign of emotion other than that of curiosity, being too young no doubt to realise the dreadful thing that had happened, for their total age amounted to no more than sixteen years), never to return, but the Lynch millenium was retarded by almost one year and a half, assuming that during that time all were spared, and so could not be expected before roughly two years from the date of Liz's departure, instead of in a mere five months time, as would have been the case if Liz together with the rest of the family had been spared, and even five or six days sooner if the infant had been spared also, as he was to be sure, but at his mother's expense, with the result that the goal towards which the whole family was striving receded to the tune of a good nineteen months, if not more, assuming all the others to be spared in the meantime.

But all the others were not spared, in the meantime.

For two months had not passed, since the death or Liz, when to the amazement of the entire family Ann

retired to the privacy of her room and gave birth, first
to a fine bouncing baby boy, and then to an almost
equally fine bouncing baby girl, and they did not remain
fine very long, nor did they long continue to bounce,
but at their birth they were both very fine indeed, and
remarkably resilient.

This brought the total number of souls in the
Lynch household up to thirty, and the happy day, on
which the eyes of all were set, nearer by twenty-four
days approximately, assuming that all were spared, in
the meantime.

Now the question that began on all hands openly
to be asked was this, Who had done, or whom had Ann
persuaded to do, this thing to Ann? For Ann was by
no means an attractive woman, and the painful disorder
under which she laboured was a matter of common
knowledge, not only in the Lynch household, but for
miles and miles around in every direction. Several
names were freely mentioned in this connexion.

Some said it was her cousin Sam, whose amorous
disposition was notorious, not only among the members
of his immediate family, but throughout the neighbourhood, and who made no secret of his having
committed adultery locally on a large scale, moving
from place to place in his self-propelling invalid's chair,
with widow women, with married women and with
single women, of whom some were young and attractive,
and others young but not attractive, and others attractive
but not young, and others neither young nor attractive,
and of whom some as a result of Sam's intervention
conceived and brought forth a son or a daughter or
two sons or two daughters or a son and a daughter, for
Sam had never managed triplets, and this was a sore
point with Sam, that he had never managed triplets,
and others conceived but did not bring forth, and others
did not conceive at all, though this was exceptional,
that they did not conceive at all, when Sam intervened.
And when reproached with this Sam with ready wit

replied that paralysed as he was, from the waist up, and from the knees down, he had no purpose, interest or joy in life other than this, to set out after a good dinner of meat and vegetables in his wheel-chair and stay out committing adultery until it was time to go home to his supper, after which he was at his wife's disposal. But until then, so far as one knew, he had never affronted Liz under her own roof, or, more strictly speaking, with any of the women that it sheltered, though there were not wanting those to insinuate that he was the father of his cousins Art and Con.

Others said it was her cousin Tom who, in a fit of exaltation, or in a fit of depression, had done this thing to Ann. And to those who objected to this that Tom, when in a fit of exaltation, was incapable of the least exertion, and could move neither hand nor foot, when in a fit of depression, it was replied that the exertion and the motion here involved were not the exertion and the motion from which Tom's fits debarred him, but another exertion and another motion, the suggestion being that the inhibition was not a physical inhibition, but a moral, or aesthetic, and that Tom's recurrent inability on the one hand to discharge certain offices requiring on the part of his bodily frame not the slightest expenditure of energy, such as that of keeping an eye on the kettle, or on the saucepan, and on the other to move from where he stood, or sat, or lay, or to reach out with his hand, or foot, for a tool, such as a hammer, or a chisel, or for a kitchen utensil, such as a shovel, or a bucket, was in neither case an absolute inability, but an inability limited by the nature of the office to be discharged, or the act to be performed. And it was further with cynicism urged, in support of this view, that if Tom had been asked to keep an eye, not on the kettle, or on the saucepan, but on his niece Bridie dressing up for the night, he would have done so, however great his depression at the time, and that his exaltation had often been observed to fall, with remark-

able abruptness, in the neighbourhood of a corkscrew
and a bottle of stout. For Ann, though apparently plain
and rotten with disease, had her partisans, both inside
and outside the house. And to those who objected that
neither Ann's charms, nor her powers of persuasion,
could be compared with Bridie's, or with a bottle of
stout's, it was replied that if Tom had not done this
thing in a fit of depression, or in a fit of exaltation, then
he had done it in the interval between a fit of depression
and a fit of exaltation, or in the interval between a fit
of exaltation and a fit of depression, or in the interval
between a fit of depression and another fit of depression,
or in the interval between a fit of exaltation and another
fit of exaltation, for with Tom depression and exaltation
were not of regular alternance, whatever may have been
said to the contrary, but often he emerged from one fit
of depression only to be seized soon after by another,
and frequently he shook off one fit of exaltation only
to fall into the next almost at once, and in these brief
intervals Tom would sometimes behave most strangely,
almost like a man who did not know what he was
doing.

Some said it was her uncle Jack, who it will be
remembered was weak in the head. And to those who
were not of this opinion those who were were good
enough to point out that Jack was not only weak in
the head, but married to a woman who was weak in the
chest, whereas this could not be said of Ann's chest, that
it was weak, whatever might be said of other parts of
her, for it was well known that Ann had a splendid
bosom, white and fat and elastic, and what could be
more natural, in the mind of a man like Jack, weak-
minded and tied to a weak-chested woman, than that
the thought of this splendid part of Ann, so white, so
fat and so elastic, should grow and grow, whiter and
whiter, fatter and fatter, and more and more elastic,
until all thought of those other parts of Ann (and
they were numerous), where whiteness did not dwell,

nor fatness, nor elasticity, but greyness, and even greenness, and thinness, and bagginess, were driven quite away.

Other names mentioned in this connexion were those of Ann's uncles Joe, Bill and Jim, and of her nephews, Blind Bill and Maim Mat, Sean and Simon.

That none of Ann's kith and kin, but a stranger from without, had brought Ann to this pass, was considered likely by many, and the names of many strangers from without were freely mentioned, in this connexion.

Then some four months later, when winter seemed safely past, and spring in the air by some was even felt, the brothers Joe, Bill and Jim, or a grand total of more than one hundred and ninety-three years, in the short space of one week were carried off, Joe the eldest being carried off on a Monday, and Bill his junior by one year on the following Wednesday, and Jim their junior by two years and one year respectively on the Friday following, leaving old Tom sonless, and May and Kate husbandless, and May Sharpe brotherless, and Tom and Jack and Art and Con and Sam fatherless, and Mag and Lil father-in-lawless, and Ann uncleless, and Simon and Ann and Bridie and Tom and Sean and Kate and Bill and Matt and Sam's infant by the late Liz grandfatherless, and Rose and Cerise and Pat and Larry greatgrandfatherless.

This set back the longed-for day, on which the Lynches' eyes still were fixed, though with less confidence than before, by no less than seventeen years approximately, that is to say far beyond the horizon of expectation or even hope. For old Tom, for example, grew daily worse, and was heard to say, Why was me three boys took, and me with me gripes left?, suggesting that it would have been preferable, in his opinion, if his boys, who whatever their suffering did not suffer from unremitting agony in the caecum, had been left, and he, with his gripes, taken, and many other members of the

family also grew daily worse and could not be expected
to live, very much longer.

Then they were sorry for what they had said who
had said it was her uncle Joe, and who had said it was
her uncle Bill, and who had said it was her uncle Jim,
who had done this thing to Ann, for all three had
confessed their sins, to the priest, prior to being carried
away, and the priest was an old and intimate friend of
the family. And from the corpses of the brothers in a
cloud the voices rose and hovering sank to rest among
the living, here some, there others, here some again,
there others again, until hardly one living but had his
voice, and not one voice but was at rest. And of those
who had been in agreement, many were now in
disagreement, and of those who had been in disagreement, many now were in agreement, though some
that had agreed agreed still, and some that had
disagreed still disagreed. And so new friendships were
formed, and new enmities, and old friendships preserved,
and old enmities. And all was agreement and
disagreement and amity and enmity, as before, only
redistributed. And not one voice but was either for
or against, no, not one. But all was objection and
answer and answer and objection, as before, only in
other mouths. Not that many did not go on saying what
they had always said, for many did. But still more did
not. And the reason for that was perhaps this, that not
only were those who had said what they had said of
Jim, of Bill and of Joe, now by the deaths of Joe, of
Bill and of Jim incapacitated from going on doing so
and obliged to find something new to say, because Bill,
Joe and Jim, for all their foolishness, were not so
foolish as to allow themselves to be carried away without
owning up to the priest to what they had done to
Ann, if they had done it, but also a great number of
those who had never said anything of Jim, of Joe and
of Bill, in this connexion, unless it was that they had
not done this thing to Ann, and who were therefore in

no way by the deaths of Joe, of Jim and of Bill incapacitated from going on saying what they had always
said, in this connexion, nevertheless preferred, when
they heard some of those who had always spoken
against them, and against whom they had always spoken,
now speaking with them, to cease saying what they had
always said, in this connexion, and to begin saying
something quite new, in order that they might continue
to hear speaking against them, and themselves to speak
against, the greatest possible number of those who, prior
to the deaths of Bill, of Joe and of Jim, had always
spoken against them, and against whom they had always
spoken.   For it is a strange thing, but apparently
true, that those who speak speak rather for the
pleasure of speaking against than for the pleasure
of speaking with, and the reason for that is
perhaps this, that in agreement the voice can not
be raised perhaps quite so high as it can in
disagreement.

This little matter of the food and the dog, Watt
pieced it together from the remarks let fall, every now
and then, in the evening, by the twin dwarfs Art and
Con. For it was they who led the famished dog, every
evening, to the door. They had done this since the age
of twelve, that is to say for the past quarter of a century,
and they continued to do so all the time that Watt
remained in Mr Knott's house, or rather all the time
that he remained on the ground floor, for when Watt
was moved to the first floor, then Watt lost touch with
the ground floor, and saw no more the dog, nor them
who brought it. But surely it was still Art and Con who
led the dog, every evening, at nine o'clock, to Mr Knott's
backdoor, even when Watt was no longer there to witness
it, for they were sturdy little fellows, and wrapped up
in their work.

The dog in service when Watt entered Mr Knott's
service was the sixth dog that Art and Con had
employed, in this manner, in twenty-five years.

The dogs employed to eat Mr Knott's occasional remains were not long-lived, as a rule. This was very natural. For besides what the dog got to eat, every now and then, on Mr Knott's backdoorstep, it got so to speak nothing to eat. For if it had been given food other than the food that Mr Knott gave it, from time to time, then its appetite might have been spoilt, for the food that Mr Knott gave it. For Art and Con could never be certain, in the morning, that there would not be waiting for their dog, in the evening, on Mr Knott's backdoorstep, a pot of food so nourishing, and so copious, that only a thoroughly famished dog could get it down. And this was the eventuality for which it was their duty to be always prepared.

Add to his that Mr Knott's food was a little on the rich and heating side, for a dog.

Add to this that the dog was seldom off the chain, and so got no exercise worth mentioning. This was inevitable. For if the dog had been set free, to run about, as it pleased, then it would have eaten the horsedung, on the road, and all the other nasty things that abound, on the ground, and so ruined its appetite, perhaps for ever, or worse still would have run away, and never come back.

The name of this dog, when Watt entered Mr Knott's service, was Kate. Kate was not at all a handsome dog. Even Watt, whom his fondness for rats prejudiced against dogs, had never seen a dog that he less liked the look of than Kate. It was not a large dog, and yet it could not be called a small dog. It was a medium-sized dog, of repulsive aspect. It was called Kate not as might be supposed after Jim's Kate, so soon to be made a widow, but after quite a different Kate, a certain Katie Byrne, who was a kind of cousin of Joe's wife May, so soon to be made a widow too, and this Katie Byrne was a great favourite with Art and Con, to whom she always brought a gift of tobacco twist, when she came on a visit, and Art and Con were great chewers of tobacco twist, and never had enough, never never had enough tobacco twist, for their liking.

Kate died while Watt was still on the ground floor, and was replaced by a dog called Cis. Watt did not know whom this dog was called after. If he had enquired, if, coming out into the open, he had said, Con, or, Art, Kate I know was called after your relative, Katie Byrne, but after whom is Cis called?, then he might have learnt what he so desired to know. But there were limits to what Watt was prepared to do, in pursuit of information. There were times when he was half tempted to believe, as he observed the effect that this name had on Art and Con, notably when associated with certain injunctions, that it was the name of a friend of theirs, a near and dear friend, and that it was in honour of this near and dear friend that they had given the dog the name of Cis rather than some other name. But this was a mere conjecture, and at other times Watt was more inclined to believe that if the dog was called Cis, it was not on account of some living person's being called Cis, no, but simply because the dog had to be called something, to distinguish it, for itself, and for others, from all the other dogs, and that Cis was as good a name as any other, and indeed prettier than many.

Cis was still alive when Watt left the ground floor, for the first floor. What became of her later, and of the dwarfs, he had no idea. For once on the first floor Watt lost sight of the ground floor, and interest in the ground floor. This was indeed a merciful coincidence, was it not, that at the moment of Watt's losing sight of the ground floor, he lost interest in it also.

It was part of Watt's duties to receive Art and Con, when they called in the evening with the dog, and, when there was food for the dog, to witness the dog's eating the food, until not an atom remained. But after the first few weeks Watt abruptly ceased, on his own responsibility, to discharge this office. From then on, when there was food for the dog, he put it outside the door, on the doorstep, in the dog's dish, and he lit a light in the passage window, so that the doorstep should not be in darkness, even on the darkest night, and he contrived, for the dog's dish, a little lid that could be fastened down, by means of clasps, of clasps that clasped tight the sides, of the dish. And Art and Con grew to know that when the dog's dish was not on the doorstep, waiting for them, then there was no food for Kate, or Cis. They did not need to knock, and enquire, no, the bare doorstep was enough. And they even grew to know that when there was no light in the passage window, then there was no food, for the dog. And they learned also not to advance any further, in the evening, than the place whence they could see the passage window, and then to advance further only if there was a light, in the window, and always to go away, without advancing any further, if there was none. This was unfortunately of small practical assistance to Art and Con, for coming as one did, suddenly, round a corner of the bushes, on the backdoor, one did not see the passage window, which was beside the backdoor, until one was so close to the backdoor that one could have touched it with one's stick, if one had wished. But Art and Con gradually learned to tell, from no less a distance than ten or fifteen paces, whether there was a light in the passage window, or not. For the light, though hidden by the corner, shone through the passage window and made a glow, in the air, a glow that could be seen, especially when the night was dark, from no less a distance than ten or fifteen paces. Thus all that Art and Con had to do, when the night was favourable, was to advance a little way along the avenue, until they reached the place whence the light, if it was burning, must be visible, as a glow, a feeble glow, in the air, and thence to go on, towards the backdoor, or to go back, towards the gate, as the case might be. In the height of summer to be sure, only the doorstep bare,

or surmounted by the dog's dish, could tell Art and Con
and Kate, or Cis, whether there was food for the dog,
or not. For in the height of summer Watt did not set a
light, in the passage window, when there was food for
the dog, no, for in the height of summer the doorstep
was not dark until coming up to ten thirty, or eleven,
at night, but burning with all the raging dying summer
light, for it looked west, the backdoorstep. And to set
a light in the passage window, under these conditions,
would have been a mere waste of oil. But for more than
three quarters of the year Art's and Con's task was
greatly lightened as a result of Watt's refusal to be
present when the dog ate the food, and of the measures
he was obliged to take, in consequence. Then Watt, if
he had put out the plate, a little after eight, took it in
again, a little before ten, and washed it up, in readiness
for the morrow, before he locked up for the night and
went up to his bed, holding the lamp high above his
head, to guide his feet, on the stairs, the stairs that
never seemed the same stairs, from one night to another,
and now were steep, and now shallow, and now long,
and now short, and now broad, and now narrow, and
now dangerous, and now safe, and that he climbed,
among the moving shadows, every night, shortly after
ten o'clock.

This refusal, by Knott, I beg your pardon, by
Watt, to assist at the eating, by the dog, of Mr Knott's
remains, might have been supposed to have the gravest
consequences, both for Watt and for Mr Knott's
establishment.

Watt expected something of this kind. And yet
he could not have done otherwise, than he did. It
was in vain that he had no love for dogs, greatly prefer-
ring rats, he could not have done otherwise, believe it
or not, than he did. As is was, nothing happened, but
all went on, as before, apparently. No punishment fell
on Watt, no thunderbolt, and Mr Knott's establishment
swam on, through the unruffled nights and days, with

all its customary serenity. And this was a great source
of wonder, to Watt, that he had infringed, with
impunity, such a venerable tradition, or institution.
But he was not so foolish as to found in this a principle
of conduct, or a precedent of rebelliousness, ho no, for
Watt was only too willing to do as he was told, and as
custom required, at all times. And when he was forced
to transgress, as in the matter of witnessing the dog's
meal, then he was at pains to transgress in such a way,
and to surround his transgression with such precautions,
such delicacies, that it was almost as though he had not
transgressed at all. And perhaps this was counted to
him for grace. And he stilled the wonder the trouble
in his mind, by reflecting that if he went unpunished
for the moment, he would not perhaps always go
unpunished, and that if the hurt to Mr Knott's establishment did not at once appear, it would perhaps one day
appear, a little bruise at first, and then a bigger, and
then a bigger still, until, growing, growing, it blackened
the entire body.

For reasons that remain obscure Watt was, for a
time, greatly interested, and even fascinated, by this
matter of the dog, the dog brought into the world, and
maintained there, at considerable expense, for the sole
purpose of eating Mr Knott's food, on those days on
which Mr Knott was not pleased to eat it himself, and
he attached to this matter an importance, and even a
significance, that seem hardly warranted. For otherwise
would he have gone into the matter at such length?
And would he have gone into the Lynch family at such
length if, in thought, he had not been obliged to pass,
from the dog, to the Lynches, as to one of the terms of
the relation that the dog wove nightly, the other of
course being Mr Knott's remains. But much more than
with the Lynches, or with Mr Knott's remains, Watt's
concern, while it lasted, was with the dog. But it did
not last long, this concern of Watt's, not very long, as
such concerns go. And yet it was a major concern, of

that period, while it lasted. But once Watt had grasped, in its complexity, the mecanism of this arrangement, how the food came to be left, and the dog to be available, and the two to be united, then it interested him no more, and he enjoyed a comparative peace of mind, in this connexion. Not that for a moment Watt supposed that he had penetrated the forces at play, in this particular instance, or even perceived the forms that they upheaved, or obtained the least useful information concerning himself, or Mr Knott, for he did not. But he had turned, little by little, a disturbance into words, he had made a pillow of old words, for a head. Little by little, and not without labour. Kate eating from her dish, for example, with the dwarfs standing by, how he had laboured to know what that was, to know which the doer, and what the doer, and what the doing, and which the sufferer, and what the sufferer, and what the suffering, and what those shapes, that were not rooted to the ground, like the veronica, but melted away, into the dark, after a while.

Erskine was for ever running up the stairs and down them again. Not so Watt, who came down only once a day, when he got up, to begin his day, and only once a day went up, when he lay down, to begin his night. Unless when, in his bedroom, in the morning, or in the kitchen, in the evening, he left something behind, that he could not do without. Then of course he went back, up, or down, to fetch this thing, whatever it was. But this was very rare. For what could Watt leave behind, that he could not do without, for a day, for a night? His handkerchief perhaps. But Watt never used a handkerchief. His slopbag. No, he would not have gone back down all the way expressly for his slopbag. No, there was so to speak nothing that Watt could forget, that he could not do without, for the fourteen or fifteen hours that his day lasted, for the ten or nine hours that his night lasted. And yet every now and then he did forget something, some tiny little thing, so that he was obliged to return and fetch it, for he could not have got on, through his day, through his night, without it. But this was very rare. And otherwise he stayed quietly where he was, on the second floor in his little bedroom by night, and by day on the ground floor in the kitchen mostly, or wherever else his duties might take him, or in the pleasure garden up and down, or in a tree, or sitting on the ground against a tree or bush, or on a rustic seat. For to the first floor his duties never took him, at this period, nor to the second, once he had made his bed, and swept clean his little room, which he did every morning the first thing, before coming down, on an empty stomach. Whereas Erskine never did a tap on the ground floor, but all his duties were on the first floor. Now Watt did not know, nor care to ask, in what exactly these duties consisted. But whereas Watt's ground floor duties kept him quietly on the ground floor, Erskine's first floor duties did not keep Erskine quietly on the first floor, but for ever he was flying up the stairs from the first floor to the second floor and down them again from the second floor to the first floor and down the stairs from the first floor to the ground floor and up them again from the ground floor to the first floor, for no reason that Watt could see, though to be sure this was a matter in which Watt could not be expected to see very far, because he did not know, and did not care to ask, in what exactly Erskine's duties on the first floor consisted. Now this is not to say that Erskine did not spend a great deal of his time quietly on the first floor, for he did, but only that the number of times in the day that he went flying up and down again and down and up again seemed to Watt extraordinary. And what further seemed to Watt extraordinary was the shortness of time that Erskine spent up, when he flew up, before flying down again, and the shortness of time that he spent down, when he flew down, before flying up again, and of course the rapidity of his flight, as though he were

always in a hurry to get back. And if it were asked
how Watt, who was never on the second floor from
morning to night, could know how long Erskine spent
on the second floor, when he went there in this way,
the answer to that would perhaps be this, that Watt,
from where he sat in the bottom of the house, could
hear Erskine hasten up the stairs to the top of the
house, and then hasten down them again to the middle
of the house, almost without pause. And the reason
for that was perhaps this, that the sound came down
the kitchen chimney.

Watt did not care to enquire in so many words
into the meaning of all this, for he said, All this will
be revealed to Watt, in due time, meaning of course
when Erskine went, and another came. But he was not
easy until he had said, in short and isolated phrases,
or fragments of phrases, separated by considerable
periods of time from one another, Perhaps Mr Knott
sends him now upstairs, and now downstairs, on this
errand and on that, saying, But hasten back to me,
Erskine, don't delay, but hasten back to me. But what
kind of errand? Perhaps to fetch him something that
he has forgotten, and that suddenly he feels the need
of, such as a nice book, or piece of cotton wool or tissue
paper. Or perhaps to look out of a top window, to
make sure that nobody is coming, or to have a quick
look round below stairs, to make sure that no danger
threatens the foundations. But am I not here, below
stairs, somewhere about, on the alert? But it may be
that Mr Knott has more confidence in Erskine, who has
been here longer than I, than in me, who have not been
here so long as Erskine. And yet that does not seem like
Mr Knott, to be ever wanting this or that and sending
Erskine flying to see to it. But what do I know of
Mr Knott? Nothing. And what to me may seem most
unlike him, and what to me may seem most like him,
may in reality be most like him, most unlike him,
for all I can tell. Or perhaps Mr Knott sends Erskine

flying up and down in this way, simply in order to be
rid of him if only for a few moments. Or perhaps
Erskine, finding the first floor trying, is obliged to run
upstairs every now and then for a breath of the second
floor, and then every now and then downstairs for a
breath of the ground floor, or even garden, just as in
certain waters certain fish, in order to support the middle
depths, are forced to rise and fall, now to the surface
of the waves and now to the ocean bed. But do such
fish exist? Yes, such fish exist, now. But trying in
what way? Perhaps who knows Mr Knott propagates
a kind of waves, of depression, or oppression, or perhaps
now these, now those, in a way that it is impossible to
grasp. But that does not at all agree with my conception
of Mr Knott. But what conception have I of Mr Knott?
None.

Watt wondered if Arsene, Walter, Vincent and
the others had passed through the same phase as that
through which Erskine then was passing, and he wondered if he Watt would pass through it too, when his time
came. Watt could not easily imagine Arsene ever behav-
ing in such a way, nor himself either for that matter.
But there were many things that Watt could not easily
imagine.

Sometimes in the night Mr Knott pressed a bell
that sounded in Erskine's room, and then Erskine got
up and went down. This Watt knew, for from his bed
where he lay not far away he would hear the bell sound
ting! and Erskine get up and go down. He would hear
the sound of the bell because he was not asleep, or only
half asleep, or sleeping only lightly. For it is rare that
the sound of a bell not far away is not heard by the
only half asleep, the only lightly sleeping. Or he would
hear, not the sound of the bell, but the sound of Erskine
getting up and going down, which came to the same
thing. For would Erskine have got up and gone down
if the bell had not sounded? No. He might have got
up, without the bell's sounding, to do his number one,

or number two, in his great big white chamber pot. But
get up and go down, without the bell's sounding, no. At
other times, when Watt was sleeping deeply, or plunged
in meditation, or otherwise engrossed, then of course the
bell might sound and sound and Erskine get up and get
up and go down and go down and Watt be not a whit
the wiser. But that did not matter. For Watt had
heard the bell sound, and Erskine get up and go down,
often enough to know that sometimes in the night Mr
Knott pressed a bell and that then Erskine, doubtless
in obedience to the summons, got up and went down.
For were there other fingers in the house, and other
thumbs, than Mr Knott's and Erskine's and Watt's,
that might have pressed the bell? For by what but
by a finger, or by a thumb, could the bell have been
pressed? By a nose? A toe? A heel? A projecting
tooth? A knee? An elbow? Or some other prominent
bony or fleshy process? No doubt. But whose, if not
Mr Knott's? Watt had not pressed a bell with any part
of him, of that he was morally certain, for there was no
bell in his room that he could have pressed. And if
he had got up and gone down, to where the bell was,
and he did not know where the bell was, and pressed it
there, could he have got back into his room, and into
his bed, and sometimes even fallen into a light sleep,
in time to hear, from where he lay, in his bed, the bell
sound? The fact was that Watt had never seen a bell,
in any part of Mr Knott's house, or heard one, under
any other circumstances than those that so perplexed
him. On the ground floor there was no bell of any kind,
he could vouch for that, or so cunningly dissembled
that no trace appeared, on the walls, or the doorposts.
There was the telephone, to be sure, in a passage. But
what sounded in Erskine's room, in the night, was not
a telephone, Watt was sure of that, but a bell, a simple
bell, a simple little probably white electric bell, of the
kind that one presses until it sounds ting! and then lets
spring back, to the position of silence. Similarly

Erskine, if he had pressed the bell, must have pressed
it in his own room, and indeed from where he lay, in
his bed, as was manifest from the noise that Erskine
made in getting out of bed, immediately the bell rang.
But was it likely that there was a bell in Erskine's room,
that he could press, from his bed, when there was no
bell of any kind in any part of Watt's room? And even
if there was a bell in Erskine's room, that he could
press without leaving his bed, what interest could
Erskine have in pressing it, when he knew that at the
sound of the bell he must leave his warm bed and go
downstairs, inadequately clothed? If Erskine wished
to leave his snug bed and go downstairs, half naked,
could he not have done so without pressing a bell
beforehand? Or was Erskine out of his mind? And he
himself Watt was he not perhaps slightly deranged?
And Mr Knott himself, was he quite right in his head?
Were they not all three perhaps a little off the
hooks?

The question of who pressed the bell that sounded
in Erskine's room, in the night, was a great source of
worry to Watt, for a time, and kept him awake at night,
on the qui vive. If Erskine had been a snorer, and the
sound of the bell coincided with the sound of a snore,
then the mystery, it seemed to Watt, would have been
dissipated, as the mist, by the sun. But there, Erskine
was not a snorer. And yet to look at him, or hear him
sing his song, you would have taken him for a snorer, a
great snorer. And yet he was not a snorer. So the
sound of the bell came always on the stillness. But on
further reflexion it seemed to Watt that the bell's
coinciding with the snore would not have dissipated the
mystery, but left it entire. For might not Erskine
simulate a snore, at the very moment that he reached
out with his arm and pressed the bell, or might he not
simulate a long series of snores culminating in the snore
that he simulated as he pressed the bell, in order to
deceive Watt and make him think that it was not he

Erskine who pressed the bell, but Mr Knott, in some other part of the house? So the fact finally that Erskine did not snore, and that the sound of the bell came always on the silence, made Watt think, not that the bell might be pressed by Erskine, as at first it had made him think, no, but that the bell must be pressed by Mr Knott. For if Erskine pressed the bell, and did not wish it known, then he would utter a snore, or in some other way dissemble, as he pressed the bell, in order to make Watt think that it was not he Erskine who pressed the bell, but Mr Knott. But then it occurred to Watt that Erskine might press the bell not caring whether it were known or not, that it was he who did so, and that in that case he would not trouble to utter a snore, or otherwise dissemble, as he pressed the bell, but let the sound of the bell come on the stillness, for Watt to make of what he would.

Watt decided in the end that an examination of Erskine's room was essential, if his mind was to be pacified, in this connexion. Then he would be able to put the matter from him, and forget it, as one puts from one and forgets the peel of an orange, or of a banana.

Watt might have asked Erskine, he might have said, Tell me, Erskine, is there a bell in your room, or is there not? But this would have put Erskine on his guard, and Watt did not desire that. Or Erskine might have answered, Yes!, when the true answer was, No!, or, No!, when the true answer was, Yes!, or he might have answered truly, Yes!, or, No!, and Watt been unable to believe him. And then Watt would have been no better off than before, but rather worse, for he would have set Erskine on his guard.

Now Erskine's room was always locked, and the key in Erskine's pocket. Or rather, Erskine's room was never unlocked, nor the key out of Erskine's pocket, longer than two or three seconds at a stretch, which was the time that Erskine took to take the key from his pocket, unlock his door on the outside, glide into his room, lock his door again on the inside and slip the key back into his pocket, or take the key from his pocket, unlock his door on the inside, glide out of his room, lock the door again on the outside and slip the key back into his pocket. For if Erskine's room had been *always* locked, and the key *always* in Erskine's pocket, then Erskine himself, for all his agility, would have been hard set to glide in and out of his room, in the way he did, unless he had glided in and out by the window, or the chimney. But in and out by the window he could not have glided, without breaking his neck, nor in and out by the chimney, without being crushed to death. And this was true also of Watt.

The lock was of a kind that Watt could not pick. Watt could pick simple locks, but he could not pick obscure locks.

The key was of a kind that Watt could not counterfeit. Watt could counterfeit simple keys, in a workshop, in a vice, with a file and solder, filing down and building up another and quite different simple key, until the two simplicities were quite alike. But Watt could not counterfeit obscure keys.

Another reason why Watt could not counterfeit Erskine's key was this, that he could not obtain possession of it, even for a moment.

Then how did Watt know that Erskine's key was not a simple key? Why, for having turned and twisted his little wire in the hole.

Then Watt said, Obscure keys may open simple locks, but simple keys obscure locks never. But Watt had hardly said this when he regretted having done so. But then it was too late, the words were said and could never be forgotten, never undone. But a little later he regretted them less. And a little later he did not regret them at all. And a little later they pleased him again, no less than when they had first sounded, so gentle, so cajoling, in his skull. And then again a little later

he regretted them again, most bitterly. And so on.
Until there were few degrees of remorse, few of com-
placency, but more particularly of remorse, with which
Watt was not familiar, with reference to these words.
And this is perhaps worthy of mention, because it was
with Watt a common experience, where words were
concerned. And though it sometimes happened that a
moment's pensiveness was sufficient to fix his attitude,
once and for all, towards words when they sounded, so
that he liked them, or disliked them, more or less,
with an inalterable like or dislike, yet this did not
happen often, no, but thinking now this, now that, he
did not in the end know what to think, of the words
that had sounded, even when they were plain and modest
like the above, of a meaning so evident, and a form so
inoffensive, that made no matter, he did not know what
to think of them, from one year's end to the next,
whether to think poorly of them, or highly of them,
or with indifference.

    And if Watt had not known this, that Erskine's
key was not a simple key, then I should never have
known it either, nor the world. For all that I know
on the subject of Mr Knott, and of all that touched
Mr Knott, and on the subject of Watt, and of all that
touched Watt, came from Watt, and from Watt alone.
And if I do not appear to know very much on the subject
of Mr Knott and of Watt, and on the subject of all
that touched them, it is because Watt did not know
a great deal on these subjects, or did not care to tell.
But he assured me at the time, when he began to spin
his yarn, that he would tell all, and then again, some
years later, when he had spun his yarn, that he had
told all. And as I believed him then and then again, so
I continued to believe him, long after the yarn was
spun, and Watt gone. Not that there is any proof that
Watt did indeed tell all he knew, on these subjects, or
that he set out to do so, for how could there be, I knowing nothing on these subjects, except what Watt told me,

For Erskine, Arsene, Walter, Vincent and the others had all vanished, long before my time. Not that Erskine, Arsene, Walter, Vincent and the others could have told anything of Watt, except perhaps Arsene a little, and Erskine a little more, for they could not, but they might have told something of Mr Knott. Then we would have had Erskine's Mr Knott, and Arsene's Mr Knott, and Walter's Mr Knott, and Vincent's Mr Knott, to compare with Watt's Mr Knott. That would have been a very interesting exercise. But they all vanished, long before my time.

This does not mean that Watt may not have left out some of the things that happened, or that were, or that he may not have foisted in other things that never happened, or never were. Mention has already been made of the difficulties that Watt encountered in his efforts to distinguish between what happened and what did not happen, between what was and what was not, in Mr Knott's house. And Watt made no secret of this, in his conversations with me, that many things described as happening, in Mr Knott's house, and of course grounds, perhaps never happened at all, or quite differently, and that many things described as being, or rather as not being, for these were the more important, perhaps were not, or rather were all the time. But apart from this, it is difficult for a man like Watt to tell a long story like Watt's without leaving out some things, and foisting in others. And this does not mean either that I may not have left out some of the things that Watt told me, or foisted in others that Watt never told me, though I was most careful to note down all at the time, in my little notebook. It is so difficult, with a long story like the story that Watt told, even when one is most careful to note down all at the time, in one's little notebook, not to leave out some of the things that were told, and not to foist in other things that were never told, never never told at all.

Nor was the key the kind of key of which an impression could be taken, in wax, or plaster, or putty, or butter, and the reason for that was this, that possession of the key could not be obtained, even for a moment.

For the pocket in which Erskine kept this key was not the kind of pocket that Watt could pick. For it was no ordinary pocket, no, but a secret one, sewn on to the front of Erskine's underhose. If the pocket in which Erskine kept this key had been an ordinary pocket, such as a coat pocket, or a trouser's pocket, or even a waistcoat pocket, then Watt, by picking the pocket when Erskine was not looking, might have obtained possession of the key for long enough to record its impression in wax, or plaster, or putty, or butter. Then when he had recorded the impression he could have put the key back in the same pocket as the pocket from which he had taken it, having first taken care to wipe it clean, with a damp cloth. But to pick a pocket sewn on to the front of a man's underhose, even when the man was looking the other way, without arousing suspicion, was not, Watt knew, in his power.

Now if Erskine had been a lady... But there, Erskine was not a lady.

And if it were asked how it is known that the pocket in which Erskine kept this key was sewn on to the front of his underhose, the answer to that would be this, that one day when Erskine was doing his number one against a bush, Watt, who as Lachesis would have it was doing his number one too against the same bush, but on the other side, caught a glimpse, through the bush, for it was a deciduous bush, of the key, gleaming among the flap buttons.

And so always, when the impossibility of my knowing, of Watt's having known, what I know, what Watt knew, seems absolute, and insurmountable, and undeniable, and uncoercible, it could be shown that I know, because Watt told me, and that Watt knew, because someone told him, or because he found out for himself. For I know nothing, in this connexion, but what Watt told me. And Watt knew nothing, on this subject, but what he was told, or found out for himself, in one way or in another.

Watt might have broken the door down, with an axe, or a crow, or a small charge of explosive, but this might have aroused Erskine's suspicions, and Watt did not want that.

So that what with one thing and another, and with Watt's not wishing this, and with Watt's not wanting that, it seemed that Watt, as he was then, could never get into Erskine's room, never never get into Erskine's room, as it was then, and that for Watt to get into Erskine's room, as they were then, Watt would have to be another man, or Erskine's room another room.

And yet, without Watt's ceasing to be what he was, and without the room's ceasing to be what it was, Watt did get into the room, and there learned what he wished to know.

Ruse a by, he said, and as he said, Ruse a by, he blushed, until his nose seemed a normal colour, and hung his head, and twisted and untwisted his big red bony hands.

There was a bell in Erskine's room, but it was broken.

The only other object of note in Erskine's room was a picture, hanging on the wall, from a nail. A circle, obviously described by a compass, and broken at its lowest point, occupied the middle foreground, of this picture. Was it receding? Watt had that impression. In the eastern background appeared a point, or dot. The circumference was black. The point was blue, but blue! The rest was white. How the effect of perspective was obtained Watt did not know. But it was obtained. By what means the illusion of movement in space, and it almost seemed in time, was given, Watt could not

say. But it was given. Watt wondered how long it
would be before the point and circle entered together
upon the same plane. Or had they not done so already,
or almost? And was it not rather the circle that was
in the background, and the point that was in the foreground? Watt wondered if they had sighted each other,
or were blindly flying thus, harried by some force of
merely mechanical mutual attraction, or the playthings
of chance. He wondered if they would eventually pause
and converse, and perhaps even mingle, or keep steadfast on their ways, like ships in the night, prior to the
invention of wireless telegraphy. Who knows, they might
even collide. And he wondered what the artist had
intended to represent (Watt knew nothing about painting), a circle and its centre in search of each other, or
a circle and its centre in search of a centre and a circle
respectively, or a circle and its centre in search of its
centre and a circle respectively, or a circle and its centre
in search of a centre and its circle respectively, or a circle
and a centre not its centre in search of its centre and its
circle respectively, or a circle and a centre not its centre
in search of a centre and a circle respectively, or a circle
and a centre not its centre in search of its centre and
a circle respectively, or a circle and a centre not its
centre in search of a centre and its circle respectively,
in boundless space, in endless time (Watt knew nothing
about physics), and at the thought that it was perhaps
this, a circle and a centre not its centre in search of
a centre and its circle respectively, in boundless space,
in endless time, then Watt's eyes filled with tears that
he could not stem, and they flowed down his fluted
cheeks unchecked, in a steady flow, refreshing him
greatly.

Watt wondered how this picture would look
upside down, with the point west and the breach north,
or on its right side, with the point north and the breach
east, or on its left side, with the point south and the
breach west.

So he took it from its hook and held it before
his eyes, at arm's length, upside down, and on its right
side, and on its left side.

But in these positions the picture pleased Watt
less than it had when on the wall. And the reason for
that was perhaps this, that the breach ceased to be
below. And the thought of the point slipping in from
below at last, when it came home at last, or to its new
home, and the thought of,the breach open below perhaps
for ever in vain, these thoughts, to please Watt as they
did, required the breach to be below, and nowhere else.
It is by the nadir that we come, said Watt, and it is
by the nadir that we go, whatever that means. And the
artist must have felt something of this kind too, for the
circle did not turn, as circles will, but sailed steadfast
in its white skies, with its patient breach for ever below.
So Watt put it back on its hook, in the position in
which he had found it.

Watt did not of course wonder all these things
at the time, but some he wondered at the time, and the
others subsequently. But those that he wondered at
the time, he again wondered subsequently, together with
those that he did not wonder at the time, over and
over again. And many other things in this connexion
also, of which some at the time, and the others subsequently, Watt wondered subsequently also, time
without number.

One of these had to do with the property. Did
the picture belong to Erskine, or had it been brought
and left behind by some other servant, or was it part
and parcel of Mr Knott's establishment?

Prolonged and irksome meditations forced Watt
to the conclusion that the picture was part and parcel
of Mr Knott's establishment.

The question to this answer was the following,
of great importance in Watt's opinion: Was the picture
a fixed and stable member of the edifice, like Mr Knott's
bed, for example, or was it simply a manner of paradigm,

here to-day and gone to-morrow, a term in a series, like the series of Mr Knott's dogs, or the series of Mr Knott's men, or like the centuries that fall, from the pod of eternity?

A moment's reflexion satisfied Watt that the picture had not been long in the house, and that it would not remain long in the house, and that it was one of a series.

There were times when Watt could reason rapidly, almost as rapidly as Mr Nackybal. And there were other times when his thought moved with such extreme slowness that it seemed not to move at all, but to be at a standstill. And yet it moved, like Galileo's cradle. Watt was greatly worried by this disparity. And indeed it contained cause for worry.

Watt had more and more the impression, as time passed, that nothing could be added to Mr Knott's establishment, and from it nothing taken away, but that as it was now, so it had been in the beginning, and so it would remain to the end, in all essential respects, any significant presence, at any time, and here all presence was significant, even though it was impossible to say of what, proving that presence at all times, or an equivalent presence, and only the face changing, but perhaps the face ever changing, even as perhaps even Mr Knott's face ever slowly changed.

This supposition, as far as the picture was concerned, was to be strikingly confirmed, before long. And of the numberless suppositions elaborated by Watt, during his stay in Mr Knott's house, this was the only one to be confirmed, or for that matter infirmed, by events (if one may speak here of events), or rather the only passage to be confirmed, the only passage of the long supposition, the long dwindling supposition, that constituted Watt's experience in Mr Knott's house, and of course grounds, to be confirmed.

Yes, nothing changed, in Mr Knott's establishment, because nothing remained, and nothing came or went, because all was a coming and a going.

Watt seemed highly pleased with this tenth rate xenia. Spoken as he spoke it, back to front, it had a certain air, it is true.

But what preoccupied Watt most of all, towards the end of his stay on the ground floor, was the question as to how long he would remain, on the ground floor, and in his then bedroom, before being transferred to the first floor, and to Erskine's bedroom, and then how long he would remain, on the first floor, and in Erskine's bedroom, before leaving the place for ever.

Watt did not for a moment doubt that the ground floor went with his bedroom, and the first floor with Erskine's. Yet what could be more uncertain, than such a correspondence? As there seemed no measure between what Watt could understand, and what he could not, so there seemed none between what he deemed certain, and what he deemed doubtful.

Watt's feeling in this matter was that he would serve Mr Knott for one year on the ground floor, and then for another year on the first floor.

In support of this monstrous assumption he assembled the following considerations.

If the period of service, first on the ground floor, and then on the first floor, was not one year, then it was less than one year, or more than one year. But if it was less than one year, then there was want, seasons passing, or a season, or a month, or a week, or a day, wholly or in part, on which the light of Mr Knott's service had not shone, nor its dark brooded, a page of the discourse of the earth unturned. For in a year all is said, in any given latitude. But if it was more than one year, then there was surfeit, seasons passing, or a season, or a month, or a week, or a day, wholly or in part, twice through the beams the shadows of the service of Mr Knott, a fragment of rigmarole reread. For the new year says nothing new, to the man fixed in space. Therefore on the ground floor one year, and on the first another, for the light of the day of the ground floor was not as the light of the day of the first floor (notwithstanding their proximity), nor were the lights of their nights the same lights.

But even Watt could not hide from himself for long the absurdity of these constructions, which assumed the period of service to be the same for every servant, and invariably divided into two phases of equal duration. And he felt that the period and distribution of service must depend on the servant, on his abilities, and on his needs; that there were short-time men and long-time men, ground floor men and first floor men; that what one might exhaust, what might exhaust one, in two months, another might not, might not another, in ten years; and that to many on the ground floor the nearness of Mr Knott must long be a horror, and long a horror to others on the first his farness. But he had hardly felt the absurdity of those things, on the one hand, and the necessity of those others, on the other (for it is rare that the feeling of absurdity is not followed by the feeling of necessity), when he felt the absurdity of those things of which he had just felt the necessity (for it is rare that the feeling of necessity is not followed by the feeling of absurdity). For the service to be considered was not the service of one servant, but of two servants, and even of three servants, and even of an infinity of servants, of whom the first could not out till the second up, nor the second up till the third in, nor the third in till the first out, nor the first out till the third in, nor the third in till the second up, nor the second up till the first out, every going, every being, every coming consisting with a being and a coming, a coming and a going, a going and a being, nay with all the beings and all the comings, with all the comings and all the goings, with all the goings and all the beings, of all the servants that had ever served Mr Knott, of all the servants that ever would serve Mr Knott. And in this long chain of consistence, a chain stretching from the long dead to the far unborn, the notion of the arbitrary could only survive as the notion of a pre-established arbitrary.   For take any three or four servants, Tom, Dick, Harry and another, if Tom serves two years on the first floor, then Dick serves two years on the ground floor, and then Harry comes, and if Dick serves ten years on the first floor, then Harry serves ten years on the ground floor, and then the other comes, and so on for any number of servants, the period of service of any given servant on the ground floor coinciding always with the period of service on the first floor of his predecessor, and terminating with the arrival of his successor on the premises.   But Tom's two years on the first floor are not *because of* Dick's two years on the ground floor, or of Harry's coming then, and Dick's two years on the ground floor are not *because of* Tom's two years on the first floor, or of Harry's coming then, and Harry's coming then is not *because of* Tom's two years on the first floor, or of Dick's two years on the ground floor, and Dick's ten years on the first floor are not *because of* Harry's ten years on the ground floor, or of the other's coming then, and Harry's ten years on the ground floor are not *because of* Dick's ten years on the first floor, or of the other's coming then, and the other's coming then is not *because of* (tired of underlining this cursed preposition) Dick's ten years on the first floor, or of Harry's ten years on the ground floor, no, that would be too horrible to contemplate, but Tom's two years on the first floor, and Dick's two years on the ground floor, and Harry's coming then, and Dick's ten years on the first floor, and Harry's ten years on the ground floor, and the other's coming then, are because Tom is Tom, and Dick Dick, and Harry Harry, and that other that other, of that the wretched Watt was persuaded.   For otherwise in Mr Knott's house, and at Mr Knott's door, and on the way to Mr Knott's

door, and on the way from Mr Knott's door, there
would be a languor, and a fever, the languor of the
task done but not ended, the fever of the task ended
but not done, the languor and the fever of the going of
the coming too late, the languor and the fever of the
coming of the going too soon. But to Mr Knott, and
with Mr Knott, and from Mr Knott, were a coming
and a being and a going exempt from languor, exempt
from fever, for Mr Knott was harbour, Mr Knott was
haven, calmly entered, freely ridden, gladly left.
Driven, riven, bidden, by the storms without, the
storms within? The storms without! The storms within!
Men like Vincent and Walter and Arsene and Erskine
and Watt! Haw! No. But in the stress, in the threat,
in the call of storm, in the need, in the having, in the
losing of refuge, calm and freedom and gladness. Not
that Watt felt calm and free and glad, for he did not,
and had never done so. But he thought that perhaps
he felt calm and free and glad, or if not calm and free
and glad, at least calm and free, or free and glad, or
glad and calm, or if not calm and free, or free and glad,
or glad and calm, at least calm, or free, or glad, without
knowing it. But why Tom Tom? And Dick Dick?
And Harry Harry? Because Dick Dick and Harry
Harry? Because Harry Harry and Tom Tom? Because
Tom Tom and Dick Dick? Watt saw no objection.
But it was a conception of which for the moment he
had no need, and conceptions of which for the moment
Watt had no need Watt did not for the moment unfurl,
but left standing, as one does not unfurl, but leaves
standing, in readiness for a rainy day, one's umbrella
in one's umbrella stand. And the reason why Watt
for the moment had no need of this conception was
perhaps this, that when one's arms are full of waxen
lilies, then one does not stop to pick, or smell, or
chuck, or otherwise acknowledge, a daisy, or a primrose,
or a cowslip, or a buttercup, or a violet, or a dandelion,
or a daisy, or a primrose, or any other flower of the

field, or any other weed, but treads them down, and when the weight is past, and past the bowed head buried blinded in the white sweetness, then little by little under the load of petals the bruised stems straighten, those that is that have been fortunate enough to escape rupture. For it was not the Tomness of Tom, the Dickness of Dick, the Harryness of Harry, however remarkable in themselves, that preoccupied Watt, for the moment, but their Tomness, their Dickness, their Harryness then, their then-Tomness, then-Dickness, then-Harryness; nor the ordaining of a being to come by a being past, of a being past by a being to come (no doubt in itself a fascinating study), as in a musical composition bar a hundred say by say bar ten and bar say ten by bar a hundred say, but the interval between them, the ninety bars, the time taken to have been true, the time taken to be proved true, whatever that is. Or of course false, whatever that means.

So at first, in mind as well as body, Watt laboured at the ancient labour.

And so Watt, having opened this tin with his blowlamp, found it empty.

As it turned out, Watt was never to know how long he spent in Mr Knott's house, how long on the ground floor, how long on the first floor, how long altogether. All he could say was that it seemed a long time.

Thinking then, in search of rest, of the possible relations between such series as these, the series of dogs, the series of men, the series of pictures, to mention only these series, Watt remembered a distant summer night, in a no less distant land, and Watt young and well lying all alone stone sober in the ditch, wondering if it was the time and the place and the loved one already, and the three frogs croaking Krak!, Krek! and Krik!, at one, nine, seventeen, twenty-five, etc., and at one, six, eleven, sixteen, etc., and at one, four, seven, ten, etc., respectively, and how he heard

Krak! — — — — — —
Krek! — — — — Krek! — —
Krik! — — Krik! — — Krik! —

Krak! — — — — — —
— — Krek! — — — — Krek!
— Krik! — — Krik! — — Krik!

Krak! — — — — — —
— — — — Krek! — — —
— — Krik! — — Krik! —

Krak! — — — — — —
— Krek! — — — — Krek! —
Krik! — — Krik! — — Krik! —

Krak! — — — — — —
— — — — Krek! — — —
— Krik! — — Krik! — — Krik!

Krak! — — — — — —
Krek! — — — — Krek! — —
— — Krik! — — Krik! — —

Krak! — — — — — —
— — Krek! — — — — Krek!
Krik! — — Krik! — — Krik! —

Krak! — — — — — —
— — — — Krek! — —
— Krik! — — Krik! — — Krik!

Krak! — — — — — —
— Krek! — — — — Krek! —
— — Krik! — — Krik! —

Krak! — — — — — —
— — — Krek! — — — —
Krik! — — Krik! — — Krik! —

Krak! — — — — — — —
Krek! — — — — Krek! — —
— Krik! — — Krik! — — Krik!

Krak! — — — — — — —
— — Krek! — — — — Krek!
— — Krik! — — Krik! — —

Krak! — — — — — — —
— — — — Krek! — — —
Krik! — — Krik! — — Krik! —

Krak! — — — — — — —
— Krek! — — — — Krek! —
— Krik! — — Krik! — — Krik!

Krak! — — — — — — —
— — — Krek! — — — —
— — Krik! — — Krik! — —

Krak!
Krek!
Krik!

The fishwoman pleased Watt greatly. Watt was
not a woman's man, but the fishwoman pleased him
greatly. Other women would perhaps please him more,
later. But of all the women who had ever pleased him
up till then, not one could hold a candle to this fishwoman, in Watt's opinion.   And Watt pleased the
fishwoman. This was a merciful coincidence, that they
pleased each other. For if the fishwoman had pleased
Watt, without Watt's pleasing the fishwoman, or if
Watt had pleased the fishwoman, without the fishwoman's pleasing Watt, then what would have become
of Watt, or of the fishwoman? Not that the fishwoman
was a man's woman, for she was not, being of an
advanced age and by nature also denied those properties
that attract men to women, unless it was perhaps the

remains of a distinguished carriage, acquired from the
habit of carrying her basket of fish on her head, over
long distances. Not that a man, without possessing any
of those properties that attract women to men, may not
be a woman's man, nor that a woman, without possessing
any of those properties that attract men to women, may
not be a man's woman, for they may. And Mrs Gorman
had had several admirers, both before and after Mr Gorman, and even during Mr Gorman, and Watt at least
two well defined romances, in the course of his celibate.
Watt was not a man's man either, possessing as he did
none of those properties that attract men to men, though
of course he had had male friends (what wretch has
not?) on more than one occasion. Not that Watt might
not have been a man's man, without possessing any of
those properties that attract men to men, for he might.
But it happened that he was not. As to whether
Mrs Gorman was a woman's woman, or not, that is
one of those things that is not known. On the one hand
she may have been, on the other she may not. But it
seems probable that she was not. Not that it is by
any means impossible for a man to be both a man's
man and a woman's man, or for a woman to be both
a woman's woman and a man's woman, almost in the
same breath. For with men and women, with men's
men and women's men, with men's women and women's
women, with men's and women's men, with men's and
women's women, all is possible, as far as can be ascertained, in this connexion.
    Mrs Gorman called every Thursday, except when
she was indisposed. Then she did not call, but stayed
at home, in bed, or in a comfortable chair, before the
fire, if the weather was cold, and by the open window,
if the weather was warm, and, if the weather was neither
cold nor warm, by the closed window or before the
empty hearth. So Thursday was the day that Watt
preferred, to all other days. Some prefer Sunday,
others Monday, others Tuesday, others Wednesday,

others Friday, others Saturday, But Watt preferred
Thursday, because Mrs Gorman called on Thursday.
Then he would have her in the kitchen, and open for
her a bottle of stout, and set her on his knee, and wrap
his right arm about her waist, and lean his head upon
her right breast (the left having unhappily been removed
in the heat of a surgical operation), and in this position
remain, without stirring, or stirring the least possible,
forgetful of his troubles, for as long as ten minutes,
or a quarter of an hour. And Mrs Gorman too, as with
her left hand she stirred the greypink tufts, and with
her right at studied intervals raised the bottle to her
lips, was in her own small way at peace too, for a time.
      From time to time, hoisting his weary head,
from waist to neck his weary hold transferring, Watt
would kiss, in a despairing manner, Mrs Gorman on
or about the mouth, before crumpling back into his
post-crucified position. And these kisses, when their
first feverish force began to fail, that is to say very
shortly following their application, it was Mrs Gorman's
invariable habit to catch up, as it were, upon her own
lips, and return, with tranquil civility, as one picks
up a glove, or newspaper, let fall in some public place,
and restores it with a smile, if not a bow, to its rightful
proprietor. So that each kiss was in reality two kisses,
first Watt's kiss, velleitary, anxious, and then Mrs Gorman's, unctious and urbane.
      But Mrs Gorman did not always sit on Watt,
for sometimes Watt sat on Mrs Gorman. Some days
Mrs Gorman was on Watt all the time, other days Watt
was on Mrs Gorman throughout. Nor were there lacking
days when Mrs Gorman began by sitting on Watt, and
ended by having Watt sitting on her, or when Watt
began by sitting on Mrs Gorman, and ended by having
Mrs Gorman sitting on him. For Watt was apt to tire,
before the time came for Mrs Gorman to take her leave,
of having Mrs Gorman sitting on him, or of sitting
himself on Mrs Gorman. Then, if it was Mrs Gorman

on Watt, and not Watt on Mrs Gorman, then he would
urge her gently off his lap, to her feet, on the floor,
and he himself rise, until they who but a moment before
had both been seated, she on him, he on the chair,
now stood, side by side, on their feet, on the floor.
And then together they would sink to rest, Watt and
Mrs Gorman, the latter on the chair, the former on the
latter. But if was not Mrs Gorman on Watt, but Watt
on Mrs Gorman, then he would climb down from off
her knees, and raise her gently by the hand to her feet,
and take her place (bending his knees) on the chair, and
draw her down (spreading his thighs) among his lap.
And so little could Watt support, on certain days, on
the one hand the pressure of Mrs Gorman from above,
and on the other the thrust of Mrs Gorman from below,
that no fewer than two, or three, or four, or five, or six,
or seven, or eight, or nine, or ten, or eleven, or even
twelve, or even thirteen, changes of position were found
necessary, before the time came for Mrs Gorman to
take her leave. Which, allowing one minute for the
interversion, gives an average session of fifteen seconds,
and, on the moderate basis of one kiss, lasting one
minute, every minute and a half, a total for the day of
one kiss only, one double kiss, begun in the first session
and consummated in the last, for during the interversions
they could not kiss, they were so busy interverting.

Further than this, it will be learnt with regret,
they never went, though more than half inclined to do so
on more than one occasion. Why was this? Was it the
echo murmuring in their hearts, in Watt's heart, in
Mrs Gorman's, of past passion, ancient error, warning
them not to sully not to trail, in the cloaca of clonic
gratification, a flower so fair, so rare, so sweet, so frail?
It is not necessary to suppose so. For Watt had not the
strength, and Mrs Gorman had not the time, indispensable to even the most perfunctory coalescence.
The irony of life! Of life in love! That he who has
the time should lack the force, that she who has the

force should lack the time! That a trifling and in all
probability tractable obstruction of some endocrinal
Bandusia, that a mere matter of forty-five or fifty
minutes by the clock, should as effectively as death
itself, or as the Hellespont, separate lovers. For if Watt
had had a little more vigour Mrs Gorman would have
just had the time, and if Mrs Gorman had had a little
more time Watt could very likely have developed, with
a careful nursing of his languid tides, a breaker not
unworthy of the occasion. Whereas as things stood,
with Watt's strength, and Mrs Gorman's time, limited
as they were, it is difficult to see what more they
could have done than what they did, than sit on each
other, turn about, kissing, resting, kissing again and
resting again, until it was time for Mrs Gorman to
resume her circuit.

What was this in Mrs Gorman, what this in
Watt, that so appealed to Watt, so melted Mrs Gorman?
Between what deeps the call, the counter-call? Between
Watt not a man's man and Mrs Gorman not a woman's
woman? Between Watt not a woman's man and Mrs Gorman not a man's woman ? Between Watt not
a man's man and Mrs Gorman not a man's
woman ? Between Watt not a woman's man and
Mrs Gorman not a woman's woman ? Between
Watt neither a man's nor a woman's man and Mrs Gorman neither a man's nor a woman's woman? In his
own vitals, nucleant, he knew them clasped, the men
that were not men's, that were not women's men. And
Mrs Gorman was doubtless the theatre of a similar
conglutination. But that meant nothing. And were
they not perhaps rather drawn, Mrs Gorman to Watt,
Watt to Mrs Gorman, she by the bottle of stout, he by
the smell of fish? This was the view towards which,
in later years, when Mrs Gorman was no more than a
fading memory, than a dying perfume, Watt inclined.

Mr Graves came to the back door three times a
day. In the morning, when he arrived, to fetch the

key of his shed, and at midday, to fetch his pot of tea, and in the afternoon, to fetch his bottle of stout and return the teapot, and in the evening, to return the key and the bottle.

Watt conceived for Mr Graves a feeling little short of liking. In particular Mr Graves's way of speaking did not displease Watt. Mr Graves pronounced his *th* charmingly. Turd and fart, he said, for third and fourth. Watt liked these venerable saxon words. And when Mr Graves, drinking on the sunny step his afternoon stout, looked up with a twinkle in his old blue eye, and said, in mock deprecation, Tis only me turd or fart, then Watt felt he was perhaps prostituting himself to some purpose.

Mr Graves had much to say on the subject of Mr Knott, and of Erskine, Arsene, Walter, Vincent and others, whose names he had forgotten, or never known. But nothing of interest. He quoted as well from his ancestors' experience as from his own. For his father had worked for Mr Knott, and his father's father, and so on. Here then was another series. His family, he said, had made the garden what it was. He had nothing but good to say of Mr Knott and of his young gentlemen. This was the first time that Watt had been assimilated to the class of young gentlemen. But Mr Graves might just as well have been speaking of tavern companions.

But Mr Grave's chief subject of conversation was his domestic troubles. He did not, it appeared, get on well with his wife, and had not, for some time past. Indeed he did not get on with his wife at all. Mr Graves seemed to have reached the age at which the failure to get on with one's wife is more generally a cause of satisfaction than of repining. But it greatly discouraged Mr Graves. All his married life he had got on with his wife, like a house on fire, but now for some time past he had been quite unable to do so. This was very distressing also to Mrs Graves, that her husband could not get on with her any more, for there was nothing that Mrs Graves loved better than to be got on well with.

Watt was not the first to whom Mr Graves had unbosomed himself, in this connexion. For he had unbosomed himself to Arsene, many years before, when his trouble was green, and Arsene had given advice, which Mr Graves had followed to the letter. But nothing had ever come of it.

Erskine too had been admitted, by Mr Graves, to his confidence, and Erskine had been most generous with his advice. It was not the same advice as Arsene's, and Mr Graves had acted on it, to the best of his ability. But nothing had come of it.

Now to Watt Mr Graves did not say, in so many words, Tell me wat to do, Mr Watt, in order tat I may get on wid me wife, as in former times. And it was perhaps as well that he did not, for Watt would have been unable to reply, to such a question. And this silence would perhaps have been misconstrued by Mr Graves, and made to mean that it was all the same to Watt whether Mr Graves got on with his wife, or whether he did not.

The question was nevertheless implied, and indeed blatantly. For the first time that Mr Graves ended the relation of his trouble, he did not go away, but remained where he was, silent and expectant, floccillating his hard hat (Mr Graves always took off his hard hat, even in the open air, when in speech with his betters), and looking up at Watt, who was standing on the step. And as Watt's face wore its habitual expression, which was that of Judge Jeffreys presiding the Ecclesiastical Commission, Mr Graves's hopes ran high, of hearing something to his advantage. Unfortunately Watt was thinking of birds at the time, their missile flights, their canorous reloadings. But soon tiring of this he turned back into the house, closing the door behind him.

But it was not long before Watt began to put out the key, overnight, by the step, under a stone, and to put out the pot of tea at midday, under a cosy, and to put out the bottle of stout in the afternoon, with a corkscrew, in the shade. And in the evening, when Mr Graves had gone home, then Watt would take in the teapot, and the bottle, and the key, which Mr Graves had put back, where he had found them. But a little later Watt ceased to take in the key. For why take in the key, at six, when it must be put out, at ten? So the key's nail, in the kitchen, knew the key no more, but only Mr Graves's pocket, and the stone. But if Watt did not take in the key, in the evening, when Mr Graves was gone, but only the teapot and the bottle, yet he never failed, when he took in the teapot and the bottle, to look under the stone, and make sure the key was there.

Then one bitter night Watt left his warm bed and went down, and took in the key, and he wrapped it in a snippet of blanket, that he had snipped, from his own blanket. And then he put it out again, under the stone. And when he looked the next evening he found it, as he had left it, in its blanket, under the stone. For Mr Graves was a very understanding man.

Watt wondered if Mr Graves had a son, as Mr Gall had, to step into his shoes, when he was dead. Watt thought it most probable. For does one get on with one's wife, all one's married life, like a house on fire, without having a least one son, to step into one's shoes, when one dies, or retires?

Sometimes in the vestibule Watt would catch a glimpse of Mr Knott, or in the garden, stock still, or moving slowly about.

One day Watt, coming out from behind a bush, almost ran into Mr Knott, which for an instant troubled Watt greatly, for he had not quite finished adjusting his dress. But he need not have been troubled. For Mr Knott's hands were behind his back, and his head

bowed down, towards the ground. Then Watt in his
turn looking down at first saw nothing but the short
green grass, but when he had looked a little longer he
saw a little blue flower and close by a fat worm burrow-
ing into the earth. So this was what had attracted
Mr Knott's attention, perhaps. So there for a short
time they stood together, the master and the servant, the
bowed heads almost touching (which gives Mr Knott's
approximate height, does it not, assuming that the
ground was level), until the worm was gone and only
the flower remained. One day the flower would be
gone and only the worm remain, but on this particular
day it was the flower that remained, and the worm
that went. And then Watt, looking up, saw that
Mr Knott's eyes were closed, and heard his breathing,
soft and shallow, like the breathing of a child asleep.

Watt did not know whether he was glad or sorry
that he did not see Mr Knott more often. In one sense
he was sorry, and in another glad. And the sense in
which he was sorry was this, that he wished to see
Mr Knott face to face, and the sense in which he was
glad was this, that he feared to do so. Yes indeed, in
so far as he wished, in so far as he feared, to see Mr Knott
face to face, his wish made him sorry, his fear glad,
that he saw him so seldom, and at such a great distance
as a rule, and so fugitively, and so often sideways on,
and even from behind.

Watt wondered if Erskine was better served, in
this matter, than he.

But as time, as time will, drew on, and Watt's
period of service on the ground floor approached its
term, then this wish and this fear, and so this sorrow
and this gladness, like so many other wishes and fears,
so many other sorrows and gladnesses, grew duller and
duller and gradually ceased to be felt, at all. And the
reason for that was perhaps this, that little by little
Watt abandoned all hope, all fear, of ever seeing
Mr Knott face to face, or perhaps this, that Watt, while

continuing to believe in the possibility of his seeing one
day Mr Knott face to face, came to regard its realization
as one to which no importance could be attached, or
perhaps this, that as Watt's interest in what has been
called the spirit of Mr Knott increased, his interest in
what is commonly known as the body diminished (for
it is frequent, when one thing increases in one place,
for another in another to diminish), or perhaps some
quite different reason, such as mere fatigue, having
nothing to do with any of these.

Add to this that the few glimpses caught of
Mr Knott, by Watt, were not clearly caught, but as it
were in a glass, not a looking-glass, a plain glass, an
eastern window at morning, a western window at evening.

Add to this that the figure of which Watt sometimes caught a glimpse, in the vestibule, in the garden,
was seldom the same figure, from one glance to the next,
but so various, as far as Watt could make out, in its
corpulence, complexion, height and even hair, and of
course in its way of moving and of not moving, that
Watt would never have supposed it was the same, if
he had not known that it was Mr Knott.

Watt had never heard Mr Knott either, heard
him speak, that is to say, or laugh, or cry. But once
he thought he heard him say Tweet! Tweet! to a little
bird, and once he heard him make a strange noise,
PLOPF PLOPF *Plopf* Plopf *plopf* plopf plop plo pl.
This was in the flower garden.

Watt wondered if Erskine was any better off in
this respect. Did he and his master converse? Watt
had never heard them do so, as he surely would have
done, if they had done so. In an undertone perhaps.
Yes, perhaps they conversed in undertones, the master
and the servant, in two undertones, the master's
undertone, the servant's undertone.

One day towards the end of Watt's stay on the
ground floor, the telephone rang and a voice asked
how Mr Knott was. Here was a teaser, to be sure. The

voice said further, A friend. It might have been a
high male voice, or it might have been a deep female
voice.

Watt stated this incident as follows:

A friend, sex uncertain, of Mr Knott telephoned
to know how he was

Cracks soon appeared in this formulation.

But Watt was too tired to repair it. Watt dared
not tire himself further.

How often he had poohpoohed it, this danger
of tiring himself further. Poohpooh, he had said, poohpooh, and set to, to repair the cracks. But not now.

Watt was now tired of the ground floor, the
ground floor had tired Watt out.

What had he learnt? Nothing.

What did he know of Mr Knott? Nothing.

Of his anxiety to improve, of his anxiety to
understand, of his anxiety to get well, what remained?
Nothing.

But was not that something?

He saw himself then, so little, so poor. And now,
littler, poorer. Was not that something?

So sick, so alone.

And now.

Sicker, aloner.

Was not that something?

As the comparative is something. Whether more
than its positive or less. Whether less than its super-
lative or more.

Red, bluer, yellowist, that old dream was ended,
half ended, ended. Again.

A little before morning.

But at last he awoke to find, on arising, on
descending, Erskine gone, and, on descending a little
further, a strange man in the kitchen.

He did not know when this was. It was when
the yew was dark green, almost black. It was on a
morning white and soft, and the earth seemed dressed

for the grave. It was to the sound of bells, of chapel bells, of church bells. It was on a morning that the milkboy came singing to the door, shrilly to the door his tuneless song, and went singing away, having measured out the milk, from his can, to the jug, with all his usual liberality.

The strange man resembled Arsene and Erskine, in build. He gave his name as Arthur. Arthur.

regret, at ever having left his mansion at all, and the vow, the hollow vow, never to leave his mansion again, never never to leave his mansion again, on any account. So we knew resistance too, resistance to the call of the kind of weather we liked, but seldom simultaneously. Not that our resisting simultaneously had any bearing on our meeting, our conversing, for it had not. For when we both resisted we no more met, no more conversed, than when the one resisted, the other yielded. But ah, when we yielded both, then we met, and perhaps conversed, in the little garden.

It is so easy to accept, so easy to refuse, when the call is heard, so easy, so easy. But to us, in our windowlessness, in our bloodheat, in our hush, to us who could not hear the wind, nor see the sun, what call could come, from the kind of weather we liked, but a call so faint as to mock acceptance, mock refusal? And it was of course impossible to have any confidence in the meteorological information of our attendants. So it is not to be wondered at if, through sheer ignorance of what was going on without, we spent indoors, now Watt, now I, now Watt and I, many fleeting hours that might have fled, just as well, if not better, certainly not worse, from us with us as we walked, Watt, or I, or Watt and I, and perhaps even went through some of the forms of conversation, in the little garden. No, but what is to be wondered at is this, that to us both, disposed to yield, each in his separate soundless unlit warmth, the call should come, and coax us out, as often as it did, as sometimes it did, into the little garden. Yes, that we should have ever met, and spoken and listened together, and that my arm should ever have rested on his arm, and his on mine, and our shoulders ever touched, and our legs moved in and out, together over more or less the same ground, parallelly the right legs forward, the left ones back, and then without hesitation the reverse, and that, leaning forward, breast to breast, we should ever have embraced (oh, exceptionally, and of course never on the mouth), that seemed to me, the last time I remembered, strange, strange. For we never left our mansions, never, unless at the call of the kind of weather we liked, Watt never left his for me, I never left mine for him, but leaving them independently at the call of the kind of weather we liked we met, and sometimes conversed, with the utmost friendliness, and even tenderness, in the little garden.

No truck with the other scum, cluttering up the passageways, the hallways, grossly loud, blatantly morose, and playing at ball, always playing at ball, but stiffly, delicately, out from our mansions, and through this jocose this sniggering muck, to the kind of weather we liked, and back as we went.

The kind of weather we liked was a high wind and a bright sun mixed (1). But whereas for Watt the important thing was the wind, the sun was the important thing for Sam. With the result that though the sun though bright were not so bright as it might have been, if the wind were high Watt did not audibly complain, and that I, when illuminated by rays of appropriate splendour, could forgive a wind which, while strong, might with advantage have been stronger. It is thus evident that the occasions were few and far between on which, walking and perhaps talking in the little garden, we walked there and perhaps talked with equal enjoyment. For when on Sam the sun shone bright, then in a vacuum panted Watt, and when Watt like a leaf was tossed, then stumbled Sam in deepest night. But ah, when exceptionally the desired degrees of ventilation and radiance were united, in the little garden, then we were peers in peace, each in his own way, until the wind fell, the sun declined.

---

(1) Watt liked the sun at this time, or at least supported it. Nothing is known about this volte-face. He seemed pleased that all the shadows should move, not only himself.

Not that the garden was so little, for it was not, being of ten or fifteen acres in extent. But it seemed little to us, after our mansions.

In it great pale aspens grew, and yews ever dark, with tropical luxuriance, and other trees, in lesser numbers.

They rose from the wild pathless grass, so that we walked much in shade, heavy, trembling, fierce, tempestuous.

In winter there were the thin shadows writhing, under our feet, in the wild withered grass.

Of flowers there was no trace, save of the flowers that plant themselves, or never die, or die only after many seasons, strangled by the rank grass. The chief of these was the pissabed.

Of vegetables there was no sign.

There was a little stream, or brook, never dry, flowing, now slow, now with torrential rapidity, for ever in its narrow ditch. Unsteadily a rustic bridge bestrode its dark waters, a rustic humpbacked bridge, in a state of extreme dilapidation.

It was through the crown of this construction that one day Watt, treading more heavily than was his wont, or picking his steps with less than his usual care, drove his foot, and part of his leg. And he would certainly have fallen, and perhaps been carried away by the subfluent flood, had I not been at hand to bear him up. For this trifling service, I remember, I received no thanks. But we set to work at once, Watt from the one bank, I from the other, with stout boughs and withes of willow, to repair the havoc. We lay at full length on our stomachs, I at my full length on my stomach, and Watt at his on his, partly (for security) on our banks, partly on the up slopes of the stages, and worked with diligence with arms outstretched until our task was done, and the place mended, and as good as before, if not better. Then, our eyes meeting, we smiled, a thing we did rarely, when together. And when we had lain a little thus, with this exceptional smile, on our faces, then we began to draw ourselves forward, and upward, and persisted in this course until our heads, our noble bulging brows, met, and touched, Watt's noble brow, and my noble brow. And then we did a thing we seldom did, we embraced. Watt laid his hands on my shoulders, and I laid mine on his (I could hardly do otherwise), and then I touched Watt's left cheek with my lips, and then Watt touched my left cheek with his (he could scarcely do less), the whole coolly, and above us tossed the overarching boughs.

We were attached, you see, to the little bridge. For without it how should we have passed from one part of the garden to the other, without wetting our feet, and perhaps catching a chill, liable to develop into pneumonia, with very likely fatal results.

Of seats, on which to sit down, and rest, there was not the slightest vestige.

Shrubs and bushes, properly so called, were absent from the scene. But thickets rose at every turn, brakes of impenetrable density, and towering masses of brambles, of a beehive form.

Birds of every kind abounded, and these it was our delight to pursue, with stones and clods of earth. Robins, in particular, thanks to their confidingness, we destroyed in great numbers. And larks' nests, laden with eggs still warm from the mother's breast, we ground into fragments, under our feet, with peculiar satisfaction, at the appropriate season, of the year.

But our particular friends were the rats, that dwelt by the stream. They were long and black. We brought them such titbits from our ordinary as rinds of cheese, and morcels of gristle, and we brought them also bird's eggs, and frogs, and fledgelings. Sensible of these attentions, they would come flocking round us at our approach, with every sign of confidence and affection, and glide up our trouserlegs, and hang upon our breasts. And then we would sit down in the midst of them, and give them to eat, out of our hands, of a nice fat frog, or a baby thrush. Or seizing suddenly a plump young rat, resting in our bosom after its repast, we would feed it to its mother, or its father, or its brother, or its sister, or to some less fortunate relative.

It was on these occasions, we agreed, after an exchange of views, that we came nearest to God.

When Watt spoke, he spoke in a low and rapid voice. Lower voices, voices more rapid, have been heard, will be heard, than Watt's voice, no doubt. But that there ever issued from the mouth of man, or ever shall again, except in moments of delirium, or during the service of the mass, a voice *at once* so rapid and so low, is hard to believe. Watt spoke also with scant regard for grammar, for syntax, for pronunciation, for enunciation, and very likely, if the truth were known, for spelling too, as these are generally received. Proper names, however, both of places and of persons, such as Knott, Christ, Gomorrha, Cork, he articulated with great deliberation, and from his discourse these emerged, palms, atolls, at long intervals, for he seldom specified, in a most refreshing manner . The labour of composition, the uncertainty as to how to proceed, or whether to proceed at all, inseparable from even our most happy improvisations, and from which neither the songs of birds, nor even the cries of quadrupeds, are exempt, had here no part, apparently. But Watt spoke as one speaking to dictation, or reciting, parrot-like, a text, by long repetition become familiar. Of this impetuous murmur much fell in vain on my imperfect hearing and understanding, and much by the rushing wind was carried away, and lost for ever.

This garden was surrounded by a high barbed wire fence, greatly in need of repair, of new wire, of fresh barbs. Through this fence, where it was not overgrown by briars and giant nettles, similar gardens, similarly enclosed, each with its pavilion, were on all sides distinctly to be seen. Now converging, now diverging,

these fences presented a striking irregularity of contour.
No fence was party, nor any part of any fence. But their
adjacence was such, at certain places, that a broad-
shouldered or broad-basined man, threading these narrow
straits, would have done so with greater ease, and with
less jeopardy to his coat, and perhaps to his trousers,
sideways than frontways. For a big-bottomed man, on
the contrary, or a big-bellied man, frontal motion would
be an absolute necessity, if he did not wish his stomach
to be perforated, or his arse, or perhaps both, by a
rusty barb, or by rusty barbs. A big-bottomed big-
bosomed woman, an obese wet-nurse, for example, would
be under a similar necessity. While persons at once
broad-shouldered and big-bellied, or broad-basined and
big-bottomed, or broad-basined and big-bellied, or
broad-shouldered and big-bottomed, or big-bosomed and
broad-shouldered, or big-bosomed and broad-basined,
would on no account, if they were in their right senses,
commit themselves to this treacherous channel, but turn
about, and retrace their steps, unless they wished to be
impaled, at various points at once, and perhaps bleed
to death, or be eaten alive by the rats, or perish from
exposure, long before their cries were heard, and still
longer before the rescuers appeared, running, with the
scissors, the brandy and the iodine. For were their cries
not heard, then their chances of rescue were small, so
vast were these gardens, and so deserted, in the ordinary
way.

  Some time passed, after Watt's transfer, before
we met again. I walked in my garden as usual, that is
to say when I yielded to the call of the kind of weather
I liked, and similarly Watt walked in his. But as it
was no longer the same garden, we did not meet. When
finally we did meet, again, in the way described below,
it was clear to us both, to me, to Watt, that we might
have met much sooner, if we had wished. But there,
the wish to meet was lacking. Watt did not wish to
meet me, I did not wish to meet Watt. This is not to

say that we were opposed to meeting, to resuming our walks, our talks, as before, for we were not, but only that the wish to do so was not felt, by Watt, by me.

Then one fine day, of unparallelled brightness and turbulence, I found my steps impelled, as though by some external agency, towards the fence; and this impulsion was maintained, until I could go no further, in that direction, without doing myself a serious, if not fatal, injury; then it left me and I looked about, a thing I never used to do, on any account, in the ordinary way. How hideous is the semi-colon. I say an external agency; for of my own volition, which, if not robust, did nevertheless possess, at that period, a kind of kittenish tenacity, I should never have gone near the fence, under any circumstances; for I was very fond of fences, of wire fences, very fond indeed; not of walls, nor palissades, nor opacious hedges, no; but to all that limited motion, without limiting vision, to the ditch, the dyke, the barred window, the bog, the quicksand, the paling, I was deeply attached, at that time, deeply deeply attached. And (which renders, if possible what follows even more singular that it would be otherwise), so, I believe, was Watt. For when, before his transfer, we walked together in our garden, on no single occasion did we go near the fence, as we surely must have done, if chance had led us, at least once or twice. Watt did not guide me, nor I him, but of our own accord, as though by mutual tacit consent, we never went nearer to the fence than a hundred yards, or a quarter of a mile. Sometimes we saw it afar, faintly the old sagging strands, the leaning posts, trembling in the wind, at the end of a glade. Or we saw a big black bird perched in the void, perhaps croaking, or preening its feathers.

Being now so near the fence, that I could have touched it with a stick, if I had wished, and so looking about me, like a mad creature, I perceived, beyond all possibility of error, that I was in the presence of one of those channels or straits described above, where the

limit of my garden, and that of another, followed the
same course, at so short a remove, the one from the
other, and for so considerable a distance, that it was
impossible for doubts not to arise, in a reasonable mind,
regarding the sanity of the person responsible for the
lay-out. Continuing my inspection, like one deprived
of his senses, I observed, with a distinctness that left no
room for doubt, in the adjoining garden whom do you
think but Watt, advancing backwards towards me. His
progress was slow and devious, on account no doubt of
his having no eyes in the back of his head, and painful
too, I fancy, for often he struck against the trunks of
trees, or in the tangles of underwood caught his foot,
and fell to the ground, flat on his back, or into a great
clump of brambles, or of briars, or of nettles, or of
thistles. But still without murmur he came on, until
he lay against the fence, with his hands at arm's length
grasping the wires. Then he turned, with the intention
very likely of going back the way he had come, and I
saw his face, and the rest of his front. His face was
bloody, his hands also, and thorns were in his scalp.
(His resemblance, at that moment, to the Christ believed
by Bosch, then hanging in Trafalgar Square, was so
striking, that I remarked it.) And at the same instant
suddenly I felt as though I were standing before a great
mirror, in which my garden was reflected, and my fence,
and I, and the very birds tossing in the wind, so that I
looked at my hands, and felt my face, and glossy skull,
with an anxiety as real as unfounded. (For if anyone, at
that time, could be truly said not to resemble the Christ
supposed by Bosch, then hanging in Trafalgar Square,
I flatter myself it was I.) Why, Watt, I cried, that is a
nice state you have got yourself into, to be sure. Not
it is, yes, replied Watt. This short phrase caused me,
I believe, more alarm, more pain, than if I had received,
unexpectedly, at close quarters, a charge of small shot
in the ravine. This impression was reinforced by what
followed. Wonder I, said Watt, panky-hanky me lend

you could, blood away wipe. Wait, wait, I am coming,
I cried. And I believe, that in my anxiety to come at
Watt then, I would have launched myself against the
barrier, bodily, if necessary. Indeed I went so far, with
this purpose in view, as hastily to withdraw to a distance
of ten or fifteen paces, and to cast round for a sapling,
or a bough, susceptible of conversion, rapidly, and
without the help of any cutting instrument, into a pole,
or perch. While I was thus half-heartedly employed, I
thought I saw, in the fence, on my right, a hole, large
and irregular. Judge then of my astonishment when,
upon approach, I found I was not mistaken. It was a
hole, in the fence, a large irregular hole, caused by
numberless winds, numberless rains, or by a boar, or
by a bull, flying, pursuing, a wild boar, a wild bull,
blind with fear, blind with rage, or who knows perhaps
with carnal desire, crashing at this point, through the
fence, weakened by numberless winds, numberless rains.
Through this hole I passed, without hurt, or damage to
my pretty uniform, and found myself looking about me,
for I had not yet recovered my aplomb, in the couloir.
My senses being now sharpened to ten or fifteen times
their normal acuity, it was not long before I saw, in the
other fence, another hole, in position opposite, and
similar in shape, to that through which, some ten
or fifteen minutes before, I had made my way. So
that I said that no boar had made these holes, nor any
bull, but the stress of weather, particularly violent just
here. For where was the boar, where the bull, capable,
after bursting a hole in the first fence, of bursting a
second, exactly similar, in the second? But would not
the bursting of the first hole so reduce the infuriated
mass as to render impossible, in the course of the same
charge, the bursting of the second? Add to this that
a bare yard separated the fences, at this point, so that
the snout would be, of necessity, in contact with the
second fence, before the hind-quarters were clear of
the first, and consequently the space be lacking in

which, after the bursting of the first hole, the fresh impetus might be developed necessary to the bursting of the second. Nor was it likely that the bull, or boar, after the bursting of the first hole, had withdrawn to a point from which, proceeding as before, he might acquire the impetus necessary to the bursting of the second hole, via the first hole. For either, after the bursting of the first hole, the animal was still blind with passion, or he was so no longer. If he was so still, then the chances were indeed small of his seeing the first hole with the distinctness necessary to his passing through it with the velocity necessary to the bursting of the second hole. And if he was so no longer, but by the bursting of the first hole calmed, and his eyes opened, why then the probability was remote indeed of his desiring to burst another. Nor was it likely that the second hole, or better still Watt's hole (for there was nothing to show that the so-called second hole was not anterior to the so-called first hole, and the so-called first hole not posterior to the so-called second hole), had been burst, independently, at some quite different time, from Watt's side of the fence. For if the two holes had been independently burst, the one from Watt's side of Watt's fence, and the other from mine of mine, by two quite different infuriated boars, or bulls (for that the one had been burst by an infuriated boar, and the other by an infuriated bull, was unlikely), and at two quite different times, the one from Watt's side of Watt's fence, and the other from mine of mine, then their conjunction, at this point, was incomprehensible, to say the least. Nor was it likely that the two holes, the hole in Watt's fence and the hole in mine, had been burst, on the same occasion, by two infuriated bulls, or by two infuriated boars, or by one infuriated bull and one infuriated cow, or by one infuriated boar and one infuriated sow (for that they had been burst, simultaneously, the one by an infuriated bull and the other by an infuriated sow, or the one by an infuriated boar and

the other by an infuriated cow, was hard to believe),
charging, with hostile or libidinous intent, the one from
Watt's side of Watt's fence, the other from mine of
mine, and clashing, the holes once burst, at the spot
where now I stood, trying to understand. For this
implied the bursting of the holes, by the bulls, or by the
boars, or by the bull and cow, or by the boar and sow,
at exactly the same moment, and not first one, and then
an instant later the other. For if first one, and then an
instant later the other, then the bull, the cow, the boar,
the sow, first through its fence, and thrusting with its
head against the other, must have prevented, willy nilly,
through this other, at this particular point, the passage
of the bull, the cow, the bull, the boar, the sow, the
boar, hastening to meet it, with all the fury of hate,
the fury of love. Nor could I find, though I went down
on my knees, and parted the wild grasses, any trace,
whether of combat or of copulation. No bull then had
burst these holes, nor any boar, nor any two bulls, nor
any two boars, nor any two cows, nor any two sows, nor
any bull and cow, nor any boar and sow, no, but the
stress of weather, rains and winds without number, and
suns, and snows, and frosts, and thaws, particularly
severe just here. Or was it not after all just possible,
through the two fences thus weakened by exposure,
for a single exceptionally powerful infuriated or terrified
bull, or cow, or boar, or sow, or even some other wild
animal, to have passed, whether from Watt's side of
Watt's fence, or from mine of mine, as though the two
fences were but one?

Turning now to where I had last had the pleasure
of seeing Watt, I saw that he was there no longer, nor
indeed in any of the other places, and they were numerous, visible to my eye. But when I called, Watt! Watt!,
then he came, awkwardly buttoning his trousers, which
he was wearing back to front, out from behind a tree,
and then backwards, guided by my cries, slowly, pain-
fully, often falling, but as often picking himself up, and

without murmur, towards where I stood, until at last,
after so long, I could touch him again, with my hand.
Then I reached out with my hand, through the hole, and
drew him, through the hole, to my side, and with a
cloth that I had in my pocket wiped his face, and his
hands, and then taking a little box of ointment that I
had in my pocket from my pocket I anointed his face,
and his hands, and then taking a little handcomb from
my pocket I straightened his tufts, and his whiskers,
and then taking a little clothesbrush from my pocket I
brushed his coat, and his trousers. Then I turned him
round, until he faced me. Then I placed his hands, on
my shoulders, his left hand on my right shoulder, and
his right hand on my left shoulder. Then I placed my
hands, on his shoulders, on his left shoulder my right
hand, and on his right shoulder my left hand. Then I
took a single pace forward, with my left leg, and he a
single pace back, with his right leg (he could scarcely
do otherwise). Then I took a double pace forward with
my right leg, and he of course with his left leg a double
pace back. And so we paced together between the fences,
I forwards, he backwards, until we came to where the
fences diverged again. And then turning, I turning, and
he turning, we paced back the way we had come, I
forwards, and he of course backwards, with our hands
on our shoulders, as before. And so pacing back the
way we had come, we passed the holes and paced on,
until we came to where the fences diverged again. And
then turning, as one man, we paced back the way
we had paced back the way we had come, I looking
whither we were going, and he looking whence we were
coming. And so, up and down, up and down, we paced
between the fences, together again after so long, and
the sun shone bright upon us, and the wind blew wild
about us.

To be together again, after so long, who love the
sunny wind, the windy sun, in the sun, in the wind, that
is perhaps something, perhaps something.

For us moving so between the fences, before they diverged, there was just room.

In Watt's garden, in my garden, we should have been more at our ease. But it never occured to me to go back into my garden with Watt, or with him to go forward into his. But it never occured to Watt to go back with me into his garden, or with me to go forward into mine. For my garden was my garden, and Watt's garden was Watt's garden, we had no common garden any more. So we walked to and fro, neither in his garden, in the way described.

So we began, after so long a time, to walk together again, and to talk, from time to time.

As Watt walked, so now he talked, back to front.

The following is an example of Watt's manner, at this period:

Day of most, night of part, Knott with now. Now till up, little seen so oh, little heard so oh. Night till morning from. Heard I this, saw I this then what. Thing quiet, dim. Ears, eyes, failing now also. Hush in, mist in, moved I so.

From this it will perhaps be suspected:

that the inversion affected, not the order of the sentences, but that of the words only;

that the inversion was imperfect;

that ellipse was frequent;

that euphony was a preoccupation;

that spontaneity was perhaps not absent;

that there was perhaps more than a reversal of discourse;

that the thought was perhaps inverted.

So to every man. soon or late, comes envy of the fly, with all the long joys of summer before it.

The utterance was as rapid, and as muffled, as before.

These were sounds that at first, though we walked face to face, were devoid of significance for me.

Nor did Watt follow me. Pardon beg, he said, pardon, pardon beg.

Thus I missed I suppose much I suspect of great interest touching I presume the first or initial stage of the second or closing period of Watt's stay in Mr Knott's house.

For Watt's sense of chronology was strong, in a way, and his dislike of battology was very strong.

Often my hands left his shoulders, to make a note in their little notebook. But his never left mine, unless I detached them personally.

But soon I grew used to these sounds, and then I understood as well as before, that is to say a great part of what I heard.

So all went well until Watt began to invert, no longer the order of the words in the sentence, but that of the letters in the word.

This further modification Watt carried through with all his usual discretion and sense of what was acceptable to the ear, and aesthetic judgement. Nevertheless to one, such as me, desirous above all of information, the change was not a little disconcerting.

The following is an example of Watt's manner, at this period:

Ot bro, lap rulb, krad klub. Ot murd, wol fup, wol fup. Ot niks, sorg sam, sorg sam. Ot lems, lats lems, lats lems. Ot gnut, trat stews, trat stews.

These were sounds that at first, though we walked breast to breast, made little or no sense to me.

Nor did Watt follow me. Geb nodrap, he said, geb nodrap, nodrap.

Thus I missed I suppose much I presume of great interest touching I suspect the second stage of the second or closing period of Watt's stay in Mr Knott's house.

But soon I grew used to these sounds, and then I understood as well as before.

So all went well until Watt began to invert, no

longer the order of the letters in the word, but that of
the sentences in the period.

The following is an example of Watt's manner
at this period:

*Of nought. To the source. To the teacher. To
the temple. To him I brought. This emptied heart.
These emptied hands. This mind ignoring. This body
homeless. To love him my little reviled. My little
rejected to have him. My little to learn him forgot.
Abandoned my little to find him.*

These were sounds that at first, notwithstanding
our proximity, were not perfectly clear to me.

Nor did Watt follow me. Beg pardon, pardon, he
said, beg pardon.

Thus I missed I presume much I suppose of great
interest touching I presume the third stage of the second
or closing period of Watt's stay in Mr Knott's house.

But soon I grew used to these sounds, and then I
understood as well as before.

So all went well until Watt began to invert, no
longer the order of the sentences in the period, but that
of the words in the sentence together with that of the
letters in the word.

The following is an example of Watt's manner at
this period:

*Deen did taw? Tonk. Tog da taw? Tonk. Luf
puk saw? Hap! Deen did tub? Ton sparp. Tog da
tub? Ton wonk.*

These were sounds that at first, though we
walked belly to belly, were so much wind to me.

Nor did Watt follow me. Nodrap geb, he said,
nodrap, nodrap geb.

Thus I missed I suspect much I presume of great
interest touching the fourth stage of the second or
closing period of Watt's stay in Mr Knott's house.

But soon I grew used to these sounds.

Then all went well until Watt began to invert, no
longer the order of the words in the sentence together

with that of the letters in the word, but that of the words
in the sentence together with that of the sentences in
the period.

The following is an example of Watt's manner
at this period:

*Say he'd, No, waistcoat the, vest the, trousers
the, socks the, shoes the, shirt the, drawers the, coat
the, dress to ready things got had when. Say he'd, Dress.
Say he'd, No, water the, towel the, sponge the, soap
the, salts the, glove the, brush the, basin the, wash to
ready things got had when. Say he'd, Wash. Say he'd,
No, water the, towel the, sponge the, soap the, razor
the, powder the, brush the, bowl the, shave to ready
things got had when. Say he'd, Shave.*

These were sounds that at first, though we walked
pubis to pubis, seemed so much balls to me.

Nor did Watt follow me. Pardon, pardon beg,
he said, pardon beg.

Thus I missed I presume much I suspect touching
I suppose the fifth stage of the second or closing period
of Watt's stay in Mr Knott's house.

But soon I grew used to these sounds.

Until Watt began to invert, no longer the order
of the words in the sentence together with that of the
sentences in the period, but that of the letters in the
word together with that of the sentences in the period.

The following is an example of this manner:

*Lit yad mac, ot og. Ton taw, ton tonk. Ton dob,
ton trips. Ton vila, ton deda. Ton kawa, ton pelsa.
Ton das, ton yag. Os devil, rof mit.*

This meant nothing to me.

Geb nodrap, nodrap, said Watt, geb nodrap.

Thus I missed I presume much I suppose of great
interest touching I suspect the fifth, no, the sixth stage
of the second or closing period of Watt's stay in Mr
Knott's house.

But in the end I understood.

Then Watt began to invert, no longer the order

of the letters in the word together with that of the sentences in the period, but that of the letters in the word together with that of the words in the sentence together with that of the sentences in the period.

For example:

Dis yb dis, nem owt. Yad la, tin fo trap. Skin, skin, skin. Od su did ned taw? On. Taw ot klat tonk? On. Tonk ot klat taw? On. Tonk ta kool taw? On. Taw ta kool tonk? Nilb, mun, mud. Tin fo trap, yad la. Nem owt, dis yb dis.

It took me some time to get used to this.

Nodrap, nodrap geb, said Watt, nodrap geb.

Thus I missed I suppose much I suspect of great interest touching I presume the seventh stage of the second or closing period of Watt's stay in Mr Knott's house.

Then he took it into his head to invert, no longer the order of the words in the sentence, nor that of the letters in the word, nor that of the sentences in the period, nor simultaneously that of the words in the sentence and that of the letters in the word, nor simultaneously that of the words in the sentence and that of the sentences in the period, nor simultaneously that of the letters in the word and that of the sentences in the period, nor simultaneously that of the letters in the word and that of the words in the sentence and that of the sentences in the period, ho no, but, in the brief course of the same period, now that of the words in the sentence, now that of the letters in the word, now that of the sentences in the period, now simultaneously that of the words in the sentence and that of the letters in the word, now simulaneously that of the words in the sentence and that of the sentences in the period, now simultaneously that of the letters in the word and that of the sentences in the period, and now simultaneously that of the letters in the word and that of the words in the sentence and that of the sentences in the period.

I recall no example of this manner.

These were sounds that at first, though we walked glued together, were so much Irish to me.

Nor did Watt follow me. Beg nodrap, he said, nodrap, pardon geb.

Thus I missed I suppose much I presume of great interest touching I suspect the eighth or final stage of the second or closing period of Watt's stay in Mr Knott's house.

But soon I grew used to these sounds, and then I understood as well as ever, that is to say fully one half of what won its way past my tympan.

For my own hearing now began to fail, though my myopia remained stationary. My purely mental faculties on the other hand, the faculties properly so called of

?	?
?	?
?	?

were if possible more vigorous than ever.

To these conversations we are indebted for the following information.

One day they were all four in the garden, Mr Knott, Watt, Arthur and Mr Graves. It was a beautiful summer's day. Mr Knott was moving slowly about, disappearing now behind a bush, emerging now from behind another. Watt was sitting on a mound. Arthur was standing on the lawn, talking to Mr Graves. Mr Graves was leaning on a fork. But the great mass of the empty house was hard by. A bound, and they were all in safety.

Arthur said:

Do not despair, Mr Graves. Some day the clouds will roll away, and the sun, so long obnubilated, burst forth, for you, Mr Graves, at last.

Not a kick in me, Mr Arter, said Mr Graves.

Oh Mr Graves, said Arthur, do not say that.

When I says a kick, said Mr Graves, I means a — . He made a gesture with his fork.

Have you tried Bando, Mr Graves, said Arthur.
A capsule, before and after meals, in a little warm
milk, and again at night, before turning in. I had tried
everything, and was thoroughly disgusted, when a
friend spoke to me of Bando. Her husband was never
without it, you understand. Try it, she said, and come
back in five or six years. I tried it, Mr Graves, and it
changed my whole outlook on life. From being a
moody, listless, constipated man, covered with squames,
shunned by my fellows, my breath fetid and my appetite
depraved (for years I had eaten nothing but high fat
rashers), I became, after four years of Bando, vivacious,
restless, a popular nudist, regular in my daily health,
almost a father and a lover of boiled potatoes. Bando.
Spelt as pronounced.

Mr Graves said he would give it a trial.

The unfortunate thing about Bando, said Arthur,
is that it is no longer to be obtained in this unfortunate
country. I understand that inferior products, such as
Ostreine and Spanish Flies, may still be wheedled out
of some of the humaner chemists, up and down the
city, in the ten minutes or a quarter of an hour
immediately following their midday meal. But for
Bando, even on a Saturday afternoon, you will grovel in
vain. For the State, taking as usual the law into its own
hands, and duly indifferent to the sufferings of
thousands of men, and tens of thousands of women,
all over the country, has seen fit to place an embargo
on this admirable article, from which joy could stream,
at a moderate cost, into homes, and other places of
rendez-vous, now desolate. It cannot enter our ports,
nor cross our northern frontier, if not in the form of a
casual, hasardous and surreptitious dribble, I mean
piecemeal in ladies' underclothing, for example, or
gentlemen's golfbags, or the hollow missal of a broad-
minded priest, where on discovery it is immediately
seized, and confiscated, by some gross customs official
half crazed with seminal intoxication and sold, at ten

added, with his usual candour, and to the great merriment of the Grants Committee, that he thought he could rely on O'Connor to live on the country. To none of these items was any exception found, though the absence of others, usual in such cases, as for example that corresponding to accomodation for the night, caused no little surprise. Invited, through the College Bursar, to account for this omission, Louit replied, through the College Bursar, that being a person of great bodily fastidiousness it was his intention to pass his nights, as long as he remained in that part of the country, in the sweet-smelling hay, or the sweet-smelling straw, as the case might be, of the local barns. This explanation provoked further great hilarity among the members of the committee. And the frankness was admired by many with which Louit, on his return, confessed to having found, in the course of his excursion, three barns in all, of which two contained empty bottles and the third the skeleton of a goat. But in other quarters this and cognate statements were viewed in another and less friendly light. For Ernest, looking very pale and ill, returned to his rooms three weeks before he was due. Invited, through the College Bursar, to produce the boots for the purchase of which fifteen shillings had been allotted to him from the slender College funds, Louit replied, through the same channel, that in the late afternoon of November the twenty-first, in the vicinity of Handcross, they had unfortunately been sucked off his feet by a bog, which in the fading light, and the confusion of his senses consequent on prolonged inanition, he had mistaken for a field of late onions. To the hope then politely expressed that O'Connor had enjoyed his brief outing, Louit with grateful acknowledgement replied that he had been reluctantly obliged, on the same occasion, to hold O'Connor head downward in the morass, until his faithful heart had ceased to beat, and then roast him, in his skin, which he could not bring himself to remove, over a fire of flags and cotton-blossoms. He took no credit for this, O'Connor in his place would have done the same for him. The bones of his old pet, complete save for the medullars, were now in his rooms, in a sack, and might be inspected any afternoon, Sundays excepted, between the hours of two forty-five and three fifteen. The College Bursar now wondered, on behalf of the committee, if it would be convenient to Mr Louit to give some account of the impetus imparted to his studies by his short stay in the country. Louit replied that he would have done so with great pleasure if he had not had the misfortune to mislay, on the very morning of his departure from the west, between the hours of eleven and midday, in the gentlemen's cloakroom of Ennis railway-station, the one hundred and five loose sheets closely covered on both sides with shorthand notes embracing the entire period in question. This represented, he added, an average of no less than five pages, or ten sides, per day. He was now exerting himself to the utmost, and indeed he feared greatly beyond his strength, with a view to recuperating his MS, which, qua MS, could not be of the smallest value to any person other than himself and, eventually, humanity. But it was his experience of railway-station cloakrooms, and in particular those exploited by the western lines, that anything left there at all resembling paper, with the exception perhaps of visiting-cards, postage-stamps, betting-slips and perforated railway-tickets, was invariably swallowed up and lost, for ever. So in his efforts, greatly hampered by lack of strength, and absence of funds, to recover his property, his anticipations were of failure, rather than of success. And such a loss would be irreparable, for of the countless observations made during his tour, and of the meditations arising thence, hastily under the most adverse conditions committed to paper, he had to his great regret little or no remembrance. To the relation of these painful events, that is to say the loss of his boots, his dog, his labour, his money, his health and perhaps even the

esteem of his academical superiors, Louit had nothing
to add, if not that he looked forward to waiting on the
committee, at their mutual convenience, with proof that
his mission had not been altogether in vain. The day
and hour having been appointed, Louit was seen advancing, leading by the hand an old man dressed in
kilt, plaid, brogues and, in spite of the cold, a pair of
silk socks made fast to the purple calves by an un-
pretentious pair of narrow mauve suspenders, and
holding a large black felt hat under his arm. Louit
said, This, gentlemen, is Mr Thomas Nackybal, native
of Burren. There he has spent all his life, thence he
was loath to remove, thither he longs to return, to kill
his pig, his solitary perennial companion. Mr Nackybal
is now in his seventy-sixth year, and has never, in all
that time, received any instruction other than that
treating of such agricultural themes, indispensable to the
exercise of his profession, as the rock-potato, the clover-
thatch, every man his own fertiliser, turf versus com-
bustion and the fly-catching pig, with the result that
he cannot, nor ever could, read or write, or, without
the assistance of his fingers, and his toes, add, subtract,
multiply or divide the smallest whole number to, from,
by or into another. So much for the mental Nackybal.
The physical — . Stay, Mr Louit, said the President,
holding up his hand. One moment, Mr Louit, if you
please. A thousand, sir, if you wish, said Louit. On
the dais they were five, Mr O'Meldon, Mr Magershon,
Mr Fitzwein, Mr de Baker and Mr MacStern, from left
to right. They consulted together. Mr Fitzwein said,
Mr Louit, you would not have us believe that this man's
mental existence is exhausted by the bare knowledge,
emerging from a complete innocence of the rudiments, of
what is necessary for his survival. That, replied Louit,
is the bold claim I make for my friend, in whose mind,
save for the pale music of the innocence you mention,
and, in some corner of the cerebellum, where all agricultural ideation has its seat, dumbly flickering, the

knowledge of how to extract, from the ancestral half-acre of moraine, the maximum of nourishment, for himself and his pig, with the minimum of labour, all, I am convinced, is an ecstasy of darkness, and of silence. The committee, whose eyes had not left Louit while he spoke these words, transferred them now to Mr Nackybal, as though the conversation were of his complexion. They then began to look at one another, and much time passed, before they succeeded in doing so. Not that they looked at one another long, no, they had more sense than that. But when five men look at one another, though in theory only twenty looks are necessary, every man looking four times, yet in practice this number is seldom sufficient, on account of the multitude of looks that go astray. For example, Mr Fitzwein looked at Mr Magershon, on his right. But Mr Magershon is not looking at Mr Fitzwein, on his left, but at Mr O'Meldon, on his right. But Mr O'Meldon is not looking at Mr Magershon, on his left, but, craning forward, at Mr MacStern, on his left but three at the far end of the table. But Mr MacStern is not craning forward looking at Mr O'Meldon, on his right but three at the far end of the table, but is sitting bolt upright looking at Mr de Baker, on his right. But Mr de Baker is not looking at Mr MacStern, on his left, but at Mr Fitzwein, on his right. Then Mr Fitzwein, tired of looking at the back of Mr Magershon's head, cranes forward and looks at Mr O'Meldon, on his right but one at the end of the table. But Mr O'Meldon, tired of craning forward looking at Mr MacStern, is now craning backward looking at Mr de Baker, on his left but two. But Mr de Baker, tired of looking at the back of Mr Fitzwein's head, is now craning forward looking at Mr Magershon, on his right but one. But Mr Magershon, tired of the sight of Mr O'Meldon's left ear, is now craning forward looking at Mr MacStern, on his left but two at the end of the table. But Mr Mac Stern, tired of looking at the back of Mr de Baker s head, is now craning forward looking at Mr Fitzwein, on his right but one. Then Mr Fitzwein, tired of craning forward looking at Mr O'Meldon, cranes forward in the other direction and looks at Mr MacStern, on his left but one at the end of the table. But Mr MacStern, tired of craning forward looking at Mr Fitzwein, is now craning backward looking at Mr Magershon, on his right but two. But Mr Magershon, tired of craning backward looking at Mr MacStern, is now craning forward looking at Mr de Baker, on his left but one. But Mr de Baker, tired of craning forward looking at Mr Magershon, is now craning backward looking at Mr O'Meldon, on his right but two at the end of the table. But Mr O'Meldon, tired of craning backward looking at Mr de Baker, is now craning forward looking at Mr Fitzwein, on his left but one. Then Mr Fitzwein, tired of craning forward looking at Mr MacStern's left ear, sits back and turning towards the only member of the committee whose eye he has not yet tried to catch, that is to say Mr de Baker, is rewarded by a view of that gentleman's hairless sinciput, for Mr de Baker, tired of craning backward looking at Mr Magershon's left ear, and having turned in vain to all the members of the committee with the exception of his left-hand neighbour, has sat forward and is now looking down the dingy corollae of Mr MacStern's right ear. For Mr MacStern, sick and tired of Mr Magershon's left ear, and having no other alternative, is now craning forward contemplating the disgusted, and indeed disgusting, right side of Mr O'Meldon's face. For sure enough Mr O'Meldon, having eliminated all his colleagues with the exception of his immediate neighbour, has sat back and is now considering the boils, the pimples and the blackheads of Mr Magershon's nape. For Mr Magershon, whom Mr de Baker's left ear has ceased to interest, has sat back and is now benefiting, not indeed for the first time that afternoon, but with a new distinctness, by Mr Fitzwein's lunch of kidney-

beans. Thus of the five times four or twenty looks
taken, no two have met, and all this craning forward
and backward and looking to the right and to the left
has led to nothing, and for all the progress made by
the committee in this matter of looking at itself, its
eyes might just as well have been closed, or turned
towards heaven. Nor is this all. For now Mr Fitzwein
will very likely say, It is a long time since I looked
at Mr Magershon, let me look at him again now, perhaps
who knows he is looking at me. But Mr Magershon,
who it will be remembered has just been looking at
Mr Fitzwein, will certainly have turned his head round
the other way, to look at Mr O'Meldon, in the hope of
finding Mr O'Meldon looking at him, for it is a long time
since Mr Magershon looked at Mr O'Meldon. But
if it is a long time since Mr Magershon looked at
Mr O'Meldon, it is not a long time since Mr O'Meldon
looked at Mr Magershon, for he has just been doing so,
has he not. And indeed he might be doing so still, for
Treasurers' eyes do not readily fall, nor turn aside, were
it not for a strange-smelling, at first not unpleasant, but
with the passage of time frankly revolting vapour arising
from among the recesses of Mr Magershon's body-linen
and issuing, with great volatility, between his nape and
his collar-band, a bold and it must be allowed successful effort on the part of that dignitary's pneumogastric
to compensate the momentary confusion of its superior
connexions. So Mr Magershon turns to Mr O'Meldon,
to find Mr O'Meldon looking, not at him, as he had
hoped (for if he had not hoped to find Mr O'Meldon
looking at him when he turned to look at Mr O'Meldon,
then he would not have turned to look at Mr O'Meldon,
but would have craned forward, or perhaps backward,
to look at Mr MacStern, or perhaps at Mr de Baker,
but more likely the former, as one less lately looked
at than the latter), but at Mr MacStern, in the hope
of finding Mr MacStern looking at him. And this is
very natural, for more time has elapsed since Mr O'Mel-

12

don's looking at Mr MacStern than since Mr O'Meldon's
looking at any of the others, and Mr O'Meldon cannot
be expected to know that since Mr MacStern's looking
at him less time has elapsed than since Mr MacStern's
looking at any of the others, for Mr MacStern has
only just finished looking at Mr O'Meldon, has he not.
So Mr O'Meldon finds Mr MacStern looking, not at
him, as he had hoped, but, in the hope of finding
Mr de Baker looking at him, at Mr de Baker.   But
Mr de Baker, for the same reason that Mr Magershon
is looking, not at Mr Fitzwein, but at Mr O'Meldon,
and that Mr O'Meldon is looking, not at Mr Magershon,
but at Mr MacStern, and that Mr MacStern is looking,
not at Mr O'Meldon, but at Mr de Baker, is looking,
not at Mr MacStern, as Mr MacStern had hoped (for if
Mr MacStern had not hoped to find Mr de Baker looking
at him, when he turned to look at Mr de Baker, then
he would not have turned to look at Mr de Baker, no,
but would have craned forward, or perhaps backward,
to have a look at Mr Fitzwein, or perhaps at Mr Magershon, but more probably the former, as one less lately
looked at than the latter), but at Mr Fitzwein, who
is now benefiting by the posterior aspect of Mr Magershon in very much the same way as but a moment before
Mr Magershon by his, and Mr O'Meldon by Mr Magershon's.   And so on.   Until of the five times eight or
forty looks taken, not one has been reciprocated, and
the committee, for all its twisting and turning, is no
further advanced, in this matter of looking at itself,
than at the now irrevocable moment of its setting out
to do so.   And this it not all.   For many, many looks
may still be taken, and much, much time still lost,
ere every eye find the eye it seeks, and into every
mind the energy flow, the comfort and the reassurance,
necessary for a resumption of the business in hand.
And all this comes of lack of method, which is all the
less excusable in a committee as committees, whether
large or small, are more often under the necessity of

looking at themselves than any other body of men, with
the possible exception of commissions. Now perhaps
one of the best methods, whereby a committee may
rapidly look at itself, and all the fret and weariness,
experienced by committees looking at themselves without
method, be averted, is perhaps this, that numbers be
given to the members of the committee, one, two, three,
four, five, six, seven, and so on, as many numbers as
there are members of the committee, so that every
member of the committee has his number, and no
number of the committee is unnumbered, and that these
numbers be carefully committed to memory by the
members of the committee, until every member of the
committee knows, with certain knowledge, not only his
own number, but the numbers of all the other members
of the committee, and that these numbers be allotted
to the members of the committee at the moment of its
formation, and maintained unchanged until the hour
of its dissolution, for if at every successive meeting of
the committee a new numeration were to be adopted,
untold confusion would ensue (from the changed numeration) and unspeakable disorder. Then it will be found
that every single member of the committee not only
has his number, but is content with the number that
he has, and willing to learn it off by heart, and not only
it, but all the other numbers too, until every number
calls at once into his mind a name, a face, a temperament,
a function, and every face a number. Then, when the
time comes for the committee to look at itself, let all
the members but number one look together at number
one, and let number one look at them all in turn, and
then close, if he cares to, his eyes, for he has done his
duty. Then of all those members but number one who
have looked together at number one, and by number
one been looked at one by one, let all but number two
look at number two, and let number two in his turn
look at them all in turn, and then remove, if his eyes
are sore, his glasses, if he is in the habit of wearing

glasses, and rest his eyes, for they are no longer required, for the moment. Then of all those members but number two, and of course number one, who have looked together at number two, and by number two been looked at one by one, let all with the exception of number three look together at number three, and let number three in his turn look at them all in turn, and then get up and go to the window and look out, if he feels like a little exercise and change of scene, for he is no longer needed, for the time being. Then of all those members of the committee with the exception of number three, and of course of numbers two and one, who have looked together at number three and by number three been looked at one by one, let all save number four look at number four, and let number four in his turn look at them one after another, and then gently massage his eyeballs, if he feels the need to do so, for their immediate role is terminated. And so on, until only two members of the committee remain, whom then let at each other look, and then bathe their eyes, if they have their eyebaths with them, with a little laudanum, or weak boracic solution, or warm weak tea, for they have well deserved it. Then it will be found that the committee has looked at itself in the shortest possible time, and with the minimum number of looks, that is to say x squared minus x looks if there are x members of the committee, and y squared minus y if there are y. But slowly two by two the eyes put forth their curious beams again, first in the direction of Mr Nackybal, and then in that of Louit, who thus emboldened continued, The physical you have before you, the feet are large and flat, and so continued, working slowly up, until he came to the head, of which, as of the rest, he said many things, some good, some fair, some very good, some poor and some excellent. Then Mr Fitzwein said, But the man is in t — t — tolerable health? Can direct his steps unaided? Can sit down, sit, stand up, stand, eat, drink, go to bed, sleep, rise and attend to his

duties, without assistance? Oh yes, sir, said Louit, and
he can deject singlehanded too. Well, well, said
Mr Fitzwein. He added, And his sexual life, talking
of dejection? That of an impoverished bachelor of
repulsive appearance, said Louit, no offence meant.
I beg your pardon, said Mr MacStern. Hence the
squint, said Louit. Well, said Mr Fitzwein, it is always
a pleasure for us, for me for one for my part, and for
my colleagues for two for theirs, to meet a moron from
a different crawl of life from our crawl, from my crawl
and from their crawl. And to that extent I suppose we
are obliged to you, Mr Louit. But I do not think we
grasp, I do not think that I grasp and I should be greatly
surprised to learn that my colloborators grasp, what
this gentleman has to do with the object of your recent
visit, Mr Louit, your recent brief and, if you will allow
me to say so, prodigal visit to the western seaboard.
To this for all reply Louit reached with his right hand
out and back for the left hand of Mr Nackybal, whom
he remembered having last seen seated, docilely and
decently seated, a little to his right, and to his rear.
If I tell you all this in such detail, Mr Graves, the
reason is, believe me, that I cannot, much as I should
like, and for reasons that I shall not go into, for they
are unknown to me, do otherwise. Details, Mr Graves,
details I detest, details I despise, as much as you, a
gardener, do. When you sow your peas, when you sow
your beans, when you sow your potatoes, when you sow
your carrots, your turnips, your parsnips and other root
vegetables, do you do so with punctilio? No, but
rapidly you open a trench, a rough and ready line, not
quite straight, nor yet quite crooked, or a series of holes,
at intervals that do not offend, or offend only for a
moment, while the holes are still open, your tired old
eye, and let fall the seed, absent in mind, as the priest
dust, or ashes, into the grave, and cover it with earth,
with the edge of your boot in all probability, knowing
that if the seed is to prosper and multiply, ten-fold,

fifteen-fold, twenty-fold, twenty-five-fold, thirty-fold, thirty-five-fold, forty-fold, forty-five-fold and even fifty-fold, it will do so, and that if it is not, it will not. As a younger man, Mr Graves, I have no doubt, you used a line, a measure, a plumb, a level, and placed your peas, your beans, your maize, your lentils, in groups of four, or five, or six, or seven, not four in one hole, and five in another, and six in a third, and seven in a fourth, no, but in every hole four, or five, or six, or seven, and your potatoes with the germs uppermost, and mixed your carrot and your turnip seed, your radish and your parsnip seed, with sand, or dust, or ashes, before committing it to the seedplot. Whereas now! And when did you cease, Mr Graves, to use a line, a measure, a plumb, a level, and so to place and so to thin your seed, before sowing it? At what age, Mr Graves, and under what circumstances? And did all go at once, Mr Graves, by the board, the line, the measure, the plumb, the level, and who knows what other mechanical aids, and the way of placing, and the manner of mixing, or did the line go first, and then some time later the measure, and then some time later the plumb (though I confess I do not see the use of the plumb), and then some time later the level, and then some time later the punctilious placing, and then some time later the meticulous mixing? Or was it by twos and threes at a time, Mr Graves, until you arrived, little by little, at your present freedom, when all you need is seed, earth, excrement, water and a stick? But neither Mr Nackybal's left hand, nor his right, was free, for with the former he was supporting the weight of his bulk now acutely inclined, whilst with the latter, invisible beneath the kilt, he was scratching, gently but firmly, learnedly, through the worn but still heating material of his winter drawers, a diffuse ano-scrotal prurit (worms? nerves? piles? or worse?) of sixty-four years standing. The faint rasp could be heard of the heel of the hand coming and going, coming and going, and this, joined to the attitude of the rapt the suffering body, and to the expression, attentive, gloating, shocked, expectant, of the face, entirely misled the committee, so that it exclaimed, What vitality! At his age! The open-air life! The single life! Ego autem! (1) (Mr Mac Stern). But now Mr Nackybal, having obtained a temporary relief, brought out, as he raised himself up, his right hand from under his skirt, and drew it, palm outwards, several times back and forth beneath his nose, a characteristic gesture. Then he resumed the pose, the decent pose, from which the sudden access of his old trouble had startled him, his hands on his knees, his old hairy mottled knotted hands on his bare old bony blue knees, the right old hairy mottled hand on the bony right bare old knee, and the left old knotted mottled hand on the left old blue old bony knee, and looking, as at some scene long familiar, or for some other reason devoid of interest, with listening lacklustre eyes out of the window, at the sky supported here and there by a cupola, a dome, a roof, a spire, a tower, a treetop. But now, the moment being come, Louit led Mr Nackybal to the foot of the dais, and there, looking him affectionately full in the face, or more exactly full in the quarter-face, that is to say roughly affectionately full in the ear, for the more Louit turned his face, his full affectionate face, towards Mr Nackybal, the more Mr Nackybal turned his, his tired red old hairy face away, said, in slow loud solemn tones, Four hundred and eight thousand one hundred and eighty-four. Mr Nackybal now, to the general surprise, transferred, from the sky, his eyes, docile, stupid, liquid, staring eyes, towards Mr Fitzwein, who after a moment exclaimed, to the further general surprise, A gazelle! A sheep! An old sheep! Mr de Baker, sir, said Louit, will you be so friendly now as to make a faithful note of what I say, and of what my friend here says, from now on?

_____

(1) A Latin expression meaning: I (Ego) also (autem).

Why of course to be sure, Mr Louit, said Mr de Baker.
I am greatly obliged to you, Mr de Baker, said Louit.
Tut tut, don't mention it, Mr Louit, said Mr de Baker.
I may count on you then, Mr de Baker, said Louit.
To be sure you may, Mr Louit, said Mr de Baker. You
are too kind, Mr de Baker, said Louit. Foh, not at all,
not at all, Mr Louit, said Mr de Baker. A goat! An old
quinch! cried Mr Fitzwein. You set my mind at rest,
Mr de Baker, said Louit. Not another word, Mr Louit,
said M. de Baker, not a word more. And relieve it at
the same time of a great load of anxiety, Mr de Baker,
said Louit. His eyes coil into my very soul, said
Mr Fitzwein. His very what?, said Mr O'Meldon. His
very soul, said Mr Magershon. Bless me, what was that!
exclaimed Mr MacStern. What do you think it was?
The angelus? said Mr de Baker. Does one remark such
things, among men of the world? said Mr Magershon.
At least it was frank, said Mr O'Meldon. Then I may
proceed without misgiving, Mr de Baker, said Louit.
You certainly may indeed as far as I personally am
concerned, Mr Louit, said Mr de Baker. And wrap it
round, as with wet bands, said M. Fitzwein. God bless
you, Mr de Baker, said Louit. And you, Mr Louit, said
Mr de Baker. No no, you, Mr de Baker, you, said Louit.
Why by all means, Mr Louit, me, if you insist, but
you too, said Mr de Baker. You mean God bless us
both, Mr de Baker? said Louit. Diable, said Mr de
Baker (the French extraction). · His face is familiar,
said Mr Fitzwein. Tom! cried Louit. Mr Nackybal
turned his face towards the call, and Louit saw that it
was stamped with anxiety. Bah! said Louit, the decisive
moment is at hand. Then, in a loud voice, he said,
Three hundred and eighty-nine th — . To me, at all
events, said Mr Fitzwein. Three hundred and eighty-
nine thousand, vociferated Louit, and seventeen. Eh?
said Mr Nackybal. Have you got that down, Mr de
Baker, said Louit. I have, Mr Louit, said Mr de Baker.
Would you be good enough to repeat, Mr de Baker, said

Louit. Certainly, Mr Louit. I repeat: Mr Louit: Three
hundred and eighty-nine thousand and seventy. Mr Nack
— . Three hundred and eighty-nine thousand and
seven*teen*, said Louit, not and seven*ty*, and seven*teen*.
Oh, I beg your pardon, Mr Louit, I heard and seventy,
said Mr de Baker. I said and seven*teen*, Mr de Baker,
said Louit, as I thought distinctly. How extraordinary,
I distinctly heard and seven*ty*, said Mr de Baker. What
did you hear, Mr MacStern? I heard and seven*teen*,
with great distinctness, said Mr MacStern. Oh you did,
did you, said Mr de Baker. The *n* is still ringing in
my ears, said Mr MacStern. And you, Mr O'Meldon,
said M. de Baker. And I what? said Mr O'Meldon.
Heard what, seven*teen* or seven*ty*? said Mr de Baker.
What did you hear, Mr de Baker? said Mr O'Meldon.
And seven*ty*, said Mr de Baker. And seven what? said
Mr O'Meldon. And seven*teeeee*, said Mr de Baker.
Naturally, said Mr O'Meldon. Ha, said Mr de Baker.
I said and seventeen, said Louit. And seven what? said
Mr Magershon. And seven*teen*, said Louit. I thought so,
said Mr Magershon. But were not sure, said Mr de
Baker. Obvioŭsly, said Mr Magershon. And you,
Mr President, said Mr de Baker. Eh? said Mr Fitzwein.
I say, And you, Mr President, said Mr de Baker. I don't
follow you, Mr de Baker, said Mr Fitzwein. Was it
seven*teen* you heard, or seven*ty*? said Mr de Baker.
I heard forty-six, said Mr Fitzwein. I said and seventeen,
said Louit. We believe you, Mr Louit, we believe you,
said Mr Magershon. Will you emend, Mr de Baker,
said Louit. Why of course with pleasure, Mr Louit,
said Mr de Baker. Thank you very much, Mr de Baker,
said Louit. Not at all, not at all, Mr Louit, said
Mr de Baker. How does it read now? said Louit.
It reads now, said Mr de Baker: Mr Louit: Three
hundred and eighty-nine thousand and seventeen.
Mr Nackybal: Eh? Has he your leave to sit down? said
Louit. Has who our leave to sit down? said Mr Magershon. He is tired standing, said Louit. Where have I

seen that face before, said Mr Fitzwein. How long will
this go on? said Mr MacStern. Is that all? said Mr Magershon. He hears better seated, said Louit. Let him lie
down, if he wishes, said Mr Fitzwein. Louit helped
Mr Nackybal to lie down and knelt down beside him.
Tom, can you hear me? he cried. Yes, sir, said
Mr Nackybal. Three hundred and eighty-nine thousand
and seventeen, cried Louit. One moment while I get
that down, said Mr de Baker. A moment passed.
Proceed, said Mr de Baker. Reply, cried Louit. Sivinty-
thray, said Mr Nackybal. Sivinty-thray? said Mr de
Baker. Perhaps he means seventy-three, said Mr O'Meldon. Does he mean seventy-three? said Mr Fitzwein.
He said seventy-three, said Louit. Did he indeed, said
Mr de Baker. My God, said Mr MacStern. His what?
said Mr O'Meldon. His God, said Mr Magershon.
Would you be good enough to read out what you have
got, Mr de Baker, said Louit. What I have got? said
Mr de Baker. What you have got down in your book,
to make sure it is correct, said Louit. Yours is not a
trusting nature, Mr Louit, said Mr de Baker. So much
depends on the accuracy of the record, said Louit.
He is right, said Mr MacStern. Where shall I begin?
said Mr de Baker. Just my words and my friend's, said
Louit. The rest doesn't interest you, said Mr de Baker.
No, said Louit. Mr de Baker said, Looking back over
my notes, I find what follows: Mr Louit: Tom, can you
hear me? Mr Nackybal: Yes, sir. Mr Louit: Three
hundred and eighty-nine thousand and seventy. Mr Nack
— . And seven*teen*, said Louit. Really, Mr de Baker,
said Mr Fitzwein. How often have you to be told?
said Mr O'Meldon. Think of sweet seventeen, said
Mr Magershon. Ha ha, very good, said Mr de Baker.
Mr Magershon said, Would it not perhaps be preferable,
with such exceptionally large and involved figures — er
— at stake, if our Treasurer would consent to take over
the record, just for to-day? I do not intend any
disparagement of our Record Secretary, who as we all

know is a superb Record Secretary, but perhaps with
such unprecedentedly high and complicated figures involved, just for one afternoon — . No no, that would
never do, said Mr Fitzwein. Mr MacStern said, Perhaps
if our Record Secretary would be so good as to transcribe
the figures, not in figures, but in words — . Yes yes,
how would that be? said Mr Fitzwein. What difference
would that make? said Mr O'Meldon. Mr MacStern
replied, Why then he would simply write down the
words that he hears, instead of their ciphered equi-
valents, which requires long practice, especially in the
case of numbers of five and six letters, I beg your pardon,
I mean figures. Perhaps after all that is an excellent
idea, said Mr Magershon. Would you be good enough
to do that, Mr de Baker, do you think? said Mr Fitzwein.
But it is my invariable habit, said Mr de Baker. No no,
I believe you, said Mr Fitzwein. Then one does not
see what is to be done, said Mr Magershon. The best
of us may make a slip, said Louit. Thank you, Mr Louit,
said M. de Baker. Pray do not mention it, Mr de Baker,
said Louit. Wonderful most wonderful, exclaimed
Mr O'Meldon. What is wonderful most wonderful? said
Mr MacStern. The two figures are related, said
Mr O'Meldon, as the cute to its roob. The cute to its
what? said Mr Fitzwein. He means the cube to its
root, said Mr MacStern. What did I say? said Mr O'Meldon. The cute to its roob, ha ha, said Mr de Baker.
What does that mean, the cube to its root ? said
Mr Fitzwein. It means nothing, said Mr MacStern.
What do you mean, it means nothing? said Mr O'Mel-
on. Mr MacStern replied, To its which root? A cube
may have any number of roots. Like the long Turkey
cucumber, said Mr Fitzwein. Not all cubes, said
Mr O'Melaon. Who spoke of all cubes? said Mr Mac
Stern. Not this cube, said Mr O'Meldon. I know nothing
of that, said Mr MacStern. I am completely in the dark,
said Mr Fitzwein. I too, said Mr Magershon. What is
wonderful most wonderful? said Mr Fitzwein. Mr O'Mel-

don replied, That Mr Ballynack — . Mr Nackybal,
said Louit. Mr O'Meldon said, That Mr Nackybal, in
his head, in the short space of thirty-five or forty
seconds, should have elicited the cube root of a number
of six figures. Mr MacStern said, Forty seconds! At least
five minutes have elapsed since the figure was first
mentioned. What is wonderful about that? said Mr Fitzwein. Perhaps our President has forgotten, said Mr Mac
Stern. Two is the cube root of eight, said Mr O'Meldon.
Indeed, said Mr Fitzwein. Yes, twice two is four and
twice four is eight, said Mr O'Meldon. So two is the
cube root of eight, said Mr Fitzwein. Yes, and eight is
the cube of two, said Mr O'Meldon. Eight is the cube
of two, said Mr Fitzwein. Yes, said Mr O'Meldon. What
is there so wonderful about that? said Mr Fitzwein.
Mr O'Meldon replied, That two should be the cube root
of eight, and eight the cube of two, has long ceased to
be a matter for surprise. What is surprising is this,
that Mr Nallyback, in his head, in so short a time,
should have elicited the cube root of a number of six
figures. Oh, said Mr Fitzwein. Is it then so difficult?
said Mr Magershon. Impossible, said Mr MacStern. Well
well, said Mr Fitzwein. A feat never yet achieved by
man, and only once by a horse, said Mr O'Meldon.
A horse ! exclaimed Mr Fitzwein. An episode in the
Kulturkampf, said Mr O'Meldon. Oh, I see, said
Mr Fitzwein. Louit did not conceal his satisfaction.
Mr Nackybal lay on his side, apparently asleep. But
Mr Nackynack is not a horse, said Mr Fitzwein. Far
from it, said Mr O'Meldon. You are sure of what you
advance? said Mr Magershon. No, said Mr O'Meldon.
There is something fishy here, said Mr MacStern. Not
horsey, fishy, ha ha, very good, said Mr de Baker.
I protest, said Louit. Against what? said Mr Fitzwein.
Against the word fishy, said Louit. Make a note of
that, Mr de Baker, said M. Fitzwein. Louit took a sheet
of paper from his pocket, and handed it to Mr O'Meldon.
Why, what in the world is this, Mr Louit ? said

Mr O'Meldon. A list of perfect cubes, said Louit, of six figures and under, ninety-nine in all, with their corresponding cubic roots. What do you want me to do with this, Mr Louit? said Mr O'Meldon. Examine my friend, said Louit. Oh, said Mr Fitzwein. In my absence, since you question our good faith, said Louit. Tut tut, Mr Louit, said Mr Magershon. Strip him naked, bandage his eyes, send me away, said Louit. You forget telepathy, or the transference of thought, said Mr MacStern. Louit said, Cover the cubes when you ask for the cubes of the roots, cover the roots when you ask for the roots of the cubes. What difference will that make? said Mr O'Meldon. You won't know the answers before him, said Louit. Mr Fitzwein left the room, followed by his assistants. Louit roused Mr Nackybal and helped him to rise. Mr O'Meldon came back, Louit's paper in his hand. I may keep this, Mr Louit, he said. Certainly, said Louit. Thank you, Mr Louit, said Mr O'Meldon. Not at all, Mr O'Meldon, said Louit. Good-evening to you both, said Mr O'Meldon. Louit said, Good-evening, Mr O'Meldon. Say good-evening nicely to Mr O'Meldon, Tom, say, Good-evening, Mr O'Meldon. Ning, said Mr Nackybal. Charming, charming, said Mr O'Meldon. Mr O'Meldon left the room. Louit and Mr Nackybal, arm in arm, followed soon after. Soon the room, empty now, was grey with shadows, of the evening. A porter came, turned on the lights, straightened the chairs, saw that all was well and went away. Then the vast room was dark, for night had fallen, again. Well, Mr Graves, the next day, believe it or not, at the same hour, in the same place, in the immense and lofty hall flooded now with light, the same persons assembled and Mr Nackybal was thoroughly examined, both in cubing and extracting, from the table that Louit had provided. The precautions recommended by Louit were adopted, except that Louit was not sent out of the room, but posted with his back to it before the open window, and that Mr Nackybal was permitted to retain many of his

underclothes. From this severe trial Mr Nackybal
emerged with distinction, having in his cubing made
only twenty-five slight mistakes out of the forty-six
cubes demanded, and in his rooting, out of the fifty-
three extractions propounded, committed a mere matter
of four trifling errors! The interval between question
and response, sometimes brief, sometimes as long as
one minute, averaged, according to Mr O'Meldon, who
had come with his stop-watch, anything from thirty-
four to thirty-five seconds. Once Mr Nackybal did not
answer at all. This was an occasion of some un-
pleasantness. Mr O'Meldon, his eyes on the sheet,
announced, Five hundred and nineteen thousand three
hundred and thirteen. A minute passed, a minute and
a quarter, a minute and a half, a minute and three-
quarters, two minutes, two minutes and a quarter, two
minutes and a half, two minutes and three quarters,
three minutes, three minutes and a quarter, three
minutes and a half, three minutes and three-quarters,
and still Mr Nackybal did not reply! Come come, sir,
said Mr O'Meldon, with acerbity, five hundred and
nineteen thousand three hundred and thirteen. Still
Mr Nackybal did not reply! Either he knows or he
doesn't, said Mr Magershon. Here Mr de Baker laughed
till the tears ran down his cheeks. Mr Fitzwein said,
If you don't hear, say you don't hear. If you don't
know, say you don't know. Don't keep us waiting here
all night. Louit turned round and said, Is the number
on the list? Silence, Mr Louit, said Mr Fitzwein. Is the
number on the list? thundered Louit, taking a stride
forward, and white, under his green, with indignation.
I accuse the Treasurer, he said, pointing his finger at
that gentleman, as though there were two, or three,
or four, of five, or even six treasurers in the room,
instead of only one, of calling out a number that is
not on the list and has no more a cube root than my
arse. Mr Louit! cried Mr Fitzwein. His what? said
Mr O'Meldon. His arse, said Mr Magershon. I accuse

him, said Louit, of attempting, with deliberate and
premeditated malevolence, to bait and bewilder an old
man who is doing his best, out of friendship to me, to —
to — who is doing his best. Annoyed by this feeble conclusion, Louit added, I call that the act of a —, —, —, —.
—, —, —, —, — — , and here followed a flow
of language so gross that a less sweet-tempered man than
Mr O'Meldon would certainly have been offended, it
was so gross and fluent. But Mr O'Meldon's temper
was of such sweetness, that when Mr Fitzwein rose,
and with indignant words began to close the session,
Mr O'Meldon rose and calmed Mr Fitzwein, explaining
how it was that he and no other was to blame, who had
taken a nought for a one, and not, as he ought, for a
nought. But you did not do this on p — p — purpose,
with malice prepense, said Mr Fitzwein. Then there was
a silence until Mr O'Meldon, hanging his head, and
swinging it slowly to and fro, and shifting his weight
from one foot to the other, replied, Oh no no no no no,
as heaven is my witness, I did not. In that case I must
ask Mr Lingard to make you an apology, said Mr Fitzwein. Oh no no no no no, no apologies, cried Mr O'Meldon. Mr Lingard? said Mr Magershon. I said Mr Lingard? said Mr Fitzwein. Certainly you did, said
Mr Magershon. What can I have been thinking of,
said Mr Fitzwein. My mother was a Miss Lingard, said
Mr MacStern. Ah to be sure, I remember, a charming
woman, said Mr Fitzwein. She died in giving me birth,
said Mr MacStern. I can well believe that, said Mr de
Baker. Charming, charming woman, said Mr Fitzwein.
When the demonstration was over, then it was question-
time. Through the western windows of the vast hall
shone the low red winter sun, stirring the air, the
chambered air, with its angry farewell shining, whilst
via the opposite or oriental apertures or lights the murmur rose, appeasing, of the myriad faint clarions of
night. It was question-time. Mr Fitzwein said, And
can he square and square-root too? Mr O' Meldon said,

If he can cube he can square, if he can cube-root he can
square-root. My question was aimed at Mr Louit, said
Mr Fitzwein. Cubing and squaring is not the point, said
Louit. How is that? said Mr Fitzwein. Louit replied,
A visualiser can cube and square in his head, seeing
the figures come and go. You stand by the extirpation
of the root? said Mr Fitzwein. Of the cube root, said
Louit. Not of the square root? said Mr Fitzwein. No,
said Louit. How is that? said Mr Fitzwein. A visualiser
can extract the square root in his head, said Louit, as
with a paper and a sheet of pencil. But not the cube
root? said Mr Fitzwein. Louit said nothing, for what
could he have said? And the fourth root? said
Mr O'Meldon. The square root of the square root, said
Louit. And the fifth root? said Mr Fitzwein. Did he
rise on the second day? said Louit. And the sixth root?
said Mr de Baker. The square root of the cube root,
or the cube root of the square root, said Louit. And
the seventh root? said Mr MacStern. Dance on the
waters? said Louit. And the eighth root? said
Mr O'Meldon. The square root of the square root of
the square root, said Louit. It was question-time. Rose
and gloom, farewell and hail, mingled, clashed, vanquished, victor, victor, vanquished, in the vast indifferent
chamber. And the ninth root? said Mr Fitzwein. The
cube root of the cube root, said Louit. And the tenth
root? said Mr de Baker. Involves the fifth, said Louit.
And the eleventh root? said Mr MacStern. Into
whiskey? said Louit. And the twelfth root? said
Mr O'Meldon. The square root of the square root of
the cube root, or the cube root of the square root of
the square root, or the square root of the cube root
of the square root, said Louit. And the thirteenth
root? said Mr Fitzwein. Enough! cried Mr Magershon.
I beg your pardon? said Mr Fitzwein. Enough, said
Mr Magershon. Who are you to say enough? said
Mr Fitzwein. Gentlemen, gentlemen, said Mr Mac
Stern. Mr Louit, said Mr O'Meldon. Sir, said Louit.

In the two columns of figures before me, this afternoon, said Mr O'Meldon, the one, or column of roots, has no number of more than two digits, and the other, or column of cubes, none of more than six. Column of cubes! cried Mr MacStern. What is the matter now? said Mr Fitzwein. How beautiful, said Mr MacStern. That is so, Mr Louit, is it not? said Mr O'Meldon. I have no ear for music, said Louit. I do not refer to that, said Mr O'Meldon. To what might you refer? said Mr Fitzwein. I refer, said Mr O'Meldon, on the one hand to the absence, in the one column, or column of roots, of any number of more than two digits, and on the other, in the other column, or column of cubes, to the absence of any number of more than six digits. That is so, Mr Louit, is it not? You have the list before you, said Louit. Column of roots is very pretty too, I think, said Mr de Baker. Yes, but not so pretty as column of cubes, said Mr MacStern. Well, perhaps not quite, but very nearly, said Mr de Baker. Mr de Baker sang

> *Said the column of cubes to the column of roots,*
> *Oh what will you have to drink?*
> *Said the column of cubes to the column of roots,*
> *Oh what will you have to drink?*
> *Said the column of cubes to the column of roots,*
> *Oh what will you have to drink?*
> *Why, thank you, sir, said the column of roots,*
> *I'll have a bottle of ink.*

Hahahaha, haha, ha, hum, said Mr de Baker. Any more questions, before I go home to bed, said Mr Fitzwein. I was raising a point, said Mr O'Meldon, when I was interrupted. Perhaps he could go on from where he left off, said Mr Magershon. The point I was raising, said Mr O'Meldon, when I was interrupted, is this, that of the two columns of figures here before me this afternoon, the one, or — . He has said this twice already, said Mr MacStern. If not three times, said

13

Mr de Baker. Go on from where you left off, said
Mr Magershon, not from where you began. Or are you
like Darwin's caterpillar? Darwin's what? said Mr de
Baker. Darwin's caterpillar? said Mr Magershon.
What was the matter with him? said Mr MacStern.
The matter with him was this, said Mr Magershon, that
when he was disturbed in the building of his hammock
— . Are we here to discuss caterpillars? said Mr O'Meldon. Raise your point for the love of God, said Mr Fitzwein, and let me get home to my wife. He added, And
children. The point I was in the act of raising, said
Mr O'Meldon, when I was so rudely interrupted, was
this, that if in the lefthand column, or column of roots,
instead of there being figures of two digits at the most,
there were figures of three digits, and even four digits,
to go no further, then in the righthand column, or
column of cubes, instead of there being figures of six
digits at the most, there would be figures of seven, eight,
nine, ten, eleven and even twelve digits. A silence
followed these words. Would there not, Mr Louit, said
Mr O'Meldon. Very likely, said Louit. Then why,
said Mr Meldon, leaning forward and bringing down
his fist with a thump on the table, why are there
not? Are there not what? said Mr Fitzwein. What
I have just said, said Mr O'Meldon. What was that?
said Mr Fitzwein. Mr O'Meldon replied, On the one
hand, in the one column — . Or column of roots, said
Mr de Baker. Mr O'Meldon continued, Figures of three
digits and even four — . To go no further, said Mr Mac
Stern. Mr O'Meldon continued, And on the other, in
the other — . Or column of cubes, said Mr Magershon.
Mr O'Meldon continued, Figures of seven — . Of eight,
said Mr de Baker. Of nine, said Mr MacStern. Of ten,
said Mr Magershon. Of eleven, said Mr de Baker. And
even of twelve, said Mr MacStern. Digits, said Mr Magershon. Why should there be? said Mr Fitzwein. Little
by little the bird, said Louit. Am I then to suppose,
Mr Louit, said Mr O'Meldon, that if I were to ask this

fellow for the cube root of say — he bent over his
paper — let us say nine hundred and seventy three
million two hundred and fifty-two thousand two hundred
and seventy-one, he could not supply it? Not this
evening, said Louit. Or, said Mr O'Meldon, reading
again from his paper, nine hundred and ninety-eight
billion seven hundred million one hundred and twenty-
nine thousand nine hundred and ninety-nine, for
example? Not just now, some other time, said Louit.
Ha, said Mr O'Meldon. Is your point now raised,
Mr O'Meldon, said Mr Fitzwein. It is, said Mr O'Meldon. I am glad to hear that, said Mr Fitzwein. You
will tell us about it later, said Mr Magershon. Where
have I seen that face before, said M. Fitzwein. Just one
more thing, said Mr MacStern. The sun has now sunk,
in the west, said Mr de Baker, turning his head, and
extending his arm, in that direction. Then the others
turned too, and looked long, at the place where the
sun had been, but a moment before. But Mr de Baker
whirled round and pointed in the opposite direction,
saying, While in the orient night is falling fast. Then
the others to those shimmering windows turned them
round, to the sky dark grey below, and lighter grey
above. For the night seemed less to fall, than to rise,
from below, like another day. But finally as from the
filling grave, or with the loved one disappearing conveyance, mark well my words, Mr Graves, with the loved
one disappearing conveyance, slowly their sighing bodies
they tore away, and Mr Fitzwein began briskly to gather
up his papers, for in that ending light he had found
the place, the ancient place, where he had seen that face
before, and so he rose and rapidly left the hall (as
though he could have rapidly left the hall without
rising), followed more leisurely by his assistants, in
this order, first Mr O'Meldon, and then Mr MacStern,
and then Mr de Baker, and then Mr Magershon, as
chance would have it, or some other force. And then
Mr O'Meldon, pausing on his way to shake Louit by the

hand, and pat Mr Nackybal on the head, with a quick
pat that he wiped off at once discreetly on his trousers,
was overtaken and left behind, first by Mr MacStern,
and then by Mr de Baker, and then by Mr Magershon.
And then Mr MacStern, halting to formulate that one
more thing, was overtaken and left behind, first by Mr
de Baker, and then by Mr. Magershon. And then Mr de
Baker, kneeling to secure his lace, which had come
undone, as laces will, was passed by Mr Magershon,
who swept on slowly alone, like something out of Poe,
towards the door, and would indeed have reached it,
and passed through it, had not a sudden thought
stiffened him in his stride, so that he stood, two feet
between the foot-following feet, on left sole and right
toe, in the uncertain equilibrium of erect consternation.
And now the order was reversed in which, following
Mr Fitzwein, now in the eleven tram, they had set out,
so that the first was last, and the last first, and
the second third, and the third second, and that
what had been, in order of march, Mr O'Meldon,
Mr MacStern, Mr de Baker and Mr Magershon, was now,
brooding, kneeling, brooding, greeting, Mr Magershon,
Mr de Baker, Mr MacStern and Mr O'Meldon.   But
hardly had Mr O'Meldon, ceasing to greet, moved on
towards Mr MacStern, when Mr MacStern, ceasing to
brood, moved on, accompanied by Mr O'Meldon, towards
Mr de Baker.   But hardly had Mr O'Meldon and
Mr MacStern, ceasing, first Mr O'Meldon, then Mr Mac
Stern, the first to greet, the second to brood, moved on
together towards Mr de Baker, when Mr de Baker,
ceasing to kneel, moved on, accompanied by Mr Meldon
and Mr MacStern, towards Mr Magershon.   But hardly
had Mr O'Meldon and Mr MacStern and Mr de Baker,
ceasing, first Mr O'Meldon, then Mr MacStern, then
Mr de Baker, the first to greet, the second to brood, the
third to kneel, moved on together towards Mr Magershon,
when Mr Magershon, ceasing to brood, moved on,
accompanied by Mr O'Meldon and Mr MacStern and

Mr de Baker, towards the door. And so through the door, after the customary coagulation, the holding back, the thrust resisting, the sideways stepping, the onward urging, and the little landing along, and down the noble stairs, and out into the court now rife with night, one by one they passed, Mr MacStern, Mr O'Meldon, Mr Magershon, and Mr de Baker, in that order, as chance would have it, or some other agency. So that who was first first and second last now was second, and who was first second and second third now was first, and who was first third and second second now was last, and who was first last and second first now was third. And soon after Mr Nackybal put on his outer clothes and went away. And soon after Louit went away. And Louit, going down the stairs, met the bitter stout porter Power coming up. And as they passed the porter raised his cap and Louit smiled. And they did well. For had not Louit smiled, then Power had not raised his cap, and had not Power raised his cap, then Louit had not smiled, but they had passed, each on his way, Louit down, Power up, the one unsmiling, and the other covered. Now the next day — .

But here Arthur seemed to tire, of his story, for he left Mr Graves, and went back, into the house. Watt was thankful for this, for he too was tired, of Arthur's story, to which he had listened with the closest attention. And he could truly say, as he did, in after times, that of all the things he ever saw or heard, during his stay in Mr Knott's establishment, he heard none so well, saw none so clear, as Arthur and Mr Graves that sunny afternoon, on the lawn, and Louit, and Mr Nackybal, and Mr O'Meldon, and Mr Magershon, and Mr Fitzwein, and Mr de Baker, and Mr MacStern, and all the things they did, and the words they said. He understood it all too, very well, though he could not vouch for the accuracy of the figures, which he had not taken the trouble to check, having no head for figures. And if the words were not the exact words employed by Arthur,

by Louit, by Mr Nackybal and the others, they were
not far out. He enjoyed this incident too, at the time,
more than he had enjoyed anything for a long time,
or would enjoy anything again, for a considerable time.
But it tired him, in the end, and he was glad when
Arthur left off, and went away. Then Watt climbed
down, from off his mound, thinking how nice it would
be to go back into the cool house gloom, and drink a
glass of milk. But he did not care to leave Mr Knott
all alone in the garden, though there was really no reason
why he should not. Then he saw the branches of a
tree in agitation, and Mr Knott climbing down among
them, from branch it almost seemed to branch, lower
and lower, until he reached the ground. Then Mr Knott
turned towards the house, and Watt followed after,
very pleased with the afternoon he had spent, on his
mound, and looking forward to the nice glass of cold
milk that he would drink, in the cool, in the gloom,
in a moment. And Mr Graves remained alone, leaning
on his fork, all alone, while the shadows lengthened.

Watt learned later, from Arthur, that the telling
of this story, while it lasted, before Arthur grew tired,
had transported Arthur far from Mr Knott's premises,
of which, of the mysteries of which, of the fixity of
which, Arthur had sometimes more, than he could bear.

Arthur was a very nice open fellow, not at all
like Erskine.

In another place, he said, from another place, he
might have told this story to its end, told the true
identity of Mr Nackybal (his real name was Tisler and
he lived in a room on the canal), told his method of
cube-rooting in his head (he merely knew by heart the
cubes of one to nine, and even this was not indispensable,
and that one gives one, and two eight, and three seven,
and four four, and five five, and six six, and seven
three, and eight two, and nine nine, and of course
nought nought), and told the delinquencies of Louit,
his fall and subsequent ascension, running Bando.

But on Mr Knott's premises, from Mr Knott's premises, this was not possible, for Arthur.

For what stopped Arthur, and made him go silent, in the middle of his story, was not really fatigue with his story, for he was not really fatigued, but the desire to return, to leave Louit and return, to Mr Knott's house, to its mysteries, to its fixity. For he had been absent longer from them, than he could bear.

But perhaps in another place, from another place, Arthur would never have begun this story.

For there was no other place, but only there where Mr Knott was, whose mysteries, whose fixity, whose fixity of mystery, so thrust forth, with such a thrust.

But if he had begun, in some other place, from some other place, to tell this story, then he would very likely have told it to the end.

For there was no place, but only there where Mr Knott was, whose peculiar properties, having first thrust forth, with such a thrust, called back so soon, with such a call.

Watt sympathised with this predicament. Had not he himself, in the beginning, resorted to similar shifts?

Was he finished with them now? Well, almost.

Fixity was not the word he would have chosen.

Watt had little to say on the subject of the second or closing period of his stay in Mr Knott's house.

In the course of the second or closing period of Watt's stay in Mr Knott's house, the information acquired by Watt, on that subject, was scant.

Of the nature of Mr Knott himself Watt remained in particular ignorance.

Of the many excellent reasons for this, two seemed to Watt to merit mention: on the one hand the exiguity of the material propounded to his senses, and on the other the decay of these. What little there was to see, to hear, to smell, to taste, to touch, like a man in a stupor he saw it, heard it, smelt it, tasted it, touched it.

In empty hush, in airless gloom, Mr Knott abode, in the large room set aside for his exclusive enjoyment, and that of his attendant. And from it this ambience followed him forth, and when he moved, in the house, in the garden, with him moved, dimming all, dulling all, stilling all, numbing all, where he passed.

The clothes that Mr Knott wore, in his room, about the house, amid his garden, were very various, very very various. Now heavy, now light; now smart, now dowdy; now sober, now gaudy; now decent, now daring (his skirtless bathing-costume, for example). Often too he wore, by his fireside, or as he mooched about the rooms, the stairs, the passage-ways of his home, a hat, or cap, or, imprisoning his rare his wanton hair, a net. And as often his head was bare.

As for his feet, sometimes he wore on each a sock, or on the one a sock and on the other a stocking, or a boot, or a shoe, or a slipper, or a sock and boot, or a sock and shoe, or a sock and slipper, or a stocking and boot, or a stocking and shoe, or a stocking and slipper, or nothing at all. And sometimes he wore on each a stocking, or on the one a stocking and on the other a boot, or a shoe, or a slipper, or a sock and boot, or a sock and shoe, or a sock and slipper, or a stocking and boot, or a stocking and shoe, or a stocking and slipper, or nothing at all. And sometimes he wore on each a boot, or on the one a boot and on the other a shoe, or a slipper, or a sock and boot, or a sock and shoe, or a sock and slipper, or a stocking and boot, or a stocking and shoe, or a stocking and slipper, or nothing at all. And sometimes he wore on each a shoe, or on the one a shoe and on the other a slipper, or a sock and boot, or a sock and shoe, or a sock and slipper, or a stocking and boot, or a stocking and shoe, or a stocking and slipper, or nothing at all. And sometimes he wore on each a slipper, or on the one a slipper and on the other a sock and boot, or a sock and shoe, or a sock and slipper,

or a stocking and boot, or a stocking and shoe, or a
stocking and slipper, or nothing at all. And sometimes
he wore on each a sock and boot, or on the one a sock
and boot and on the other a sock and shoe, or a sock
and slipper, or a stocking and boot, or a stocking and
shoe, or a stocking and slipper, or nothing at all. And
sometimes he wore on each a sock and shoe, or on the
one a sock and shoe and on the other a sock and slipper,
or a stocking and boot, or a stocking and shoe, or a
stocking and slipper, or nothing at all. And sometimes
he wore on each a sock and slipper, or on the one a
sock and slipper and on the other a stocking and boot,
or a stocking and shoe, or a stocking and slipper, or
nothing at all. And sometimes he wore on each a
stocking and boot, or on the one a stocking and boot
and on the other a stocking and shoe, or a stocking
and slipper, or nothing at all. And sometimes he wore
on each a stocking and shoe, or on the one a stocking
and shoe and on the other a stocking and slipper, or
nothing at all. And sometimes he wore on each a
stocking and slipper, or on the one a stocking and
slipper and on the other nothing at all. And sometimes
he went barefoot.

To think, when one is no longer young, when
one is not yet old, that one is no longer young, that
one is not yet old, that is perhaps something. To pause,
towards the close of one's three hour day, and consider:
the darkening ease, the brightening trouble; the pleasure
pleasure because it was, the pain pain because it shall
be; the glad acts grown proud, the proud acts growing
stubborn; the panting the trembling towards a being
gone, a being to come; and the true true no longer,
and the false true not yet. And to decide not to smile
after all, sitting in the shade, hearing the cicadas,
wishing it were night, wishing it were morning, saying,
No, it is not the heart, no, it is not the liver, no, it is
not the prostate, no it is not the ovaries, no, it is
muscular, it is nervous. Then the gnashing ends, or it

goes on, and one is in the pit, in the hollow, the longing
for longing gone, the horror of horror, and one is in
the hollow, at the foot of all the hills at last, the ways
down, the ways up, and free, free at last, for an instant
free at last, nothing at last.

But whatever he put on, in the beginning, for by
midnight he was always in his nightshirt, whatever he
put on then, on his head, on his body, on his feet, he
did not touch again, but kept on all that day, in his
room, in his house, in his grounds, until the time came
to put on his nightshirt, once again.   Yes, not one
button would he touch, to button or unbutton it, except
those that nature obliged him to, and these he habit-
ually left unbuttoned, from the moment of his putting
on his clothes, and adjusting them to his satisfaction,
to the moment of his taking them off, once more.   So
that he was not seldom to be seen, in his room, in his
house, in his grounds, in strange and unseasonable
costume, as though he were unaware of the weather,
or of the time of year.   And to see him sometimes thus,
barefoot and for boating dressed, in the snow, in the
slush, in the icy winter wind, or, when summer came
again, by his fire, charged with furs, was to wonder,
Does he seek to know again, what is cold, what is
heat?   But this was an anthropomorphic insolence of
short duration.

For except, one, not to need, and, two, a witness
to his not needing, Knott needed nothing, as far as
Watt could see.

If he ate, and he ate well; if he drank, and he
drank heartily; if he slept, and he slept sound; if he did
other things, and he did other things regularly, it was
not from need of food, or drink, or sleep, or other
things, no, but from the need never to need, never never
to need, food, and drink, and sleep, and other things.

This was Watt's first surmise of any interest on
the subject of Mr Knott.

And Mr Knott, needing nothing if not, one, not

from the bed to the fire, from the fire to the bed;
from the door to the fire, from the fire to the door;
from the fire to the door, from the door to the fire;
from the window to the bed, from the bed to the window;
from the bed to the window, from the window to the bed;
from the fire to the window, trom the window to the fire;
from the window to the fire, from the fire to the window;
from the bed to the door, from the door to the bed;
from the door to the bed, from the bed to the door;
from the door to the window, from the window to the
fire; from the fire to the window, from the window to
the door; from the window to the door, from the door
to the bed; from the bed to the door, from the door
to the window; from the fire to the bed, from the bed
to the window; from the window to the bed, from the
bed to the fire; from the bed to the fire, from the fire
to the door; from the door to the fire, from the fire
to the bed; from the door to the window, from the
window to the bed; from the bed to the window, from
the window to the door; from the window to the door,
from the door to the fire; from the fire to the door,
from the door to the window; from the fire to the bed,
from the bed to the door; from the door to the bed,
from the bed to the fire; from the bed to the fire, from
the fire to the window; from the window to the fire,
from the fire to the bed; from the door to the fire,
from the fire to the window; from the window to the
fire, from the fire to the door; from the window to
the bed, from the bed to the door; from the door to
the bed, from the bed to the window; from the fire
to the window, from the window to the bed; from the
bed to the window, from the window to the fire; from
the bed to the door, from the door to the fire; from
the fire to the door, from the door to the bed.

This room was furnished solidly and with taste.

This solid and tasteful furniture was subjected by
Mr Knott to frequent changes of position, both absolute
and relative.   Thus it was not rare to find, on the

Sunday, the tallboy on its feet by the fire, and the
dressing-table on its head by the bed, and the nightstool on its face by the door, and the washhand-stand
on its back by the window; and, on the Monday, the
tallboy on its back by the bed, and the dressing-table
on its face by the door, and the night-stool on its back
by the window, and the washhand-stand on its feet by
the fire; and, on the Tuesday, the tallboy on its face
by the door, and the dressing-table on its back by the
window, and the nightstool on its feet by the fire, and
the washhand-stand on its head by the bed; and, on
the Wednesday, the tallboy on its back by the window,
and the dressing-table on its feet by the fire, and the
nightstool on its head by the bed, and the washhand-
stand on its face by the door; and, on the Thursday,
the tallboy on its side by the fire, and the dressing-table
on its feet by the bed, and the nightstool on its head
by the door, and the washhand-stand on its face by the
window; and, on the Friday, the tallboy on its feet
by the bed, and the dressing-table on its head by the
door, and the nightstool on its face by the window,
and the washhand-stand on its side by the fire; and,
on the Saturday, the tallboy on its head by the door,
and the dressing-table on its face by the window, and
the nightstool on its side by the fire, and the washhand-
stand on its feet by the bed; and, on the Sunday week,
the tallboy on its face by the window, and the dressing-
table on its side by the fire, and the nightstool on its
feet by the bed, and the washhand-stand on its head by
the door; and, on the Monday week, the tallboy on
its back by the fire, and the dressing-table on its side
by the bed, and the nightstool on its feet by the door,
and the washhand-stand on its head by the window;
and, on the Tuesday week, the tallboy on its side by
the bed, and the dressing-table on its feet by the door,
and the nightstool on its head by the window, and the
washhand-stand on its back by the fire; and, on the
Wednesday week, the tallboy on its feet by the door,

and the dressing-table on its head by the window, and
the nightstool on its back by the fire, and the washhand-
stand on its side by the bed; and, on the Thursday
week, the tallboy on its head by the window, and the
dressing-table on its back by the fire, and the nightstool
on its side by the bed, and the washhand-stand on its
feet by the door; and, on the Friday week, the tallboy
on its face by the fire, and the dressing-table on its back
by the bed, and the nightstool on its side by the door,
and the washhand-stand on its feet by the window;
and, on the Saturday week, the tallboy on its back
by the bed, and the dressing-table on its side by the door,
and the nightstool on its feet by the window, and the
washhand-stand on its face by the fire; and, on the
Sunday fortnight, the tallboy on its side by the door,
and the dressing-table on its feet by the window, and
the nightstool on its face by the fire, and the washhand-
stand on its back by the bed; and, on the Monday fortnight, the tallboy on its feet by the window, and the
dressing-table on its face by the fire, and the nightstool
on its back by the bed, and the washhand-stand on its
side by the door; and, on the Tuesday fortnight, the
tallboy on its head by the fire, and the dressing-table
on its face by the bed, and the nightstool on its back
by the door, and the washhand-stand on its side by the
window; and, on the Wednesday fortnight, the tallboy
on its face by the bed, and the dressing-table on its back
by the door, and the nightstool on its side by the window,
and the washhand-stand on its head by the fire; and,
on the Thursday fortnight, the tallboy on its back by
the door, and the dressing-table on its side by the
window, and the nightstool on its head by the fire, and
the washhand-stand on its face by the bed; and, on the
Friday fortnight, the tallboy on its side by the window,
and the dressing-table on its head by the fire, and the
nightstool on its face by the bed, and the washhand-
stand on its back by the door, for example, not at all
rare, to consider only, over a period of nineteen days

only, the tallboy, the dressing-table, the nightstool and the washhand-stand, and their feet, and heads, and faces, and backs and unspecified sides, and the fire, and the bed, and the door, and the window, not at all rare.

For the chairs also, to mention only the chairs also, were never still.

For the corners also, to mention only the corners also, were seldom vacant.

Alone the bed maintained the illusion of fixity, the bed so tasteful, the bed so solid, that it was round, and clamped to the ground.

Mr Knott's head, Mr Knott's feet, in nightly displacements of almost one minute, completed in twelve months their circuit of this solitary couch. His coccyx also, and adjacent gear, performed their little annual revolution, as appeared from an examination of the sheets (changed regularly on Saint Patrick's Day), and even of the mattress.

Of the strange doings above stairs, that had so preoccupied Watt during his time below stairs, no explanation was to be had. But they did not preoccupy Watt any longer.

From time to time Mr Knott disappeared from his room, leaving Watt alone. Mr Knott was there one moment, and the next gone. But on these occasions Watt, unlike Erskine, did not feel impelled to institute a search, above stairs and below, assassinating with his tread the quiet house, and pestering his colleague in the kitchen, no, but he remained quietly where he was, not wholly asleep, not wholly awake, until Mr Knott came back.

Watt suffered neither from the presence of Mr Knott, nor from his absence. When he was with him, he was content to be with him, and when he was away from him, he was content to be away from him. Never with relief, never with regret, did he leave him at night, or in the morning come to him again.

This ataraxy covered the entire house-room, the pleasure-garden, the vegetable-garden and of course Arthur.

So that when the time came for Watt to depart, he walked to the gate with the utmost serenity.

But he was no sooner in the public road than he burst into tears. He stood there, he remembered, with bowed head, and a bag in each hand, and his tears fell, a slow minute rain, to the ground, which had recently been repaired. He would not have believed such a thing possible, if he had not been there himself. The humidity thus lent to the road surface must, he reckoned, have survived his departure by as long as two minutes at least, if not three. Fortunately the weather was fine.

Watt's room contained no information. It was a small, dingy, and, though Watt was a man of some bodily cleanliness, fetid compartment. Its one window commanded a very fine view of a race-course. The painting, or coloured reproduction, yielded nothing further. On the contrary, as time passed, its significance diminished.

From Mr Knott's voice nothing was to be learnt. Between Mr Knott and Watt no conversation passed. From time to time, for no apparent reason, Mr Knott opened his mouth in song. From bass to tenor, all male registers were employed by him, with equal success. He did not sing well, in Watt's opinion, but Watt had heard worse singers. The music of these songs was of an extreme monotony. For the voice, save for an occasional raucous sally, both up and down, to the extent of a tenth, or even an eleventh, did not leave the pitch at which, having elected to begin, it seemed obliged to remain, and finally to end. The words of these songs were either without meaning, or derived from an idiom with which Watt, a very fair linguist, had no acquaintance. The open a sound was predominant, and the explosives k and g. Mr Knott talked often to himself too, with great variety and vehemence of intonation

and gesticulation, but this so softly that it came, a wild
dim chatter, meaningless to Watt's ailing ears.   This
was a noise of which Watt grew exceedingly fond.   Not
that he was sorry when it ceased, not that he was glad
when it came again, no.   But while it sounded he was
gladdened, as by the rain on the bamboos, or even
rushes, as by the land against the waves, doomed to
cease, doomed to come again.   Knott was also addicted
to solitary dactylic ejaculations of extraordinary vigour,
accompanied by spasms of the members.   The chief of
these were :   Exelmans !   Cavendish !   Habbakuk !
Ecchymose !

      With regard to the so important matter of
Mr Knott's physical appearance, Watt had unfortunately
little or nothing to say.   For one day Mr Knott would
be tall, fat, pale and dark, and the next thin, small,
flushed and fair, and the next sturdy, middlesized,
yellow and ginger, and the next small, fat, pale and fair,
and the next middlesized, flushed, thin and ginger, and
the next tall, yellow, dark and sturdy, and the next fat,
middlesized, ginger and pale, and the next tall, thin,
dark and flushed, and the next small, fair, sturdy
and yellow, and the next tall, ginger, pale and fat, and
the next thin, flushed, small and dark, and the next
fair, sturdy, middlesized and yellow, and the next dark,
small, fat and pale, and the next fair, middlesized,
flushed and thin, and the next sturdy, ginger, tall and
yellow, and the next pale, fat, middlesized and fair, and
the next flushed, tall, thin and ginger, and the next
yellow, small, dark and sturdy, and the next fat, flushed,
ginger and tall, and the next dark, thin, yellow, and
small, and the next fair, pale, sturdy and middlesized,
and the next dark, flushed, small and fat, and the next
thin, fair, yellow and middlesized, and the next pale,
sturdy, ginger and tall, and the next flushed, fair, fat
and middlesized, and the next yellow, ginger, tall and
thin, and the next sturdy, small, pale and dark, and
the next tall, fat, yellow, and fair, and t.ie next small,

                                                        14

pale, thin and ginger, and the next middlesized, flushed,
dark and sturdy, and the next fat, small, ginger and
yellow, and the next middlesized, thin, dark and pale,
and the next tall, fair, sturdy and flushed, and the next
middlesized, dark, yellow and fat, and the next thin,
pale, tall and fair, and the next ginger, sturdy, small
and flushed, and the next dark, tall, fat and yellow,
and the next fair, small, pale and thin, and the next
sturdy, ginger, middlesized and flushed, and the next
yellow, fat, small and fair, and the next pale, middlesized, thin and ginger, and the next flushed, tall, dark
and sturdy, and the next fat, yellow, ginger and middlesized, and the next dark, thin, pale and tall, and the
next fair, flushed, sturdy and small, and the next ginger,
yellow, tall and fat, and the next thin, dark, pale and
small, and the next flushed, sturdy, fair and middlesized, and the next yellow, dark, fat and small, and the
next pale, fair, middlesized and thin, and the next
sturdy, tall, flushed and ginger, and the next middlesized, fat, yellow and fair, and the next tall, pale, thin
and ginger, and the next small, flushed, dark and sturdy,
and the next fat, tall, fair and pale, and the next small,
thin, ginger and flushed, and the next middlesized,
dark, sturdy and yellow, and the next small, ginger,
pale and fat, and the next thin, flushed, middlesized
and dark, and the next fair, sturdy, tall and yellow, and
the next dark, middlesized, fat and pale, and the next
fair, tall, flushed and thin, and the next sturdy, ginger,
small and yellow, and the next flushed, fat, tall and
fair, and the next yellow, small, thin and ginger, and
the next pale, middlesized, dark and sturdy, and the
next fat, flushed, ginger and small, and the next dark,
thin, yellow and middlesized, and the next fair, pale,
sturdy and tall, and the next dark, flushed, middlesized
and fat, and the next thin, fair, yellow and tall, and
the next pale, sturdy, ginger and small, and the next
flushed, dark, fat and tall, and the next yellow, fair,
small and thin, and the next sturdy, middlesized, pale

and ginger, and the next small, fat, flushed and fair,
and the next middlesized, yellow, thin and ginger, and
the next tall, pale, dark and sturdy, and the next fat,
middlesized, ginger and flushed, and the next tall,
thin, dark and yellow, and the next small, fair, sturdy
and pale, or so it seemed to Watt, to mention only
the figure, stature, skin and hair.

For daily changed, as well as these, in carriage,
expression, shape and size, the feet, the legs, the hands,
the arms, the mouth, the nose, the eyes, the ears, to
mention only the feet, the legs, the hands, the arms, the
mouth, the nose, the eyes, the ears, and their carriage,
expression, shape and size.

For the port, the voice, the smell, the hairdress,
were seldom the same, from one day to the next, to
mention only the port, the voice, the smell, the hairdress.

For the way of hawking, the way of spitting,
were subject to daily fluctuation, to consider only the
way of hawking, and of spitting.

For the belch was never the same, two days running, to go no further than the belch.

Watt had no hand in these transformations, and
did not know at what hour of the twenty-four they
were carried out. He suspected, however, thay they
were carried out between the hours of midnight, when
Watt ended his day by helping Mr Knott into his nightdress (1), and then into bed, and eight in the morning,

---

(1) For the guidance of the attentive reader, at a loss to
understand how these repeated investments, and divestments, of
the nightdress, did not finally reveal to Watt Mr Knott's veritable
aspect, it is perhaps not superfluous here to note, that Mr Knott's
attitude to his nightdress was not that generally in vogue. For Mr
Knott did not do as most men, and many women, do, who, before
putting on their nightclothes, at night, take off their dayclothes,
and again, when morning comes, once again, before they dream
of putting on their dayclothes are careful to pull off their soiled
nightclothes, no, but he went to bed with his nightclothes over
his dayclothes, and he rose with his dayclothes under his nightclothes.

when Watt began his day by helping Mr Knott out of his bed, and then out of his nightdress. For if Mr Knott had modified his appearance during Watt's hours of attendance, then it was unlikely that he could have done so without attracting Watt's attention, if not at the time, at least in the hours following. So Watt suspected that it was in the depths of the night, when the risk of disturbance was small, that Mr Knott organised his exterior for the day to come. And what went far to strengthen this suspicion in the heart of Watt was this, that when sometimes, in the small hours of the morning, unable or unwilling to sleep he rose and went to the window, to look at the stars, which he had once known familiarly by name, when dying in London, and breathe the night air, and listen to the night sounds, of which he was still extremely curious, he sometimes saw, between him and the ground, lightening the darkness, greyening the leaves and, in wet weather, tinseling the rain, a fascia of white light.

None of Mr Knott's gestures could be called characteristic, unless perhaps that which consisted in the simultaneous obturation of the facial cavities, the thumbs in the mouth, the forefingers in the ears, the little fingers in the nostrils, the third fingers in the eyes and the second fingers, free in a crisis to promote intellection, laid along the temples. And this was less a gesture than an attitude, sustained by Mr Knott for long periods of time, without visible discomfort.

Other traits, other little ways, little ways of passing the little days, Watt remarked in Mr Knott, and could have told if he had wished, if he had not been tired, so very tired, by all he had told already, tired of adding, tired of subtracting to and from the same old things the same old things.

But he could not bear that we should part, never to meet again (in this world), and I in ignorance of how Mr Knott put on his boots, or his shoes, or his slippers, or his boot and shoe, or his boot and slipper,

or his shoe and slipper, when he did so, when he did
not merely put on a boot, or a shoe, or a slipper. So,
taking his hands from my shoulders, and laying them
on my wrists, he told how Mr Knott, when he felt
the time come, taking on a cunning air would begin to
sidle sidle up to the boots, up to the shoes, up to the
boot and shoe, up 'to the boot and slipper, up to the
shoe and slipper, sidle sidle little by little with an
artless air little by little nearer and nearer to where
they lay, in the rack, till he was near enough, pouncing,
to secure them. And then, while he put on the one,
the black boot, the brown shoe, the black slipper, the
brown boot, the black shoe, the brown slipper, on the
one foot, he held the other tight, lest it should escape,
or put it in his pocket, or put his foot upon it, or put
it in a drawer, or put it in his mouth, till he might
put it on, on the other foot.

Continuing then, when he had told me this, then
he loosed my hands from his shoulders, and backwards
through the hole went back, to his garden, and left me
alone, alone with only my poor eyes to follow him,
this last of many times to follow him, over the deep
threshing shadows backwards stumbling, towards his
habitation. And often he struck against the trunks of
trees, and in the tangles of underwood caught his foot,
and fell to the ground, on his back, on his face, on his
side, or into a great clump of brambles, or of briars,
or of thistles, or of nettles. But ever he picked himself
up and unmurmuring went on, towards his habitation,
until I saw him no more, but only the aspens. And
from the hidden pavilions, his and mine, where by
this time dinner was preparing, the issuing smokes by
the wind were blown, now far apart, but now together,
mingled to vanish.

IV

As Watt told the beginning of his story, not first, but second, so not fourth, but third, now he told its end. Two, one, four, three, that was the order in which Watt told his story. Heroic quatrains are not otherwise elaborated.

As Watt came, so he went, in the night, that covers all things with its cloak, especially when the weather is cloudy.

It was summer, he thought, because the air was not quite cold. As for his coming, so now for his going, it seemed a kindly summer's night. And it came at the end of a day that was like the other days, for Watt. For of Mr Knott he could not speak.

In the room, passably lit by the moon, and large numbers of stars, Mr Knott continued, apparently very much as usual, to lie, kneel, sit, stand and walk. to utter his cries, mutter and be silent. And by the open window Watt sat, as his custom was in suitable weather, heard dully the first night sounds, saw dully the first night lights, human and celestial.

At ten the steps came, clearer, clearer, fainter, fainter, on the stairs, on the landing, on the stairs again, and through the open door the light, from darkness slowly brightening, to darkness slowly darkening, the steps of Arthur, the light of poor Arthur, little by little mounting to his rest, at his habitual hour.

At eleven the room darkened, the moon having climbed behind a tree. But the tree being small, and the moon's ascension rapid, this transit was brief, and this obscuration.

As by the steps the light, growing, dying, Watt knew that it was ten, so he knew, when the room darkened, that it was eleven, or thereabouts.

But when he thought it was midnight, or thereabouts, and he had put Mr Knott into his nightdress, and then into his bed, then he went down to the kitchen, as he did every night, to drink his last glass of milk, to smoke his last quarter of cigar.

But in the kitchen a strange man was sitting, in the gloaming of the expiring range, on a chair.

Watt asked this man who he was, and how he had got in. He felt it was his duty to do this.

My name is Micks, said the stranger. One moment I was out, and the next I was in.

So the moment was come. Watt lifted the cork lid from his glass, and drank. The milk was turning. He lit his cigar, and puffed. It was an inferior cigar.

I come from — , said Mr Micks, and he described the place whence he came. I was born at — , he said, and the site and circumstances of his ejection were unfolded. My dear parents, he said, and Mr and Mrs Micks, heroic figures, unique in the annals of cloistered fornication, filled the kitchen. He said further, At the age of fifteen, My beloved wife, My beloved dog, Till at last. Happily Mr Micks was childless.

Watt listened for a time, for the voice was far from unmelodious. The fricatives in particular were pleasing. But as from the proscript an encountered

nightsong, so it faded, the voice of Micks, the pleasant
voice of poor Micks, and was lost, in the soundless tumult
of the inner lamentation.

When Watt had finished his milk, and smoked
his cigar, until it burned his lips, he left the kitchen.
But in a short time he reappeared, to Micks, with in
each hand a small bag, that is to say, two small bags
in all.

Watt preferred, when travelling, two small bags
to one large bag. Indeed he preferred, when moving
from place to place, two small bags, one in each hand,
to one small bag, now in one hand and now in the other.
No bag, big or small, in either hand, that of course is
what he would have liked best of all, when on his
travels. But what then would have become of his
effects, his toilet necessities and change of body linen?

One of these bags was the grousebag, already
perhaps mentioned. In spite of the straps, and buckles,
with which it was generously provided, Watt held it
by the neck, as though it were a sandbag.

The other of these bags was another and similar
grousebag. It also Watt held by the neck, as though
it were a club.

These bags were three quarters empty.

Watt wore a greatcoat, still green here and there.
This coat, when last weighed by Watt, weighed between
fifteen and sixteen pounds, avoirdupois, or a little more
than a stone. Of this Watt was certain, having weighed
himself on a machine, first with the coat on, and then
with it off, lying on the ground, at his feet. But that
was a long time ago, and the coat might have put on
weight, since then. Or it might have lost weight. This
coat was of such length, that Watt's trousers, which
he wore very baggy, in order to conceal the shapes of
his legs, were hidden by it from view. This coat was
of a very respectable age, as such coats go, having
been bought at secondhand, for a small sum, from a
meritorious widow, by Watt's father, when Watt's

father was a young man, and motoring in its infancy,
that is to say some seventy years before. This coat had
not, since then, at any time been washed, except im-
perfectly by the rain, and the snow, and the sleet, and
of course occasional fleeting immersion in canal water,
nor dry-cleaned, nor turned, nor brushed, and it was
no doubt to these precautions that its preservation, as
a unit, was due. The material of this coat, though
liberally scored and contunded, especially in the rear,
was so thick, and so strong, that it remained exempt
from perforation, in the strict meaning of the word,
nor was its thread elsewhere exposed, than at the seat,
and elbows. This coat continued to button, up the
front, with nine buttons, various now in shape, and
colour, but without exception of such exceptional size
as to remain, once buttoned, buttoned. Aloft in the
flowerhole brooded the remains of a factitious murrey
chrysanthemum. Patches of velvet clung to the collar.
The skirts were not divided.

Watt wore, on his head, a block hat, of a pepper
colour. This excellent hat had belonged to his grandfather, who had picked it up, on a racecourse, from
off the ground, where it lay, and carried it home.
Then mustard, now it was pepper, in colour.

It was to be observed that the colours, on the one
hand of this coat, on the other of this hat, drew closer
and closer, the one to the other, with every passing
lustre. Yet how different had been their beginnings!
The one green! The other yellow! So it is with time,
that lightens what is dark, that darkens what is light.

It was to be expected that, once met, they would
not stay, no, but continue, each as it must, to age, until
the hat was green, the coat yellow, and then through
the last circles paling, deepening, swooning cease, the
hat to be a hat, the coat to be a coat. For so it is with
time.

Watt wore, on his feet, a boot, brown in colour,
and a shoe, happily of a brownish colour also. This

boot Watt had bought, for eight pence, from a one-legged man who, having lost his leg, and a fortiori his foot, in an accident, was happy to realize, on his discharge from hospital, for such a sum, his unique remaining marketable asset. He little suspected that he owed this good fortune to Watt's having found, some days before, on the sea-shore, the shoe, stiff with brine, but otherwise shipshape.

This shoe and this boot were so close in colour, the one to the other, and so veiled, as to their uppers, in the first place by the trousers, and in the second by the greatcoat, that they might almost have been taken, not for a shoe on the one hand, and on the other for a boot, but for a true pair, of boots, or of shoes, had not the boot been blunt, and the shoe sharp, at the toe.

In this boot, a twelve, and in this shoe, a ten, Watt, whose size was eleven, suffered, if not agony, at least pain, with his feet, of which each would willingly have changed places with the other, if only for a moment.

By wearing, on the foot that was too small, not one sock of his pair of socks, but both, and on the foot that was too large, not the other, but none, Watt strove in vain to correct this asymmetry. But logic was on his side, and he remained faithful, when involved in a journey of any length, to this distribution of his socks, in preference to the other three.

Of Watt's coat and waistcoat, of his shirt his vest and his drawers, much might be written, of great interest and significance. The drawers, in particular, were remarkable, from more than one point of view. But they were hidden, coat and waistcoat, shirt and underclothes, all hidden, from the eye.

Watt wore no tie, nor any collar. Had he had a collar, he would no doubt have found a tie, to go with it. And had he had a tie, he might perhaps have procured a collar, to carry it. But having neither tie, nor collar, he had neither collar, nor tie.

Thus dressed, and holding in either hand a bag,
Watt stood in the kitchen, and the expression on his
face became gradually of such vacancy that Micks,
raising in amaze an astonished hand to a thunderstruck
mouth, recoiled to the wall, and there stood, in a
crouching posture, his back pressed against the wall,
and the back of the one hand pressed against his
parted lips, and the back of the other pressed against
the palm of the one. Or it may have been something
else that caused Micks to recoil in this way, and to
crouch against the wall, with his hands to his face, in
this way, something other than the face of Watt. For
it is hard to believe that the face of Watt, dreadful
and all as it was at the time, was dreadful and all
enough to cause a powerful lymphatic man like Micks
to recoil to the wall with his hands to his face, as if
to ward off a blow, or press back a cry, in the way
he did, and to turn pale, for he turned pale, very
properly. For Watt's face, dreadful and all as it undoubtedly was, especially when it wore this particular
expression, was scarcely as dreadful and all as all that.
Nor was Micks a little girl, or an innocent little choirboy,
no, but a big placid man, who had seen something of
the world, both at home, and abroad. What may it
then have been, if not Watt's face, that so repelled
Micks, and drained his cheeks, of their natural high
colour? The greatcoat? The hat? The shoe and boot?
Yes, the shoe and boot perhaps, taken together, so
brown, so peeping, so sharp and blunt, heel to heel
in obscene attention splayed, and so brown, such a
brown. Or was it not perhaps something that was not
Watt, nor of Watt, but behind Watt, or beside Watt,
or before Watt, or beneath Watt, or above Watt, or
about Watt, a shade uncast, a light unshed, or the grey
air aswirl with vain entelechies?

But if Watt's mouth was open, and his jaw sunk,
and his eyes glassy, and his head sunk, and his knees
bent, and his back bent, his mind was busy, busy

wondering which was best, to shut the door, from which
he felt the draught, on the nape, of his neck, and set
down his bags, and sit down, or to shut the door, and
set down his bags, without sitting down, or to shut
the door, and sit down, without setting down his bags,
or to set down his bags, and sit down, without shutting
the door, or to shut the door, from which he felt the
blast, on the nape, of his neck, without setting down
his bags, or sitting down, or to set down his bags.
without bothering to shut the door, or sit down, or to
sit down, without troubling to set down his bags, or
shut the door, or to leave things as they were, the bags
pulling at his hands, the floor pushing at his feet, and
the air puffing, through the door, on the nape, of his
neck. And the conclusion of Watt's reflexions was this,
that if one of these things was worth doing, all were
worth doing, but that none was worth doing, no, not
one, but that all were unadvisable, without exception.
For he would not have time to rest, and grow warm.
For the sitting down was a standing up again, and the
load laid down another load to raise, and the door
shut another door to open, so hard upon the last, so
soon before the next, as to prove, very likely, in the
long run, more fatiguing, than refreshing. And he
said also, by way of a rider, that even if he had the
whole night before him, in which to rest, and grow
warm, on a chair, in the kitchen, even then it would
be a poor resting, and a mean warming, beside the rest
and warmth that he remembered, the rest and warmth
that he awaited, a very poor resting indeed, and a paltry
warming, and so in any case very likely a source, in the
long run, less of gratification, than of annoyance. But
his fatigue was so great, at the end of this long day, and
his bedtime so long past, and the desire for rest so
strong in consequence, and the desire for warmth, that
he stooped, very likely with the intention of setting
down his bags, on the floor, and of shutting the door,
and of sitting down at the table, and of putting his

at a great distance, poured down on Watt, and on
the hortulan beauties through which he moved, with
regret, in his heart, for his neglect of Micks, to Watt's
disgust a light so strong, so pure, so steady and so
white, that his progress, though painful, and uncertain,
was less painful, less uncertain, than he had appre-
hended, when setting out.

Watt was always lucky with his weather.

He walked on the grass edging, because he did not
like the feel of gravel under his feet, and the flowers,
and the long grasses, and the boughs, both of shrubs
and of trees, brushed against him in a way that he did
not find unpleasant. The lapping, against the crown,
of his hat, of some pendulous umbel, perhaps a horn's,
gave him peculiar satisfaction, and he had not gone
far, from the place, when he turned, and returned, to
the place, and stood, beneath the bough, attentive to
the drag, to and fro, to and fro, of the tassels, on the
crown, of his hat.

He remarked that there was no wind, not a
breath. And yet in the kitchen he had felt the cold
air, on the nape, of his neck.

He was overtaken, in the road, by the passing
weakness already mentioned. But it passed, and he
pursued his way, towards the railway-station.

He walked in the middle of the road, because
of the freestone, with which the path was strewn.

He met no human being, on his way. A strayed
ass, or goat, lying in the ditch, in the shadow, raised
its head, as he passed. Watt did not see the ass, or goat,
but the ass, or goat, saw Watt. And it followed him
with its eyes while he passed, little by little, down
the road, out of sight. Perhaps it thought that in the
bags there was something good to eat. When it could
see the bags no more, then it laid back its head, among
the nettles.

When Watt reached the railway-station, it was
shut. It had indeed been shut for some time, before

Watt reached it, and it was so still, when he did. For the time was now perhaps between one and two o'clock, in the morning, and the last train to call at this railway-station, at night, and the first to call, in the morning, called, the one between eleven and twelve o'clock, at night, and the other between five and six o'clock, in the morning. So this particular railway-station closed, at latest, at twelve o'clock, at night, and never opened before five o'clock, in the morning. And as the time was now probably between one and two o'clock, in the morning, the railway-station was shut.

Watt climbed the stone steps and stood before the wicket, looking through its bars. He admired the permanent way, stretching away on either hand, in the moonlight, and the starlight, as far as the eye could reach, as far as Watt's eye could have reached, if it had been inside the station. He contemplated with wonder also the ample recession of the plain, its flow so free and simple to the mountains, the crumpled umbers of its verge. His eyes then rising with the rising land fell ultimately on the mirrored sky, its coalsacks, its setting constellations, and on the eyes, ripple-blurred, staring from amidst the waters. Finally suddenly he focussed the wicket.

Watt climbed the wicket and found himself on the platform, with his bags. For he had the foresight, before climbing the wicket, to hoist his bags over the wicket and let them fall, to the ground, on the other side.

Watt's first care, now that he was safe and sound, with his bags, within the station, was to turn, and to gaze, through the wicket, the way back he had come, so recently.

Of the many touching prospects thus offered to his inspection, none touched him more than the highway, now whiter somehow than by day, and of a fairer onrush, between its hedges, and its ditches. This highway, after an unbroken course of considerable length, dipped suddenly, and was lost to view, in a deplorable confusion of vertical vegetation.

The chimneys of Mr Knott's house were not visible, in spite of the excellent visibility. On fine days they could be discerned, from the station. But on fine nights apparently not. For Watt's eyes, when he put himself out, were no worse than another's, even at this time, and the night was exceptionally fine, even for this part of the country, reputed for the fineness of its nights.

Watt had always great luck with his weather.

Watt was beginning to tire of running his eyes up and down this highway, when a figure, human apparently, advancing along its crown, arrested, and revived, his attention. Watt's first thought was that this creature had risen up out of the ground, or fallen from the sky. And his second, some fifteen or twenty minutes later, that it had perhaps gained its present position by way of first a hedge, and then a ditch. Watt was unable to say whether this figure was that of a man, or that of a woman, or that of a priest, or that of a nun. That it was not that of a boy, nor that of a girl, was shown, in Watt's opinion, by its dimensions. But to decide whether it was that of a man, or that of a woman, or that of a priest, or that of a nun, was more than Watt could do, strain as he might his eyes. If it was that of a woman, or that of a nun, it was that of a woman, or that of a nun, of unusual size, even for this part of the country, remarkable for the unusual size of its women, and its nuns. But Watt knew too well, too too well, of what dimensions certain women, and certain nuns, were capable, to conclude, from those of this night-wanderer, that this night-wanderer was not a woman, nor a nun, but a man, or a priest. As for the clothes, their testimony was of no more assistance, at that distance, and in that light, than if they had consisted of a sheet, or a sack, or a quilt, or a rug. For from head to foot extended, as far as Watt could see, and his

eyes were as good as the next man's, even at this stage,
when he gave himself the trouble to focus them, the
uninterrupted surfaces of a single garment, while on the
head there sat, asexual, the likeness of a depressed
inverted chamber-pot, yellow with age, to put it politely.
If the figure was indeed that of a woman, or that of a
nun, of unusual size, it was that of a woman, or that
of a nun, of unusual size of uncommon inelegance. But
the giant woman was often dowdy, in Watt's experience,
and the giant nun not less so. The arms did not end at
the hands, but continued, in a manner that Watt could
not determine, to near the ground. The feet, following
each other in rapid and impetuous succession, were
flung, the right foot to the right, the left foot to the left,
as much outwards as forwards, with the result that,
for every stride of say three feet in compass, the ground
gained did not exceed one. This gave to the gait a kind
or shackled smartness, most painful to witness. Watt
felt them suddenly glow in the dark place, and go out,
the words, *The only cure is diet.*

Watt waited, with impatience, for this man, if it
was a man, or for this woman, if it was a woman, or for
this priest, if it was a priest, or for this nun, if it was
a nun, to draw near, and set his mind at rest. He did
not desire conversation, he did not desire company, he
did not desire consolation, he felt no wish for an
erection, no, all he desired was to have his uncertainty
removed, in this connexion.

He did not know why he cared, what it was,
coming along the road. He did not know whether this
was a good thing, or a bad thing. It seemed to him that,
quite apart from any question of personal feeling of
grief or satisfaction, it was greatly to be deplored, that
he cared what it was, coming along the road, profoundly
to be deplored.

He realised that he could not be content with the
figure's drawing merely near, no, but that the figure
must draw very near, very near indeed. For if the

figure drew merely near, and not very near indeed, how
should he know, if it was a man, that it was not a
woman, or a priest, or a nun, dressed up as a man? Or,
if it was a woman, that it was not a man, or a priest, or
a nun, dressed up as a woman? Or, if it was a priest,
that it was not a man, or a woman, or a nun, dressed up
as a priest? Or, if it was a nun, that it was not a man,
or a woman, or a priest, dressed up as a nun? So Watt
waited, with impatience, for the figure to draw very near
indeed.

Then, as Watt still waited for the figure to draw
very near indeed, he realised that it was not necessary,
not at all necessary, that the figure should draw very
near indeed, but that a moderate proximation would be
more than sufficient. For Watt's concern, deep as it
appeared, was not after all with what the figure was, in
reality, but with what the figure appeared to be, in
reality. For since when were Watt's concerns with what
things were, in reality? But he was for ever falling into
this old error, this error of the old days when,
lacerated with curiosity, in the midst of substance
shadowy he stumbled. This was very mortifying, to
Watt. So Watt waited, with impatience, for the figure
to draw near.

He waited and waited, his hands curled round the
bars, of the wicket, so that his nails pricked his palms,
his bags at his feet, staring through the bars, staring at
this incomprehensible staffage, suffering greatly from
impatience. His agitation became finally so great, that
he shook the wicket, with all his might.

What so agitated Watt was this, that in the ten
minutes or half-an-hour that had elapsed, since he first
became aware of this figure, striding along, on the
crest of the road, towards the station, the figure had
gained nothing in height, in breadth or in distinctness.
Pressing forward all this time, with no abatement of its
foundered precipitation, towards the station, it had made
no more headway, than if it had been a millstone.

Watt was puzzling over this, when the figure, without any interruption of its motions, grew fainter and fainter, and finally disappeared.

Watt seemed to regard, for some obscure reason, this particular hallucination as possessing exceptional interest.

Watt picked up his bags and advanced, round the corner of a wall, on to the platform. A light was burning in the signal-box.

The signal-man, an elderly man of the name of Case, was waiting in his box, as he did every night, with the exception of the night from Sunday to Monday (strange), for the upgoing express to go up safely, through the station. Then he would set his signals and go home, to his lonely wife, leaving the station deserted.

To while away the time, and at the same time improve his mind, Mr Case was reading a book:*Songs by the Way*, by George Russell (A.E.). Mr Case, his head flung back, held this book out at arm's length. Mr Case had a very superior taste in books, for a signal-man.

Mr Case read:

?

Mr Case's heavy moustache followed the movements of his lip, as it espoused, now pouting, now revulsed, the various sonorities of which these words were composed. His nose too responded, with its bulb and nostrils. The pipe moved up and down, and from the corner of the mouth the spittle fell, unheeded, on the waistcoat, which was of corduroy.

Watt stood in the cabin as he had stood in the kitchen, his bags in his hands, his open eyes at rest, and the door open behind him. Mr Case had once caught, through the windows, of his box a glimpse of Watt, on the evening of his arrival. So he was familiar with his appearance. This stood him now in good stead.

Could you tell me what time it was, said Watt.

It was as he feared, earlier than he hoped.

Could I be admitted to a waiting-room, said Watt.

Here was a teaser, to be sure. For Mr Case might not leave his box, until he left it to go home, to his anxious wife. Nor was it possible, detaching the key from the bunch, to hand it to Watt, saying, Here, Sir, is the key of our waiting-room, I shall call for it on my way home. No. For the waiting-room opened off the booking-office, in such a way, that to reach the waiting-room it was necessary to pass through the booking-office. And the key of the door of the waiting-room did not open the door of the booking-office. Nor was it possible, slipping the two keys off the ring, to hand them to Watt, saying, Here, Sir, is the key of our waiting-room door, and here that of our booking-office door, I shall call for them on my way out. No. For the booking-office communicated with the station-master's sanctum, in such a way, that to reach the station-master's sanctum it was only necessary to traverse the booking-office. And the key of the door of the booking-office opened the door of the station-master's sanctum, in such sort, that these two doors were represented, on each bunch of station keys, on Mr Gorman's the station-master's bunch, on Mr Case's the signal-man's bunch, and on Mr Nolan's the porter's bunch, not by two keys, but by one key only.

In this way an economy of no fewer than three keys was realized, and it was Mr Gorman's the station-master's intention to reduce still further the number of station-keys by having fitted, at no distant date, and at the company's expense, to the door of the waiting-room a lock identical with the now identical locks of the doors of the booking-office and of his private sanctum. This design he had communicated, in the course of a recent conference, both to Mr Case and to Mr Nolan, and neither Mr Case nor Mr Nolan had any objections to offer. But what he had not confided, either to Mr Case or to Mr Nolan, was his determination to have fitted, in the near future, little by little, at the company's expense, to the wicket and to the doors of the signal-box, of the porters' restroom, of the luggage-office and of the ladies' and gentlemens' lavatories, locks so contrived that the key which now opened, with such perfect ease, the door of the booking-office, and the door of the station-master's sanctum, and which so soon would open, without the least difficulty, the door of the waiting-room, would open all those other doors also, one after the other, in the fulness of time. So he would leave, at his retirement, if he did not die before, or on his death, if he did not retire first, a station unique, in this respect, if not in any other, among the stations of the line.

The keys of the till, which Mr Gorman carried, the one on his watch-chain, lest his trouser's pocket should develop a hole, as trousers' pockets are so apt to do, or the key, which was minute, be drawn forth with the small change, and lost, and the other, lest his watch-chain should be lost, or stolen from him, in his trouser's pocket, these little keys Mr Gorman did not number among the station-keys. And indeed the keys of the till were not properly speaking station-keys at all. For the station-till, unlike the station-doors, did not remain in the station, all day, and all night, but left the station with Mr Gorman, when he went home in the evening, and did not return until the following morning, when Mr Gorman returned to the station.

Mr Case considered all this, or such parts as he deemed germane, weighing the for, and weighing the against, without passion. He came finally to the conclusion that he could do nothing, for the moment. When the express-train had come, and gone, and he was free to go home, to his unquiet wife, then he could do something, then he could admit Watt to the waiting-room, and leave him there. But he had no sooner come to the conclusion that he could do this, in order to oblige Watt, when he saw that he could do so only on condition that he locked the door of the booking-office, behind him. For he could not go away, leaving the door of the booking-office open, in the sleeping station. But on this condition, that Watt submitted to be locked into the booking-office, he could oblige Watt, once the express-train had come, and gone. But he had hardly decided that it would be possible for him to oblige Watt, on this condition, when he realised that, even on this condition, it would not be possible for him to oblige Watt, unless Watt consented to being locked, not only into the booking-office, but into the waiting-room also. For it was out of the question that Watt should have free access, all night long, in the sleeping station, to the station-master's sanctum's antechamber. But if he had no objection to being locked, till morning, not only into the booking-office, but into the waiting-room also, then Mr Case saw really no reason why the waiting-room should not be placed at his disposal, as soon as the express-train had passed safely by, with its passengers, and valuable freight.

Mr Case now informed Watt of what he had settled, in his mind, with reference to Watt's request, that he should be admitted to the public waiting-room. The reasons that had led Mr Case to settle this, in his mind, rather than something else, Mr Case had the delicacy to keep to himself, as being more likely to cause Watt pain, than to cause him pleasure. In the morning, said Mr Case, as soon as Mr Gorman, or Mr Nolan arrives, you will be let out, and free to come and go, as you please. Watt replied that that would indeed be something to look forward to, and a comfort to him during the night, the prospect of being enlarged, in the morning, by Mr Gorman, or Mr Nolan, and made free to come and go, as he listed. If in the meantime, said Mr Case, you care to come in, to the box, and shut the door, and take a chair, I should be happy to have you. Watt replied that it would be better if he waited outside. He would be on the platform, walking up and down, or sitting on a seat.

Watt lay on the seat, on his back, with his bags under his head, and his hat over his face. Thus the moon was in a measure kept off, and the lesser beauties of this glorious night. The problem of vision, as far as Watt was concerned, admitted of only one solution: the eye open in the dark. The results given by the closed eye were, in Watt's opinion, most unsatisfactory.

Watt first considered the matter of the express-train, so soon due to thunder, with irresistible impetus, through the sleeping station. He gave very full and close attention to this matter. Finally suddenly he ceased, as suddenly as he had begun, to think.

He lay on the seat, without thought or sensation, except for a slight feeling of chill in one foot. In his skull the voices whispering their canon were like a patter of mice, a flurry of little grey paws in the dust. This was very likely a sensation also, strictly speaking.

Mr Case was obliged to explain his insistence. But a few words were sufficient. A few words from Mr Case, and all came back to Watt. Mr Case carried a storm-lantern in his hand. From it issued a yellow beam, of extraordinary debility. Mr Case spoke of the train, with professional pride. It had left on time, it had passed on time, and it would arrive, at its destination, if nothing supervened to delay it, on time.

Here then was the explanation of the recent external commotion.

It was now fully two hours since Watt had passed water. And yet he felt no need, nay, no desire, to pass water. Not the least drop, or globule, of water could I pass, he reflected, good, bad or indifferent, if I were paid not to do so. He who hourly passed an urgent water, a delicious water, in the ordinary way. This last regular link with the screen, for he did not count as such his weekly stool, nor biannual equinoctial nocturnal emission in vacuo, he now envisaged its relaxation, and eventual rupture, with sadness, and gladness,

distinctly perceptible in an alternation of great rapidity,
for some little time, and dying blurred together away,
in due course.

Watt stood on the floor, with his bags in his
hands, and the floor was like stone under his feet, and
his faithful body did not fall, his relentless body,
suddenly on its knees, or on its coccyx, and then forward
on his face, or backward on its back, no, but it
preserved its balance, in a way not unlike the way that
its mother had taught, and the conformism of youth
confirmed.

Faintlier, faintlier came the footfalls to his ear,
until of all the faint sounds that came, by the abandoned
air, to his ear, not one was a footfall, as far as he could
judge. This was a music of which he was particularly
fond, the parted quiet closing like a groom, behind
departing footfalls, or other disturbances. But Mr Case's
way brought him behind the station, and his footfalls
came again, four or five, a little wale of stealth, to
Watt's ears, which stuck out wide on either side of his
head, like a   ?   's. Before long they would come
to Mrs Case, to her ears weary of the stepless murmurs,
stronger and stronger till they reached the grass. Few
sounds, if any, gave Mrs Case more satisfaction than
these. She was a strange woman.

Part of the waiting-room was faintly lit, by light
from without. The passage from this part to the other
was more abrupt, now that Watt had ceased to listen,
than he would have believed possible, if he had not
seen it, with his own eyes.

The waiting-room was empty of furniture, or other
objects, as far as Watt could see. Unless there was
something behind him. This did not strike him as
strange. Nor did it strike him as usual. For his
impression was, such as it was, as he drooped sigmoidal
in its midst, that this was a waiting-room of which even
the nicest degrees of strange and usual could not be
affirmed, with propriety.

Whispering it told, the mouth, a woman's, the
thin lips sticking and unsticking, how when empty they
could accommodate a larger public than when encumber-
ed with armchairs and divans, and how it was vain to
sit, vain to lie, when without the rain beat down, or
the sleet, or the snow, with or without wind, or the sun,
with greater or lesser perpendicularity. This woman's
name had been Price, her person was of an extreme
spareness, and some thirty-five years earlier she had
shot, with colours flying, the narrows of the menopause.
Watt was not displeased to hear her voice again, to
watch again the play of the pale bows of mucus. He
was not displeased either when it went away.

The waiting-room was now less empty than Watt
had at first supposed, to judge by the presence, some
two paces to Watt's fore, and as many to his right, of
what seemed to be an object of some importance. Watt
could not tell what this was, though he went so far as
to advance his head, not without torsion of the neck, in
its direction. It was not part of the ceiling, nor of a wall,
nor, though it seemed in contact with the floor, of the
floor, that was all that Watt could affirm, of this object,
and even that little he affirmed with reserve. But that
little was enough, for Watt the possibility was enough,
more than enough, that something other than he, in
this box, was not intrinsic to its limits.

A smell exceptionally foul, and yet at the same
time in some way familiar, made Watt wonder if there
were not hidden, beneath the boards, at his feet, the
decaying carcass of some small animal, such as a dog, a
cat, a rat, or a mouse. For the floor, though it felt to
Watt like stone, was in reality contabulated, all over.
This smell was of such virulence that Watt was almost
obliged to put down his bags and draw forth his pockethandkerchief, or, more exactly, his roll of toilet-paper,
from his pocket. For Watt, in order to save himself the
washing, and no doubt also for the pleasure of killing
two birds with one stone, never blew his nose, except

when the circumstances permitted of a direct digital
emunction, in anything but toilet-paper, each separate
slip, when thoroughly imbibed, being crumpled up into
a ball, and thrown away, and the hands passed through
the hair, to its great embellishment, or rubbed the one
against the other, until they shone.

This smell however was not what Watt had at
first supposed, but something quite different, for it
grew weaker and weaker, as it would not have done,
if it had been what Watt had at first supposed, and
finally ceased, altogether.

But in a short time it returned, the same smell
exactly, dilated and passed off, as before.

In this way it came and went, for some hours.

There was something about this smell that Watt
could not help but like. Yet he was not sorry, when
it went.

In the waiting-room the darkness gradually
deepened. There was no longer a dark part and a less
dark part, no, but all now was uniformly dark, and
remained so, for some time. This notable change took
place by insensible degrees.

When the waiting-room had been quite dark, for
some time, then in the waiting-room the darkness slowly
lightened, throughout, by infinitesimal stages, and continued to do so, at the same rate, until every part of
the waiting-room was faintly visible, to the dilated eye.

Watt saw now that his companion all this time
had been a chair. Its back was turned towards him.
Little by little, as the light grew, he came to know this
chair, so well, that in the end he knew it better than
many a chair he had sat on, or stood on, when the
object was beyond his reach, or shod his feet on, or
toileted his feet on, one after the other, paring and
curetting the nails, and scouring the webholes, with
a spoon.

It was a high, narrow, black, wooden chair, with
arms, and castors.

One of its feet was screwed to the floor, by means
of a clamp. Not one of the remaining feet, but all,
carried similar, if not identical irons. Not one, but all!
But the screws, which no doubt had once fixed these
to the floor, had very kindly been removed. Through
the bars, which were vertical, of the back, Watt saw
portions of a grate, heaped high with ashes, and cinders,
of a beautiful grey colour.

This chair then had been with Watt, all this
time, in the waiting-room, all these hours, of scant
light, of no light, and it was with him still, in the
exhilarating dawn. It would not be impossible, after
all, to take it away, and put it somewhere else, or sell
it by auction, or give it away.

Otherwise, as far as Watt could see, all was wall,
or floor, or ceiling.

There next emerged, without haste, from the
wall, a large coloured print of the horse Joss, standing
in profile in a field. Watt identified, first the field,
then the horse, and then, thanks to an inscription of
great   ?   , the horse Joss.   This horse, its four
hooves firmly planted on the ground, its head sunk,
seemed to consider, without appetite, the grass. Watt
pushed forward his head, to see if it was really a horse,
and not a mare, or a gelding.   But this interesting
information was hidden, just hidden, by a haunch, or
tail, of more decency than breeding.   The light was
that of approaching night, or impending storm, or both.
The grass was sparse, sere, and overrun with what Watt
took to be a species of cockle.

The horse seemed hardly able to stand, let
alone run.

This object too had not been always here, would
perhaps not be always here.

The flies, of skeleton thinness, excited to new
efforts by yet another dawn, left the walls, and the
ceiling, and even the floor, and hastened in great
numbers to the window.   Here, pressed against the

impenetrable panes, they would enjoy the light, and warmth, of the long summer's day.

A merry whistling now sounded, afar off, and the nearer it approached, the merrier it grew. For Mr Nolan's spirits always rose, as he approached the station, in the morning . They rose also, invariably, in the evening, when he left it. Thus Mr Nolan was assured, twice a day, of a rise in spirits. And when Mr Nolan's spirits rose, he could no more refrain from whistling, merrily, than a lark sing, when it rises.

It was Mr Nolan's habit, when he had flung open all the station-doors, with the air of one storming a bastille, to retire to the porters' restroom, and there drink a bottle of stout, the first of the day, over the previous evening's paper. Mr Nolan was a great reader of the evening paper. He read it five times, at his tea, at his supper, at his breakfast, with his morning stout and at his dinner. In the course of the afternoon, for he had a very gallant nature, he carried it to the ladies' house of office, and left it there, in a conspicuous position. Few pennyworths gave more joy, than Mr Nolan's evening paper.

Mr Nolan then, having unlocked and hurled, against their jambs, the wicket and the booking-office door, came to the door of the waiting-room. Had his whistle been less piercing, and his entry less resounding, he might have heard, behind the door, a disquieting sound, that of soliloquy, under dictation, and proceeded with care. But no, he turned the key and dealt, with his boot, the door a dunt that sent it flying inwards, at a great speed.

The innumerable semicircles thus brilliantly begun did not end, as on all previous mornings, in the bang that Mr Nolan loved, no, but they were all cut short, all without exception, at the same point. And the reason for that was this, that Watt, where he stood, swaying, murmuring, was nearer the waiting-room door than the waiting-room door was wide.

Mr Nolan found Mr Gorman on his doorstep, taking leave of his mother.

Now I am at liberty, said Watt, I am free to come and go, as I please.

There were four armpits, where the friezes met, four fair armpits. Watt saw the ceiling with an extreme distinctness. It was of a whiteness that he would not have believed possible, if it had been reported to him. It was a rest, after the wall. It was a rest too, after the floor. It was such a rest, after the wall, and the floor, and the chair, and the horse, and the flies, that Watt's eyes closed, a thing they never did by day in the ordinary way on any account, except very briefly now and then, to prevent themselves from becoming too dry.

Poor fellow, said Mr Gorman, shall we telephone for a policeman.

Mr Nolan was all in favour of telephoning for a policeman.

Help him to rise, said Mr Gorman, perhaps he has a bone broke.

But Mr Nolan could not bring himself to do this. He stood in the middle of the booking-office, unable to move.

You do not expect me to help him to rise, all alone, said Mr Gorman.

Mr Nolan expected nothing.

Together let us levvy him to his feet, said Mr Gorman. Then, if necessary, you will telephone for a policeman.

Mr Nolan dearly loved to telephone. It was a treat seldom vouchsafed him. But in the door of the waiting-room he stopped short, and said he could not. He was sorry, he said, but he could not.

Perhaps you are right, said Mr Gorman.

(Hiatus in MS)

Yet we cannot leave him there like that, said
Mr Gorman. The five fifty-five will be upon us — he
consulted his watch — in thirty-seven and.. (Hiatus
in MS) ..in a lower voice, And the six four will follow
hard behind. The thought of the six four seemed to
trouble him particularly, for some reason. There is
not a moment to lose, he exclaimed. He drew himself
up, threw back his head, lowered the hand that held
the watch to the level of the glans (Mr Gorman had
a very long arm) penis, laid the other to his temple
and took the time. Then suddenly flexing his knees,
and hunching his back, he cuddled the watch to his
ear, in the attitude of a child cringing away from a
blow.

It was as he feared, later than he hoped.

Run fetch a bucket of water, he said, perhaps
who knows if we souse him thoroughly he will get up
of his own free will.

Perhaps the hose — , said Mr Nolan.

The bucket, I said, said Mr Gorman, from the tap.

What bucket? said Mr Nolan.

Bloody well you know what bucket! cried
Mr Gorman, not however an impatient man as a rule.
The muck bloody bucket, blast your bloody — . He
paused. The day was Saturday. Your bloody eyes,
he said.

Watt distinguished fragments of a part:

.... *von Klippe zu Klippe geworfen*
Endlos ins .... *hinab*.

Mr Gorman and Mr Nolan advanced together,
stooping, the bucket, heavy with slime, held between
them.

Sister, sister ...... *beware of a sullen silent*
sot ...... *always musing* ...... *never thinks.*

Gently does it, said Mr Gorman.

Is that the gob? said Mr Nolan.

Gently, gently, said Mr Gorman. Have you got
a firm holt on her?

I have not, said Mr Nolan.

Don't let go whatever you do, said Mr Gorman.

Or is it a hole in his trousers? said Mr Nolan.

Never mind what it is, said Mr Gorman. Are you right?

Hold back the handle, said Mr Nolan.

To hell with the bloody handle, said Mr Gorman. Tilt the bucket when I tell you.

Tilt her with what? said Mr Nolan. With the hair on me chest?

Mr Gorman spat violently into the bucket, Mr Gorman who never spat, in the ordinary way, if not into his pockethandkerchief.

Put down the bucket, said Mr Gorman.

They put down the bucket. Mr Gorman took the time, as before.

Lady McCann will be upon us in ten minutes, said Mr Gorman.

Lady McCann was a lady who daily left the neighbourhood by the first train in the morning, and returned to it by the last at night. Her reasons for doing this were not known. On Sundays she remained in bed, receiving there the mass, and other meals and visitors.

Hell roast her, said Mr Gorman. Good-morning, Mr Gorman, lovely morning, Mr Gorman. Lovely morning!

And Arsy Cox, said Mr Nolan.

And Herring-gut Waller, said Mr Gorman.

And Cack-faced Miller, said Mr Nolan.

And Mrs Penny-a-hoist Pim, said Mr Gorman.

That old put, said Mr Nolan.

Do you know what she says to me the other day? said Mr Gorman.

What was that? said Mr Nolan.

In my private burreau, said Mr Gorman. Placing his thumb and forefinger on his cheekbones, he pushed up the long yellow-grey moustache. Shortly after the departure of the eleven twenty-four, he said. Mr Gorman, says she, winter may be in my hair, but there is still plenty of spring in my do you follow me.

(MS illegible)

The right hand firmly on the rim, said Mr Gorman, the fingers of the left curled round the —

I follow you, said Mr Nolan.

They stooped.

God knows why I give myself all this trouble, said Mr Gorman. Tilt when I say the word.

The bucket slowly rose.

Not all at one go, said Mr Gorman, there is no point in soiling the floor unnecessarily.

Mr Nolan now releasing his hold on the bucket, Mr Gorman, who did not care to wet the outside of his trousers, was obliged to do the same. Together rapidly in safety they gained the door.

I declare to God she sprang out of me hands, like as if she was alive, said Mr Nolan.

If that doesn't get him up, nothing will, said Mr Gorman.

Blood now perfused the slime. Mr Gorman and Mr Nolan were not alarmed. It was unlikely that a vital organ was touched.

Mr Case arrived. He had passed an unrefreshing night, in a sense, but his humour was excellent. He carried, in one hand, a can of hot tea, and, in the other, *Songs by the Way*, which the untoward events of the early morning had caused him to forget to leave behind, in his cabin, on the shelf, as his habit was.

He wished good-morning to, and shook hands warmly with, first Mr Gorman, and then Mr Nolan, who in their turn, and in that order, wished a very good morning to him, and shook him heartily by the hand. And then remembering, Mr Gorman and Mr Nolan, that in the heat of the morning's vicissitudes they had forgotten to wish each other good-morning, and shake each other by the hand, they did so now, most cordially, without further delay.

Mr Case's narrative was of great interest to Mr Gorman, and to Mr Nolan, there shedding light, as it did, where until now all had been dark. Much however remained to be elucidated.

You are sure it is the same? said Mr Gorman.

Mr Case picked his way, to where Watt lay. Bending he scraped, with his book, a little mire from the face.

Oh, you'll spoil your nice book, cried Mr Gorman.

The clothes seem to me the same, said Mr Case. He went to the window and turned over, with his boot, the hat. I recognise the hat, he said. He rejoined Mr Gorman and Mr Nolan in the doorway. I see the bags, he said, but I cannot say that I recognise the face. It is true, if it is the same, that I have only seen it twice before, and both times the light was poor, oh very poor. And yet I have a great memory for faces, as a rule.

Particular a face like that, said Mr Nolan.

And for arses, added Mr Case, as an afterthought. Let me once catch a fair glimpse of an arse, and I'll pick it out for you among a million.

Mr Nolan murmured something to his superior.

Grossly exaggerated, said Mr Gorman.

Otherwise my memory is poor, said Mr Case, oh very poor, as my wife could tell you.

Lady McCann joined the group. Greetings were exchanged, and salutes. Mr Gorman told her what they knew.

Do I see blood? said Lady McCann.

A mere trickle, my lady, said Mr Case, from the nose, or perhaps the lug.

Arsy Cox and Herring-gut Waller arrived together. Following the usual compliments, and prescribed motions of the head, and hands, Lady McCann informed them of what had passed.

Something must be done, said Mr Cox.

At once, said Mr Waller.

A breathless boy appeared. He said he was sent
by Mr Cole.

Mr Cole? said Lady McCann.

Of the level-crossing, my lady, said Mr Case.

Mr Cole desired to know why Mr Case's signals
were against Mr Cole's five fifty-seven, now rapidly
approaching, from the south-east.

God bless my soul, said Mr Case, what can I have
been thinking of.

But he had not reached the door, when Mr Gorman, on a sign from the boy, desired him to stay.

Mr Cole, said the boy, would also be very happy
to learn for what reasons Mr Case's signals were against
Mr Cole's six six, now hastening towards him, from
the north-west.

Return, my little man, said Lady McCann, to
him that sent you. Tell him that — has been the
scene of terrible events, but that now all is well. Repeat
now after me. The scene . . . . . of terrible . . . . .
terrible . . . . . events . . . . . but that now . . . . . all
is well . . . . . Very good. Here is a penny.

Cack-faced Miller arrived. Cack-faced Miller
never greeted anyone, orally or otherwise, and few people
ever greeted Cack-faced Miller. He knelt down beside
Watt and inserted his hand under the head. In this
touching attitude he remained for some time. He then
rose and went away. He stood on the platform, his
back to the line, his face to the wicket. The sun had
not yet risen, above the sea. It had not yet risen, but
it was rising fast. As he watched, it rose, and shone,
with its faint morning shining, on his face.

Watt now also rose, to the no small diversion
of Messrs Gorman, Nolan, Cox and Waller. Lady McCann
was less amused.

Who the devil are you, said Mr Gorman, and
what the hell do you want?

Watt found his hat and put it on.

Mr Gorman repeated his question.

Watt found his bags, first one, then the other, and settled them in his hands, in the way that irked him least. The group fell away from the door and he passed out, into the booking-office.

Who is he? said Mr Cox.

And what does he want? said Mr Waller.

Speak, said Lady McCann.

Watt halted before the ticket-window, put down his bags, once more, and knocked on the wooden shutter.

Go and see what he wants, said Mr Gorman.

When Watt saw a face on the other side of the window, he said:

Give me a ticket, if you please.

He wants a ticket, cried Mr Nolan.

A ticket to where? said Mr Gorman.

Where to? said Mr Nolan.

To the end of the line, said Watt.

He wants a ticket to the end of the line, cried Mr Nolan.

Is it a white man? said Lady McCann.

Which end? said Mr Gorman.

What end? said Mr Nolan.

Watt did not reply.

The round end or the square end? said Mr Nolan.

Watt reflected a little longer. Then he said:

The nearer end.

The nearest end, cried Mr Nolan.

There is no need to bellow, said Mr Cox.

The voice is low, but clear, said Mr Waller.

But what an extraordinary accent, said Lady McCann.

I beg your pardon, said Watt, I mean the further end.

What you want is a free pass, said Mr Nolan.

Issue him a third single to — , said Mr Gorman, and let us have done.

One and three, said Mr Nolan.

Watt counted out, in the fluted trough, one

shilling, two sixpences, three threepences, and four pennies.

What's all this? said Mr Nolan.

Three and one, said Watt.

One and three, roared Mr Nolan.

Watt put the difference in his pocket.

The train! exclaimed Lady McCann.

Quick, said Mr Cox, two there and back.

It was Mr Cox's and Mr Waller's practice, though they travelled daily, on this line, to and from the city, to buy their tickets every morning anew. One day it was Mr Cox who paid, and the next it was Mr Waller. The reasons for this are not known.

Not many minutes later the six four entered the station. It did not take up a single passenger, in the absence of Mrs Pim. But it discharged a bicycle, for a Miss Walker.

Mr Case, free now again to leave his box, joined Mr Gorman and Mr Nolan, before the wicket. The sun was now well above the visible horizon. Mr Gorman, Mr Case and Mr Nolan turned their faces towards it, as men will, in the early morning, without heeding. The road lay still, at this hour, leaden, deserted, between its hedges, and its ditches. From one of these latter a goat emerged, dragging its pale and chain. The goat hesitated, in the middle of the road, then turned away. The clatter came fainter and fainter, down the still air, and came still faintly when the pale had disappeared, beyond the rise. The trembling sea could not but be admired. The leaves quivered, or gave the impression of doing so, and the grasses also, beneath the drops, or beads, of gaily expiring dew. The long summer's day had made an excellent start. If it continued in the same manner, its close would be worth coming to see.

All the same, said Mr Gorman, life isn't such a bad old bugger. He raised high his hands and spread them out, in a gesture of worship. He then replaced

them in the pockets, of his trousers. When all is said
and done, he said.

Riley's puckaun again, said Mr Nolan, I can
smell him from here.

And they say there is no God, said Mr Case.

All three laughed heartily at this extravagance.

Mr Gorman consulted his watch.

To work, he said.

They parted. Mr Gorman went in one direction,
Mr Case in another and Mr Nolan in a third.

But they had not gone far when Mr Case hesitated,
went on, hesitated again, stopped, turned and cried:

And our friend?

Mr Gorman and Mr Nolan stopped and turned.

Friend? said Mr Gorman.

Mr Gorman was between Mr Case and Mr Nolan,
and so did not need to raise his voice.

Is it the long wet dream with the hat and bags?
cried Mr Nolan.

Mr Nolan looked at Mr Case, Mr Case at Mr Nolan,
Mr Gorman at Mr Case, Mr Gorman at Mr Nolan,
Mr Nolan at Mr Gorman, Mr Case at Mr Gorman,
Mr Gorman again at Mr Case, again at Mr Nolan, and
then straight before him, at nothing in particular. And
so they stayed a little while, Mr Case and Mr Nolan
looking at Mr Gorman, and Mr Gorman looking straight
before him, at nothing in particular, though the sky
falling to the hills, and the hills falling to the plain,
made as pretty a picture, in the early morning light,
as a man could hope to meet with, in a day's march.

ADDENDA (1)

her married life one long drawsheet

— — —

Art Conn O'Connery, called Black Velvet O'Connery, product of the great Chinnery-Slattery tradition.

— — —

the Master of the Leopardstown Halflengths

— — —

who may tell the tale
of the old man?
weigh absence in a scale?
mete want with a span?
the sum assess
of the world's woes?
nothingness
in words enclose?

— — —

judicious Hooker's heat-pimples

— — —

limits to part's equality with whole

---

(1) The following precious and illuminating material should be carefully studied. Only fatigue and disgust prevented its incorporation.

— — —

dead calm, then a murmur, a name, a murmured name, in
doubt, in fear, in love, in fear, in doubt, wind of winter in the black
boughs, cold calm sea whitening whispering to the shore, stealing,
hastening, swelling, passing, dying, from naught come, to naught
gone

— — —

Bid us sigh on from day to day,
And wish and wish the soul away,
Till youth and genial years are flown,
And all the life of life is gone.

— — —

Watt learned to accept etc. Use to explain poverty of Part III.
Watt cannot speak of what happened on first floor, because for the
greater part of the time nothing happened, without his protesting.

— — —

Note that Arsene's declaration gradually came back to Watt.

— — —

One night Watt goes on roof.

— — —

Watt snites.

— — —

Meals. Every day Mr Knott's bowl at a different place. Watt
marks with chalk.

— — —

the maddened prizeman

— — —

the sheet of dark water, the widening fret of ripples, the
deadening banks, the stillness

— — —

never been properly born

— — —

the foetal soul is full grown (Cangiamila's *Sacred Embriology*
and Pope Benedict XIV's *De Synodo Diocesana*, Bk. 7, Chap. 4,
Sect. 6.)

— — —

sempiternal penumbra

— — —

for all the good that frequent departures out of Ireland had
done him, he might just as well have stayed there

— — —

a round wooden table, of generous diameter, resting on a single massive conical frustum, filled the middle space.

— — —

zitto! zitto! dass nur das Publikum nichts merke!

— — —

on the waste, beneath the sky, distinguished by Watt as being, the one above, the other beneath, Watt. That before him, behind him, on all sides of him, there was something else, neither sky nor waste, was not felt by Watt. And it was always their long dark flowing away together towards the mirage of union that lay before him, whichever way he turned. The sky was of a dark colour, from which it may be inferred that the usual luminaries were absent. They were. The waste also, needless to say, was of a dark colour. Indeed the sky and the waste were of the same dark colour, which is hardly to be wondered at. Watt also was very naturally of the same dark colour. This dark colour was so dark that the colour could not be identified with certainty. Sometimes it seemed a dark absence of colour, a dark mixture of all colours, a dark white. But Watt did not like the words dark white, so he continued to call his darkness a dark colour plain and simple, which strictly speaking it was not, seeing that the colour was so dark as to defy identification as such.

The source of the feeble light diffused over this scene is unknown.

Further peculiarities of this soul-landscape were:

The temperature was warm.

Beneath Watt the waste rose and fell.

All was silent.

Above Watt the sky fell and rose.

Watt was rooted to the spot.

— — —

Watt will not
abate one jot
but of what

of the coming to
of the being at
of the going from
Knott's habitat

of the long way
of the short stay
of the going back home
the way he had come

of the empty heart
of the empty hands
of the dim mind wayfaring
through barren lands

of a flame with dark winds
hedged about
going out
gone out

of the empty heart
of the empty hands
of the dark mind stumbling
through barren lands

that is of what
Watt will not
abate one tot

—   —   —

die Merde hat mich wieder

—   —   —

pereant qui ante nos nostra dixerunt

—   —   —

Second picture in Erskine's room, representing gentleman
seated at piano, full length, receding profile right, naked save for
stave-paper resting on lap. With his right hand he sustains a chord
which Watt has no difficuly in identifying as that of C major in
its second inversion, while with other he prolongs pavilion of
left ear. His right foot, assisted from above by its fellow, depresses
with force the sustaining pedal. On muscles of brawny neck,
arm, torso, abdomen, loin, thigh and calf, standing out like cords
in stress of effort, Mr O'Connery had lavished all the resources
of Jesuit tactility. Beads of sweat, realized with a finish that
would have done credit to Heem, were plentifully distributed
over pectoral, subaxillary and hypogastrial surfaces. The right

nipple, from which sprang a long red solitary hair, was in a state of manifest tumescence, a charming touch. The bust was bowed over the keyboard and the face, turned slightly towards the spectator, wore expression of man about to be delivered, after many days, of particularly hard stool, that is to say the brow was furrowed, the eyes tight closed, the nostrils dilated, the lips parted and the jaw fallen, as pretty a synthesis as one could wish of anguish, concentration, strain, transport and self-abandon, illustrating extraordinary effect produced on musical nature by faint cacophony of remote harmonics stealing over dying accord. Mr O'Connery's love of significant detail appeared further in treatment of toenails, of remarkable luxuriance and caked with what seemed to be dirt. Feet also could have done with a wash, legs not what you could call fresh and sweet, buttocks and belly cried out for hipbath at least, chest in disgusting condition, neck positively filthy, and seeds might have been scattered in ears with every prospect of early germination.

That however a damp cloth had been rapidly passed at a recent date over more prominent portions of facies (latin word, meaning face) seemed not improbable.

(Latin quote)

Moustache, pale red save where discoloured by tobacco, advancing years, nervous chewing, family worries, nasal slaver and buccal froth, tumbled over ripe red lips, and forth from out ripe red jaw, and forth in same way from out ripe red dewlap, sprouted, palely red, doomed beginnings of bushy pale red beard.

— — —

like a thicket flower unrecorded

— — —

Watt's Davus complex (morbid dread of sphinxes)

— — —

One night Arthur came to Watt's room. He was agitated. He thought he had been taken for Mr Knott. He did not know if he felt honoured or not.

Walking in the garden he said, Now I am walking in the garden, not with any great pleasure it is true, but nevertheless, up and down, I am walking in the garden.

He watched his legs as under him they moved, in and out.

I stand first on one leg, he said, then on the other, so, and in that way I move forward.

Notice how without thinking you avoid the daisies, he said. What sensibility.

Halting, he contemplated the grass, at his feet.

This dewy sward is not yours, he said. He clasped his hands to his breast. He lifted them towards the maker, and giver, of all things, of him, of the daisies, of the grass. Thanks Boss, he said. He stood easy. He moved on.

This is said to be good for the health, he said.

Not many moments had elapsed since this aphorism when Arthur began to laugh, so heartily that he was obliged to lean for support against a passing shrub, or bush, which joined heartily in the joke.

When he had recovered his calm, he turned to examine the bush, or shrub. All he could say was that is was not a rush.

Now he saw, advancing towards him over the grass, an indistinct mass. A moment later it was an old man, clothed in rags.

Who can this be, I wonder, said Arthur.

A penny for a poor old man, said the old man.

Arthur gave a penny.

God bless your honour, said the old man.

Amen, said Arthur. Good-day.

I remember you when I was a boy, said the old man. I was a boy meself.

Then we was boys together, said Arthur.

You was a fine lovely boy, said the old man, and I was another.

Look at us now, said Arthur.

You was always wetting yer trousers, said the old man.

I wets them still, said Arthur.

I cleaned the boots, said the old man.

If it hadn't been you, it would have been another, said Arthur.

Yer father was very good to me.

Like father like son, said Arthur. Good-day.

I helped to lay out this darling place, said the old man.

In that case, said Arthur, perhaps you can tell me the name of this extraordinary growth.

That's what we calls a hardy laurel, said the old man.

Arthur went back into the house and wrote, in his journal:
Took a turn in the garden. Thanked God for a small mercy.

Made merry with the hardy laurel. Bestowed alms on an old man formerly employed by Knott family.

But this was not enough. So he came running to Watt.

This was the first time Watt had heard the words Knott family.

There had been a time when they would have pleased him, and the thought they tendered, that Mr Knott too was serial, in a vermicular series. But not now. For Watt was an old rose now, and indifferent to the gardener.

— — —

Watt looking as though nearing end of course of injections of sterile pus

— — —

das fruchtbare Bathos der Erfahrung

— — —

faede hunc mundum intravi, anxius vixi, perturbatus egredior, causa causarum miserere mei

— — —

change all the names

— — —

descant heard by Watt on way to station (IV):

Sop.	With	all our	heart	breathe	head	awhile	darkly	apart
Alt.	With	all our	heart	with	all	- our	heart	- - -
Ten.	With	all -	our	heart	-	-	-	- - -
Bas.	Breathe	- -	-	breathe	-	-	-	- - -

Sop.	the	air	exile	of	ended	smile	of ending	care
Alt.	breathe	breathe	- -	of -	end	-	ing - care	-
Ten.	breathe	breathe	- -	the -	-	-	ex -	-
Bas.	-	-	-	phew!	the -	-	-	ex -	-

Sop.	darkly	awhile	the exile	air	
Alt.	the - -	ex -	ile -	air	-
Ten.	ile -	- -	air -	-	
Bas.	ile -	- -	air -	-	

— — —

parole non ci appulero

— — —

Threne heard by Watt in ditch on way from station. The soprano sang :

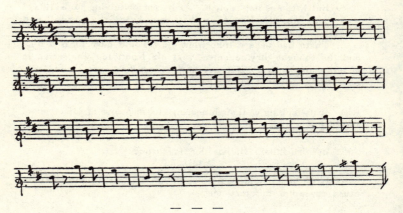

no symbols where none intended

Paris, 1945.

A Selected List of Black Cat Books

A Selecte̶̶̶̶̶̶̶̶̶̶̶̶̶̶̶̶̶̶̶̶ oks